A Short History of China

Hilda Hookham
Senior Lecturer University of London Goldsmiths' College

Longmans

LONGMANS, GREEN AND CO LTD
London and Harlow
Associated companies, branches and representatives throughout the world
© *Longmans, Green and Co Ltd 1969*
First published 1969

S B N 582 31417 8

Made and printed by offset in Great Britain by William Clowes and Sons Ltd
London and Beccles

Contents

Maps

Note on spelling

The most commonly used system of transliteration – the Wade–Giles system – has been adopted, in a simplified form, that is to say, with the elimination of all diacritical marks and hyphens. Names of people are spelt with capitals throughout, e.g. Sun Yat Sen; of places, as one word – e.g. Changan.

It is customary in China for the surname, the family name, to be written first, followed by the given names. The family name is normally of one syllable (or character), the given names are commonly of two characters. It is customary to prefix the emperor's titles with the name of the dynasty, e.g. 'Han' Wu Ti, 'Tang' Tai Tsung.

Pronunciation: vowel sounds should be given their Continental values.

Chinese terms

Li: about one-third of a mile.
Mou: about 0·165 of an acre.
Catty: about 1·1 lb.
Picul: 1 cwt.
Tael: 1⅓ ounces.

Acknowledgements

In order to keep the text simple, quotations and translations are acknowledged according to page and sequence at the end of the text.

In addition to the quotations listed, I wish to acknowledge my debt in general to the work of Drs J. Needham, Wang Ling and their associates, for their Historical Introduction in *Science and Civilisation in China* Vol. 1 (C.U.P. 1954), and to the numerous papers of Dr Needham on aspects of Chinese cultural development; to C. P. Fitzgerald's many works and in particular those referring to the Tang period; to the Studies of Professor O. Lattimore on the Asian Frontiers of China and other works on Chinese and nomad history; to J. Gernet's *Daily Life in China* (Allen & Unwin 1962) for the Sung period, and for the same period to E. Balacz's *Chinese Civilisation and Bureaucracy* (Yale U.P. 1964); to V. Purcell's *China* (Benn 1962); to E. O. Reischauer and J. K. Fairbank's *East Asia, the Great Tradition*, Vol. 1 (Houghton Mifflin 1958); to L. C. Goodrich's *Short History of the Chinese People* (Harper 1959); to W. M. McGovern *The Early Empires of Central Asia* (North Carolina 1939) for the Han period; to the works of Han Suyin, especially *China in the Year 2001* (Watts 1967); to Tung Chi Ming *Outline History of China* (Peking 1958); to the publications of the Foreign Languages Press, Peking, and to the Curators of the Museum of Chinese History, Peking.

We are grateful to the following for permission to reproduce copyright material:

George Allen and Unwin Ltd for extracts from *Chinese Poems, The Book of Songs*, and *Analects of Confucius* all by Arthur Waley; George Allen and Unwin Ltd and The Macmillan Co. Inc. for extracts from *Daily Life in China on the Eve of the Mongol Invasion* by J. Geernet, © Ernest Benn Ltd for an extract from *China Shakes the World* by J. Belden; Cambridge University Press for extracts from *Science and Civilisation in China* by Needham; author, Jonathan Cape Ltd and Charles Scribner's Sons for an extract from *Ones Company* by Peter Fleming; The Cresset Press for extracts from *China: A Short Cultural History* by Fitzgerald; author's agents for extracts from *Contemporaries of Marco Polo* by Maurice Komroff; Paragon Book Gallery Ltd for extracts from *Gems of Chinese Literature* by H. A. Giles; Penguin Books Ltd for extracts from *Marco Polo* translated by R. E. Latham; Routledge and Kegan Paul Ltd for extracts from *Life of Hsien Tsiang* translated by S. Beal; author and Victor Gollancz Ltd for extracts from *Red Star Over China* by Edgar Snow; Yale University Press for extracts from *Chinese Civilization and Bureaucracy* by Etienne Balazs, translated by H. M. Wright, edited by Arthur F. Wright.

We are grateful to the following for permission to reproduce illustrations:

British Museum: 30, 51, 54, 72, 89, 94, 105, 128, 153, 156; Werner Forman, Artia: 31, 32, 64, 65, 66, 67, 69, 100; Museum of Chinese History, Peking: 13, 39, 41, 83, 93, 96, 109, 127, 171; the Palace Museum, Peking: 102; Foreign Languages Press, Peking: 10, 15, 23, 26, 33, 34, 35, 37, 53, 71, 75, 77, 92, 96, 100, 101, 107, 108, 143, 153, 169, 205, 215; China Welfare Institute, Peking: 11, 12, 18, 19, 20, 24, 28, 29, 33, 37, 38, 39, 47, 50, 54, 74, 84, 89, 141, 142, 147, 161, 218, 222, 234; J. Needham and C.U.P.: 14; C. P. Fitzgerald and Cresset Press: 81; Sung and Yuan, and Methuen: 103; A. Waley and Allen and Unwin: 104; Radio Times Hulton Picture Library: 126; E. G. Browne and C.U.P.: 139; China Missionary Society: 151; Science Museum: 156; R. Pelissier and Secker and Warburg: 188, 208.

I am much indebted also to H. V. Bailey and staff of the Technical Workshop, University of London Goldsmiths' College, for their cooperation in the reproduction of photographic materials.

1. Prehistory and Shang to the eleventh century BC

Chinese civilisation is very ancient; it is moreover the only civilisation that had maintained cultural continuity from the second millennium BC until today. The culture of China has never at any period become extinct, as has for example that of ancient Assyria, Egypt or Greece. It is the world's oldest living civilisation.

We owe to China a number of crucial scientific developments: the use of the magnetic compass (the 'south-seeking' needle, to the Chinese), the techniques of paper manufacture and of printing, and the manufacture of gunpowder, are amongst the better known. In our own homes the walls are papered after a fashion derived from China; in happy circumstances our tables are laid with China ware; and in our gardens bloom numberless welcome migrants from the 'Flowery Land', a title by which China is known in her own literature.

Chinese scholars and philosophers have contributed to knowledge for nearly three thousand years, and many of the world's finest treasures of art come from China, including bronze-ware, paintings, ceramics and calligraphy.

The land

The China that we know today is geographically one of the largest countries of the world, and encompasses one quarter of the world's population; in area it exceeds Europe or the U.S.A. It reaches from the Pacific in the Far East to the Pamir mountains in central Asia; from the Amur and Ussuri rivers in the north-east to the Gulf of Tonking in the south. The Chinese earth provides a diversity of products and conceals important untapped resources, especially of mineral wealth. There are oil reserves in the north-west, many iron fields, abundant coal, besides gold, platinum, uranium and other minerals. This vast and variegated area, a subcontinent, has frequently in its history had periods of disunity, when feudal princes or warlords have ruled over separate regions. The periods of partition have, however, always been resolved by eventual reunification.

Although part of one of the earth's great land masses, the Eurasian continent, China is detached by immense physical features. To the north, the Gobi desert and the Mongolian plateau separate her from Siberia. To the south and west, the Tibetan plateau is bounded by the ice-peaks of the Himalayas; in the south-east are forested mountain spurs and jungle; off her shores, the South and East China Seas are sheltered by a bow of islands beyond which is the widest stretch of the Pacific Ocean. For a score of centuries China's main communication with the outer world was through the north-western corridor,

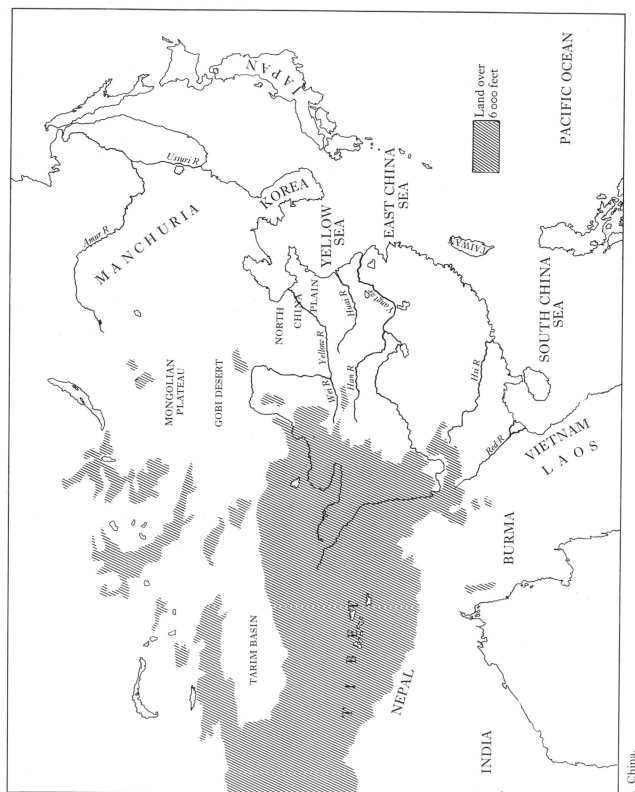

PACIFIC OCEAN

Land over
6 000 feet

MANCHURIA

Amur R

Ussuri R

JAPAN

KOREA

YELLOW
SEA

EAST CHINA
SEA

TAIWAN

NORTH
CHINA
PLAIN

Yellow R

Huai R

Yangtze

Wei R

Han R

SOUTH CHINA
SEA

Hsi R

MONGOLIAN
PLATEAU

GOBI DESERT

Red R

VIETNAM

L A O S

BURMA

TARIM BASIN

T I B E T

NEPAL

INDIA

1. China.

along the string of oases that skirted the Gobi desert and the Tarim basin and led on through central Asia to the Middle East. The relative isolation of China has been a significant factor in Chinese history; it ended only in the nineteenth century. In many ways the Chinese outlook has differed from that of other people, if not in fundamentals, at least in orientation, like their compass.

In the hinterland the deserts and mountains form an infertile, sparsely populated arc surrounding the coastal plains to the northeast, along the lower reaches of the Yellow and Yangtze rivers. Like most of China's rivers, these two majestic waters flow from west to east, cutting their way at times through deep gorges, and silting up before emptying into the sea. In the Yellow River this has caused frequent devastating floods and sometimes changes of course, so that the river has earned the title of 'China's Sorrow'. The basin of the Yellow River—the north China plain, is a fertile area with rich, easily worked soil, favourable for agriculture. This was the cradle of ancient Chinese culture; from here the Chinese spread south, to the Yangtze and beyond, absorbing other settlements. Over the centuries Chinese people and culture reached the jungles of Burma and Indo-China, and to the edges of the deserts of Mongolia and central Asia.

Rainfall in the north is irregular and comes in the right quantities only once every three or four years. Usually there is insufficiency or excess. Development in this region has therefore depended, from earliest times, upon large-scale water control projects; the success or failure of such measures has had profound influence on the social and political history of China. Because of her dependence on great centrally organised irrigation works, China has been described as a 'hydraulic society'.

To the north and west are steppelands, which gave rise to pastoral peoples, whose flocks could be maintained by moving seasonally to new pastures. In these sparsely peopled grasslands aggressive mounted nomads developed an extensive, mobile economy, in contrast to the plains and river valleys, where dense populations of settled people, spreading out from the Yellow River valley, lived by intensive agriculture, farming small plots as minutely as market gardens.

Between the Yellow River and the Yangtze is an area which separates the north, a region of dry farming, producing millet, wheat and maize as its staple crops, from the south. In the south the high rainfall produces multiple crops, with rice predominating; the terraced hillsides produce tea, and mulberry trees support the production of silk. During several periods of China's history, there has also been a political division between these regions.

Except in the north-west where there are grasslands, animal husbandry plays today an insignificant part in Chinese agriculture, for the land cannot be spared to produce fodder. The animals that are maintained—some oxen in the north and water buffalo in the south—

Reconstructed Skull of Peking Man (actually a woman's skull) from Choukoutien.

are used as plough beasts. The pig, which forages for itself, is the only animal contributing to the Chinese diet, which is mainly vegetarian.

Throughout the centuries Chinese peasant families have struggled for survival at subsistence level, on morsels of land too meagre to sustain the burden of population. The majority of the Chinese land is mountainous or semidesert; one-tenth only is cultivated, and it is here that the population is massed. The rest of the country has a sparse population.

Prehistory

About a million years ago, when northern Europe, Asia and America entered the first glacial stage, man is believed to have evolved from the ape somewhere in Afro-Asia. China is one possible cradle of mankind. The fossil remains of the Giant Ape (Gigantopithecus), one of the nearest cousins of early man, were discovered in Kwangsi province in 1956. The fossil skull of another type of ape man, who also lived in China, was unearthed at Lantian in 1964. The Lantian ape man is now regarded as the earliest human in China; he and his fellows lived about 600,000 years ago and they were amongst the first of our species to make tools.

Some remarkable and famous remains were also found at Choukoutien, a site south-west of Peking. Man's early ancestors lived here half a million years ago. These discoveries were important because they included the bones of forty-five men, women and children, and because tools were also found on the site, providing evidence about the lives of such people. We call this type *Sinanthropus pekinensis*—Peking Man. He was apelike in appearance, but he used his hands for manipulation; he had the rudiments of speech. Peking Man belonged to the Old Stone Age; he made rough stone tools by flaking flints, and clubs from branches broken from trees. Hillside caves near streams provided him with shelter. This primitive man also knew the use of fire, which was probably first obtained from natural forest fires. Another fossil skullcap of Peking Man was unearthed at Choukoutien in 1967.

Upper Cave Man was a more advanced creature, and he also inhabited Choukoutien. His stone tools had sharp blades made by an improved method of flaking; he used bone needles to sew hides for clothing. He lived chiefly by hunting and fishing, but also gathered edible roots and fruits. He could make fire by artificial means. These people probably lived about 50,000 years ago.

By about the fourth or third millennium BC, in the Neolithic Age, the ancient Chinese had learnt how to grind and polish a sharp cutting edge to their stone tools. Remains of later Neolithic people have been found in numerous sites widely scattered over China. They made needles, sickles and saws from antlers and shells. Some implements were pierced with holes, so that they could be tied together,

or so that handles could be attached. Gathering and hunting continued to be the main source of food, and bows and arrows were used as the chief hunting weapons.

Agriculture began at this stage in the middle and upper reaches of the Yellow and Yangtze Rivers; the ancient Chinese began to cultivate cereals, especially millet, and to form settlements. There is evidence of numerous villages in the North China plains inhabited by people with agricultural as well as pastoral economy; they made pit dwellings, beehive shaped huts, lined with mud blocks and roofed with reeds, half sunk into the ground for warmth.

North China was warmer in ancient times than it is today. Woolly mammoths and wild horses roamed the plains, bears and tigers lived in the hills. The domestication of animals and animal husbandry began during the Neolithic period. Animals were sometimes caught alive in hunting, and some of them would be killed immediately for food. Gradually prehistoric man learned to tend the others, and the domestication began of such creatures as dogs and pigs, and later sheep, cattle, horses and chickens.

The area of the Great Bend of the Yellow River (Huang Ho) was an important centre of Neolithic culture. Here the fertile loess soil could be worked with primitive tools, to support a substantial population. The men of this period also developed the art of making pottery for storing food and drink. Many examples of red clay pots, painted with black or purple lines, and some bowls, have been found, the most famous site being that of Yangshao. In the north China plains some very fine and smooth black pottery was made on the potter's wheel.

According to Chinese historians land and livestock were owned collectively at this period, weapons only were individually owned; farming and herding were collective activities, and the products were shared among all. There is evidence that early Chinese society was matriarchal, or at least matrilineal; for example, the Chinese character for 'surname' includes the symbol for a female.

Floor of Neolithic hut excavated at Panpo, Shensi province, evidence of the Neolithic culture flourishing in the Yellow River valley.

Neolithic basin decorated with painted fish and human face. Discovered near Sian.

The people lived in clans; neighbouring clans formed tribes which were led by elected tribal chiefs. Tribes formed alliances to guard their grazing and hunting grounds from attacks by hostile neighbours.

Legend has it that about 2000 BC one such tribal alliance had a chieftain known as Huang Ti (Yellow Emperor), one of the most powerful leaders in the Yellow River area. He was their earliest ruler, according to the ancient Chinese records. This was the period of transition from the Neolithic to the Bronze Age, when metal tools began to replace stone implements. Stock-breeding and farming were well established by this time; dams and irrigation canals were used to control the waters of the rivers and to aid cultivation. Other developments of these times included the invention of silk culture and weaving, the building of houses with timber, the construction of carriages and boats, and the written language.

As a result of the increased production of goods and the use of bronze weapons, powerful families arose and formed a ruling dynasty. The earliest of these dynasties was known as the Hsia. According to poetic tradition, the Hsia dynasty was founded by the great Yu, a possibly mythical ruler and patron of agriculture, who early in the second millennium BC pacified the floods and conserved the waters in the Yellow River valley. Yu struggled against many monsters and evil spirits who obstructed him, mobilising numbers of people to take part in the work. He raised barriers against the advance of floods and cut channels to drain off the excess waters. Legend says that Yu himself worked so tirelessly that for thirteen years he did not once enter his own home, although he is supposed on three occasions to have passed his door and heard the cries of his children. In these times the clan organisation was breaking up and being replaced by a central government. The Hsia dynasty was the earliest in China to use slaves, taken captive from enemy tribes.

Some time in the sixteenth century BC the Hsia was defeated by a neighbouring tribe called the Shang; they established control over the middle and lower territories of the Yellow River and founded the Shang dynasty.

Shang, *c.* sixteenth to eleventh century BC

Many of the legends about this period have been shown to be based on fact by archaeological finds made in recent times at the site of Anyang, a later Shang capital.

The Shang were a mainly agricultural people; they used hoes to till the soil, and they dug ditches for irrigation. Millet, rice and wheat were among their crops. Wheeled vehicles became common, and horses were used in harness, especially for war chariots and royal carts. Cloth was made from both silk and flax.

The most significant changes which took place were connected with the use of bronze (copper alloyed with 10 to 20 per cent tin). It was used to make spears, arrows, needles, knives and sacrificial vessels. These tools made possible a specialisation of skills; there was a greater division of labour, and handicrafts and trade were differentiated. A surplus of wealth was produced over and above immediate needs. This encouraged the development of exchange and trade and made possible the establishment of urban communities. Cowrie shells were used as a medium of exchange. Towns grew up where the craftsmen congregated in different quarters. Workshops of various kinds have been excavated, including one for bone implements; half the raw materials discovered there turned out to be human thigh bones; the remainder came from pigs, oxen, and deer.

Shang craftsmen have a special place in world art history; their huge bronze decorated ritual vessels, wine cups and weapons are of a standard of skill and artistry that have not been surpassed. Many Shang bronzes bear inscriptions which shed light on their society.

Slaves were widely used in production. They built great palaces for the kings, but the simple people lived, as in Neolithic times, in crude pit dwellings. The kings offered up sacrifices—human as well as animal—to their ancestors. When kings were buried, their vast tombs were filled with articles and individuals considered necessary for their well-being in the next world: excavations have revealed the remains of chariots with the skeletons of charioteers, hundreds of items in gold, jade, bronze and stone, as well as the skeletons of numerous slaves. In some cases slaves appear to have been buried alive, as in the mausoleum of an aristocratic family unearthed in Anyang County, where seventy living people were buried with the dead. In other cases headless skeletons have been found in sets of ten. The heads, also in decimal sets, have been discovered elsewhere. Living slaves were often tethered at the neck to prevent flight from their work; their hands were chained at night.

Remains of Shang city walls have been uncovered; they were made of beaten earth, and measured up to fifty-five feet thick at the base. The Shang made books of bamboo strips and wooden tablets; they also began to use a brush as well as a sharp instrument for writing. Their written language had already developed several thousand characters or ideographs closely related to the Chinese language of today. The language started with pictographs, or simplified drawings; gradually these became stylised symbols. Chinese writing usually ran from top to bottom. The writing is not phonetic and therefore does not change with dialect; the written language remained basically constant throughout the land of China, even where local spoken dialects developed wide variations. This is undoubtedly one of the factors contributing to the cultural homogeneity of the Chinese people.

The origin of the Chinese script was in divination. All important matters were decided by oracles. Flat bones like the shoulder-blades

Bronze vessel of Shang period. Tripod vessels originated in the late Neolithic period and were popular in Shang times. Such vessels were used for ritual purposes: others were cooking vessels for sacrificial food. They ranged from cups and goblets which could be held in the hand, to gigantic cauldrons weighing half a ton. Shang bronzes were remarkable for their powerful and elegant design.

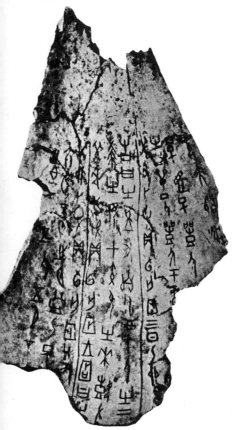

Oracle Bone (Shang period). The inscription on the left of the three panels has been interpreted 'On the day . . . a great and violent wind, and the moon was eclipsed . . . five men . . .'

of mammals, tortoise-shell or turtle shells, had questions scratched on them in the form of pictorial symbols. Such questions were about crops, the weather (was it a propitious time for sowing, or for gathering the harvest?), about sacrifices to be offered to ancestors, questions about health, setting out on journeys, hunting expeditions, about tactics to be used in war, or whether the following week (which in Shang times was a ten day period) would be a lucky one. When heated, a pattern of further cracks appeared on the bones or shells, which were interpreted as the answer of the god or ancestor. The king would undertake nothing unless the oracle had been consulted.

So-called 'dragon-bones' were sold in Peking markets up to modern times. They were ground up for medicinal use. At the end of the last century it was found that these bones came from a site near Anyang, a Shang capital, where one pit alone yielded nearly 18,000 specimens bearing inscriptions: they were in fact Shang 'oracle-bones'. The evidence of these rich finds, when deciphered, confirmed much that was previously held to be legend about the Shang, at least as far back as about 1400 BC. With the Shang dynasty therefore we enter historical times.

In the eleventh century BC, frequent wars enfeebled the Shang. The oppression of the rulers drove the slaves to revolt. When the vassal tribe of Chou under King Wu attacked the Shang, many slaves in the Shang army deserted to the attackers. Old records tell us that King Wu led his men and chariots against the Shang. 'The King of Shang had a million picked troops in formation outside the city; they came as fast as the wind with a noise like thunder, and King Wu's men were afraid. Then King Wu ordered the Patriarch to wave his white banner at the enemy, and the army of Shang fled.'

White banner or not, the Shang capital was assaulted and taken, and the Shang king ended his life in the flames that destroyed his palace.

2. Western Chou

c. Eleventh century to 770 BC

The Chou came from the west of the great bend of the Yellow River. They were culturally less advanced than the Shang; they started as illiterate people but took over many features of the earlier regime, including the form of agriculture, the mastery of bronze, and the system of writing. Their rule continued for some nine centuries, during which time great advances were made. The early part of the Chou era is known as the Western Chou, because of the situation of the capital at Hao, south-west of modern Sian.

The Chou king distributed provinces as fiefs (feudal estates) to the royal princes. These became his vassals and were in duty bound to protect the court and to contribute troops to the king's army in time of war. The vassals (feudal lords) were expected to pay a regular tribute of valuables and local products to the king's treasury; they were required to visit the capital and to reside there for stated periods. They owed the king not only tribute but homage, which had to be rendered at a strict ceremonial which emphasised their inferior position. The king alone had the right to invest a feudal lord with his fief, or to deprive him of it. Within their own states however the royal kinsmen were practically independent.

The Son of Heaven

The Chou king was the sole source of authority. He was believed to be descended from an agricultural deity, the 'Millet Ruler', and was regarded as a deputy of divine authority. He had both the title and the functions, of the 'Son of Heaven'. He alone had the power effectively to perform the ceremonies, and offer the sacrifices, which would secure the harmonious functioning of the seasons and thus abundant harvests. The chief ceremonies centred on the sacrifices to Heaven and to Earth. A round altar of Heaven, with temples, and a square altar of Earth, still stand in Peking today.

Altar of Heaven (Peking). Sacrifices by the Emperor, the Son of Heaven, were made annually to ensure good harvests; the cult continued down to the beginning of the twentieth century. This altar was constructed in the Ming period, and is today part of a public park.

One of the most important of the King's duties occurred on New Year's Day which, according to the Chinese lunar calendar, fell early in February, the beginning of spring in the Yellow River valley. The Son of Heaven on this occasion ploughed a ceremonial furrow in the precincts of the Temple, besides offering up a sacrifice.

As a king-priest, with the unique power to propitiate the forces of nature, the Son of Heaven was expected to be virtuous and disciplined in order to justify the authority which Heaven reposed in him. His example and precept were expected to ensure conformity and support from his subjects. From his moral example social blessings derived. Calamities, for which he was also held responsible, reflected on his virtue. In Chou times the idea developed that an evil ruler would lose the mandate of Heaven. The overthrow of the earlier Shang rulers was thus explained: Heaven had withdrawn its mandate from them because they had forsaken virtue; the Chou on the other hand succeeded because their virtue had secured them the mandate. (The collapse of dynasties has traditionally been ascribed to the depravity of their later members.) This convenient theory, whereby the successful rebel could presume virtue and divine patronage, meant also that the unsuccessful rebels were condemned as villains and bandits. The proof of Heavenly patronage in ancient China lay in success. A Chinese proverb says:

He who succeeds becomes Emperor;
He who fails is a bandit.

The hereditary nobility provided the counsellors, ministers and governors in times of peace, and generals in time of war. They fought in war chariots which were mounted by three men—a charioteer, the lord in the middle, and a 'righthand' man. Ordinary soldiers fought on foot around their lord's chariot. The nobles alone were educated, at least in the earlier days of Chou. Their education consisted of archery, in which contests were conducted with much ceremony; in music, poetry, arithmetic, and above all in ritual. They were taught the strict fulfilment of the ceremonial behaviour considered proper to the social status of a noble.

In ancient China the nobility practised the cult of ancestor worship. Aristocrats believed that they possessed two souls: an animal soul created at the moment of conception, which decayed with the body after death and then sank into a shadowy existence in the underworld —the Yellow Springs, and a higher soul or spirit, formed at the moment of birth, which at death ascended to the palace of the heavenly king, Shang Ti, to dwell as a subject at his court, where it supervised the destiny of descendants. This spirit, once established in Heaven, drew sustenance from the sacrifices offered in the ancestral temple, and became an influential deity, protecting the lives of living descendants in proportion to the satisfaction received from sacrifices.

This spirit could be invoked by divination to answer questions, and could intercede even in matters of life and death. Ancestral sacrifices could be offered up only by male descendants. Few greater calamities could beset the family of the noble than to have no male to continue the ancestral worship.

A poem of this period talks about the 'mighty store of blessings' which the well-sated ancestral spirit of an aristocrat could be expected to confer on its descendants:

Dynastic Hymn (from the Book of Songs)
Gifts . . .
To their shining ancestors,
Piously, making offering,
That they might be vouchsafed long life,
Everlastingly be guarded.
O, a mighty store of blessings!
Glorious and mighty, these former princes and lords
Who secure us with many blessings,
Through whose bright splendours
We greatly prosper.

The animal spirit also needed cherishing. It remained placid if the offerings of survivors at the tomb were generous. If the offerings were inadequate, the animal spirit returned as a ghost, a famished and malevolent spirit, to wreak its spite on human beings.

The ordinary people, the peasants, who were outside the clan system, had neither surnames nor ancestors to worship. Many deities were worshipped in ancient China, beside Heaven and Earth, and in this worship the common people shared. The spirits of the rivers and mountains, the spirit of the Wayside, the Rain God, the Lord of Thunder, the sun, the stars, the God of the Wind, the Count of the Yellow River, and other local features, were the objects of veneration. Each village had its own local god of the soil, each family its household gods.

Associated with ancestor worship was the very great attention which was paid to funeral and mourning rituals. Neglect of mourning rites for parents was a most serious offence. The long mourning period for parents – up to three years in some stages of Chinese history – involved a degree of withdrawal from public life as well as such matters as the wearing of coarse garments.

The final resting place of the deceased was held to be of great consequence for the descendants. Necromancers were employed to indicate not only auspicious times for burial but also to verify the suitability of the selected spot from the point of view of the local spirits of earth, wind and water. Punctiliousness in these matters would bring both peace to the departed and prosperity to the survivors. As time went on clan or surnames became general, and ancestor worship spread to humbler folk.

The Chinese have an earthy approach to manifestations which elsewhere have been regarded as supernatural. Ghosts as well as gods have many carnal traits. Traditional stories tell of 'A Cartload of Ghosts', and about a 'Man Who Sold a Ghost'. Gods and devils were humoured like spoilt children. The Chinese reach a high level of rationality when dealing with ghosts and monsters. There is a story about an artist of the Chou period who worked for a prince. He told the prince that the hardest things to paint were dogs, horses and the like, while ghosts and monsters were the easiest. 'We all know dogs and horses and see them every day; but it is hard to make an exact likeness of them. Ghosts and monsters have no definite form, and no one has ever seen them; so they are easy to paint.' The Chinese also learnt to live with their monsters on the basis of mutual toleration. China bred a more domesticated species of dragon than the carnivores of the west, much given to munching maidens. The Chinese dragon came to represent the strength and fertile beneficence of rain, and signified the water god. The dragon early became the emblem of the Son of Heaven himself; his throne was the 'dragon-throne'; no one else was entitled to use the dragon symbol. The empress was represented by the phoenix.

In ancient China survival or ruin depended primarily on the vagaries of nature, and early cults were concerned with achieving a propitious balance of the elements. The balance of nature was formulated in the doctrine of Yin and Yang, the negative and the positive, opposed but complementary and mutually dependent forces: female and male, darkness and light, moon and sun, earth and heaven, the dual forces controlling the universe. In Western Chou times, a court historian also taught that the world was made of five fundamental elements: metal, wood, water, fire and earth. A theory of the 'five elements' in nature arose from this, closely associated with the Yin/Yang doctrine.

The majority of the population in early Chou times tilled the soil and were slaves, or small farmers called commoners whose position was not far from that of slaves. They were obliged to labour on their lord's land and to pay him dues. Slaves could be sold or killed by their owners; one name for slaves in Chinese literally meant 'animal people', and they were thus treated. A proclamation surviving from Chou days classifies runaway servants with stray cattle. From a bronze inscription we learn that five slaves could be exchanged for one horse plus a hank of silk. Kings used to present their sons and ministers with lands together with the slaves working on them. They often commemorated these occasions by casting special plates and vessels on which the gift was recorded. Written accounts towards the end of the first millennium BC give details of hundreds of slaves being awarded to important officials or transferred from one to another. Lu Pu Wei of Shu, it is recorded, owned some ten thousand slaves. Towns were full

Slave traffic is recorded in this inscription on a bronze vessel of the time of King Hsiao of Chou. This reads in part: 'I am exchanging five of your slaves for a horse and a hank of silk.'

of slaves who were handicraft workers. Slaves built palaces, defence and flood control works, as well as the towns themselves.

The Chou, who were a settled agricultural people, grew wheat, maize, rice, sorghum, beans, and many other foods; fruit and other trees formed the boundaries of their plots of land. Men also hunted for food. The women looked after the silkworms, and did the weaving.

The use of bronze, which had been learnt from the Shang, reached its highest development in the Western Chou period. There are many remarkable archaeological finds dating from this time.

During the first millennium BC more intensive agriculture and stock breeding supported the rise of urban life. A divergent trend

Remains of chariot and horses found in the tomb of a nobleman, probably of Crown Prince Yuan Tu of the state of Kuo.

This drawing shows reconstruction of original appearance of the chariot, three metres long, and equipped with bronze parts. Note the 'throat and girth' harness used in ancient times in both east and west, which half choked the horse.

took place in the steppelands of the north, where the arid soil could not raise crops. In these regions stockbreeding in due course gave rise to an alternative mode of life, that of the pastoral nomad, who moved with his herds from summer to winter pastures, and who was in the short term self-sufficient. When the pastoral nomads became mounted herdsmen, equipped also with wagons, they became a serious threat to their settled neighbours in the south. Conflict between the peoples of the steppe and those of the sown lands has been a feature of Chinese history for a score of centuries. These northerners, who were culturally less advanced, were regarded by the southern Chinese as barbarians; this was a term which was applied also to all other peoples, of non-Chinese culture, whether on the Chinese borderlands or not, up to the present century.

In the eighth century BC, the Chou kingdom, weakened by internal dissension, was attacked by the Jung nomads. The records say with distaste that they grew their hair long, wore their clothes buttoned on the left side, and consumed mainly milk and meat. Other barbaric features noted were their red hair and green eyes. In 770 BC the Chou capital, Hao, was invaded and occupied by these barbarians in alliance with some rebel Chinese states, and the king was killed. His successor, King Ping, was obliged to move the capital, which was established farther east at Loyang.

3. Eastern Chou

770–221 BC

This era is traditionally divided into the 'Spring and Autumn' period, so named because of the history of the time called *Spring and Autumn Annals*, a work credited to Confucius, and the 'Warring States' period, because of the internal conflicts then raging.

Spring and Autumn Period, 770 to 476 BC

At this time the people of Chinese culture inhabited a number of states great and small, centring on the great bend of the Yellow River, (Shansi). Beyond were the peoples regarded more or less as barbarian. This concept of the Chinese core of the civilised world, has been a feature of Chinese political outlook up to the present. The Chinese very early began to call their country Chung Kuo, or the 'Middle Kingdom', the name still used today.

In the Spring and Autumn period iron replaced bronze, a near monopoly of the aristocrats, for implements and weapons. Iron was superior for making hoes, ploughs and axes. It was easier to work, and more plentiful. The use of iron tools stimulated agricultural production and the opening up of new arable land. The iron plough, drawn by oxen, permitted deeper ploughing; wasteland could be more effectively cleared, trees felled and wild beasts driven off. Agricultural production increased.

Some of the slave tillers broke away from their masters, claimed land for themselves and secured their independence. Peasant farmers who were tenants of landlords took the place of slaves.

During the centuries following the removal of the capital to Lo-yang, the vassal states grew richer and stronger, and the princes contended amongst themselves for domination; dozens of independent kingdoms emerged and the power of Chou as the common liege was increasingly challenged.

The Philosophers

Amongst the notable changes of these times was the development of a new social group, the scholars, who later became very important. The priests who had served under the Shang became superfluous in Chou times when the Son of Heaven performed the most important religious ceremonies, and when ancestor worship depended on the surviving males and not on the priest. The priests were people who could read and write. They could serve the local princes not only as scribes but could instruct them in the correct performance of ceremonies of state as well as of religion. With the decline in the authority of the Chou king, ambitious feudal princes were anxious to attract

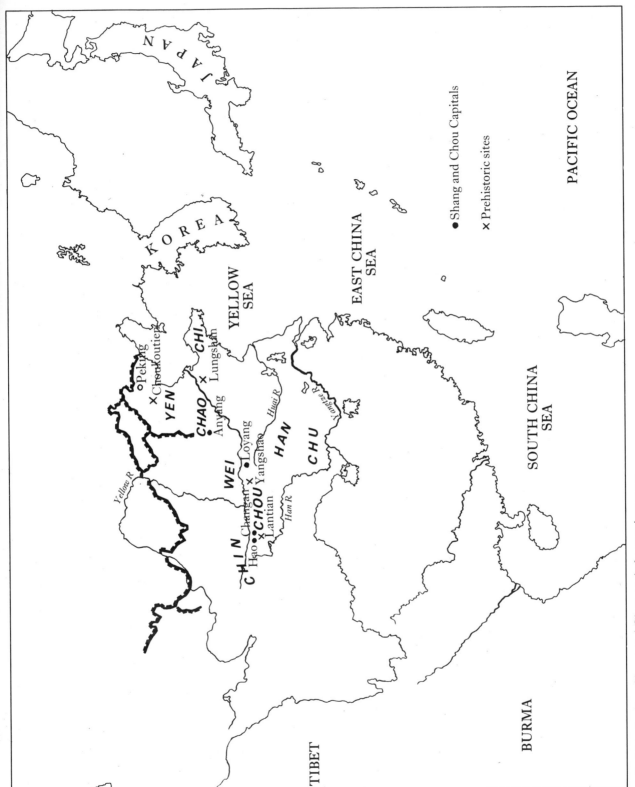

2. Prehistoric sites, Shang and Chou capitals, warring states.

such scholars, employing them as tutors for their children, entrusting them with affairs of state and the conduct of ceremonies, and benefiting from their expertise in ritual and etiquette.

The early academies of scholars go back to Chou times. The most famous was the Academy of the Gate of Chi; in the fourth century BC the king of Chi set up a magnificent building to attract scholars for lectures and discussions. Here sages from other states as well as from Chi were welcomed; they were provided with quarters and maintenance, and sometimes given official positions. This Academy later assembled some of the most outstanding scholars of the age, including Confucius. The nobility and priests lost the monopoly of education, as the poorer ones amongst them brought it to other groups. From these developed the *shih* or literati, the mandarins, of later days.

These *shih* belonged to times of great social change and conflict between the states. They inherited traditions from a past already rich in social and political experience, but were themselves faced with the disorders and disintegration of old institutions and authority.

The *shih*, professional officials, forerunners of Chinese bureacracy, wandered from state to state offering their services to the princes. Sometimes they were well received, for the rulers were anxious to add lustre to their own courts even if they were reluctant to act on the advice given to them.

Confucius

One such wanderer was a scholar from a declining aristocratic family from the state of Lu. He is known in China by his title of honour, 'Master' Kung—Kung Fu Tsu, from which the western version, Confucius is derived. For a short period he was an official in government service in charge of granaries, then of public pasturelands. But the state of Lu, like its neighbours, was torn with political dissension, and Confucius resigned his position. He spent most of his life wandering from state to state seeking in vain a ruler who would put his principles into practice. He went north to Chi, where he was well received by the king; but though he remained there several years he never received an official appointment.

Confucius (551–479 BC) attracted a number of pupils or disciples, many of whom accompanied him on his journeys. Tradition says there were three thousand of them. Confucius instructed them in six arts: rites, music, archery, chariot-driving, writing and mathematics. He taught modesty and persistence in learning. He himself was prepared to teach, and to learn from, anyone. He told his disciples: 'To learn and at due times to repeat what one has learnt, is not that after all a pleasure?' And also: 'He who learns but does not think, is lost. He who thinks but does not learn is in great danger.'

Confucius was the founder of a school of thought which triumphed over others in the later centuries and became official doctrine. He

Confucius, 551–479 BC. Traditional presentation.

Dissatisfied with state affairs, Confucius devotes himself to teaching. Stone engraving, Ming period.

built up a body of teaching based on tradition which was set down in writing by his disciples in a work known as the *Analects* – or Select Sayings – of Confucius. His point of view was not original; it was the outlook typical of the feudal times of Chou. He deplored the disorder and unrest which rent society of his day and he idealised the early Chou times which he sought to restore, believing them to be times of order and prosperity, when each man knew his place in the unified kingdom of the Son of Heaven. Confucius looked back with respect to the cult of Heaven and ancestor worship, to old standards and traditions. The myth of this golden age in China's past coloured the ideology of reformers and rebels down to the nineteenth century.

Confucius was mainly concerned with social relations, with the orderly conduct of human affairs, not with speculation about supernatural being or an afterlife. He emphasised the duties to the living rather than to the dead, advocating the doctrine of benevolence or love of one's fellow men. He taught: 'Do not do to others what you could not want done to yourself', and 'Achieve for others what you want to achieve for yourself'. Another aspect of this teaching was the emphasis on strict rules of behaviour. Confucius held that social harmony could be achieved by observances which governed the relationships of people in different strata of society. Particularly important were the rules relating to the behaviour of inferiors to superiors. Accepting the current patriarchal view of the family, considered the main pillar of society, Confucius urged the observance of family ties in a hierarchy of unconditional obedience: son to father; younger to elder brother; wife to husband. The relation of subject to ruler was that of son to father – absolute obedience, just as the ruler, the Son of Heaven, owed obedience to Heaven. Friends were bound, like brothers, by obligations, the younger to the older.

Family bonds and social order have been reinforced in China since ancient times by various systems of collective responsibility, whereby the family was held responsible for crimes committed by any individual member. Similarly, the crimes of families were visited upon neighbouring households in the community.

Women enjoyed but a meagre share of the recommended Confucian benevolence. The traditional Chinese family, which sustained the individual in times of social distress and personal disaster and suffered vicarious punishment on his account, consisted of grandparents, parents, grandchildren and servants. In this extended family of three generations, authority resided with the aged, and with the menfolk. Sons had equal rights in the inheritance of property. Marriage was a matter of family arrangement, not of individual love. Its purpose was the survival of the family, the continuation of the family name. People of the same clan or surname did not intermarry. On marriage the young wife left her own kin and lived with her husband and parents-in-law, to whom she was bound even in the case of the premature death of her husband. The Book of Songs gives an indication of the inferior status of women in China since earliest times:

Sons shall be born to him—
They will be put to sleep on couches;
They will be clothed in robes . . .

Daughters shall be born to him
They will be put to sleep on the ground
They will be clothed with wrappers.

And:

A clever man builds a city
A clever woman lays one low . . .
For disorder does not come from heaven,
But is brought about by women.

Folk wisdom however challenged the social arrogance of the male, for an ancient Chinese proverb says: 'Man thinks he knows, but a woman knows better'.

The ordered relationship of filial piety found expression in the rites or etiquette prescribed for every situation, including the decorum appropriate for such occasions as birth, marriage, death. These observances, which may strike us as empty formalities, appeared significant and valuable in times when social relationships were dissolving and when established authority was being challenged at all levels of society, from that of the slave to the Son of Heaven himself. In particular Confucius defined the behaviour proper to the 'gentleman' of his day. In Chapter 10 of the *Analects*, a section which some people regard as a description of the everyday life of the Sage himself, it says:

A gentleman does not wear facings of purple or mauve, nor in undress does he use pink or purple. In hot weather he wears an unlined gown of fine thread loosely woven, but puts on an outside garment before going out of doors. With a black robe he wears black lambskin; with a robe of undyed silk, fawn. With a yellow robe, fox fur. On his undress robe the fur cuffs are long; but the right is shorter than the left. His bedclothes must be half as long again as a man's height. . . . Apart from his court apron, all his skirts are wider at the bottom than at the waist . . .

He must not sit on a mat that is not straight . . .

There was a special emphasis on deference and its formal expression:

On entering the Palace Gate he seems to shrink into himself, as though there were not room . . . a look of confusion comes over his face, his legs seem to give way under him, and words seem to fail him. While holding up the hem of his skirt, he ascends the Audience Hall, he seems to double up and keeps in his breath. . . . On coming out after his expression relaxes into one of satisfaction and relief.

The Confucian 'vocabulary' of social attitudes includes a wide range of ceremonial 'shrinking', kowtowing, making oneself small in the presence of a superior. We ourselves observe such forms as bowing, nodding and kneeling. Music as well as ritual was favoured as a harmoniser of social relations.

Confucius asserted that a 'gentleman' need not necessarily be a person of good birth, but one whose conduct was noble, unselfish, just and considerate. No man could be considered a gentleman on grounds of birth alone, it was a matter of conduct and character. Speaking of the parasitic nobles of his time he said: 'It is difficult to expect anything from men who stuff themselves with food the whole day, while never using their minds in any way at all. Even gamblers do something, and to that degree are better than these idlers.'

Confucius has been described as 'a private person who trained the sons of gentlemen in the virtues proper to a member of the ruling class . . . his task, like that of the English trainer of gentlemen's sons in the Public Schools, was not so much to impart knowledge as to inculcate moral principles, form character, hand down unaltered and intact a great tradition from the past'. In addition Confucius was the first person in China to extend education beyond the ranks of the aristocracy. He accepted pupils regardless of class. Men of humble origin became his students. He taught them all court etiquette–the ritual that was first used in sacrifices and then extended to cover every sort of ceremony. This ritual he held to be necessary for men as social beings. It disciplined the emotions and strengthened the character, imposed controlled reactions and was conducive to social stability.

A special feature of the doctrine was its extension to rulers, who were exhorted to consider the welfare of their people and to refrain from exploitation. Good government was that which kept men happy. The ruler, like Heaven, should set an example to the people. 'The Master said: Govern the people by regulations, keep order among them by chastisements and they will flee from you, and lose all self-respect. Govern them by moral force, keep order among them by ritual and they will keep their self-respect and come to you of their own accord.' Confucius asserted that the title to rule depended not on birth but on character, ability and education. 'Employ the able;

The main hall, today, of the Confucius Temple in Chufu, Shantung province, formerly the state of Lu, home of the sage. The temple was built by the site of Confucius's home, a few years, it is said, after his death, and reconstructed in the eleventh century AD. The hall is notable for the stone carving of the dragon pillars in front.

A short distance outside Chufu are the woods where lies the tomb of Confucius.

promote the worthy' was the Confucian maxim urged upon successive generations of Chinese rulers.

According to tradition Confucius spent the last years of his life editing and compiling books which came to be known as the Classics. Much of the material in these works was old in his time, and it is not possible to say how much they owe to the Master himself. These classics include *The Book of Songs*, a collection of over three hundred poems composed during the Chou period; the poems frequently give vivid accounts of the everyday life of the people. One describes the life of a serf during the autumn and winter in the Yellow River valley some three thousand years ago:

In the ninth month we make ready the stackyards,
In the tenth month we bring in the harvest,
Millet for wine, millet for cooking, the early and the late,
Paddy and hemp, beans and wheat.
Come my husbandmen,
My harvesting is over,

In the morning gather thatch-reeds,
In the evening twist rope;
Go quickly onto the roofs.
Soon you will be beginning to sow your many grains.

The Book of History is a collection of documents and speeches of the Western Chou period. *The Spring and Autumn Annals*, gives the history mainly of the State of Lu. *The Book of Rites*, is a description of the ceremonies and ritual associated with everyday life in ancient China. *The Book of Changes* is a manual of divination; it refers to hunting and fishing, agriculture, husbandry, war, marriage, food, drink and clothing. Another classic, *The Book of Music*, has not survived. These Books, including the *Analects*, were not only read but learnt by heart by scholars in later centuries. Their emphasis on loyalty to authority made a special appeal to rulers, and Confucianism later was adopted as the orthodox doctrine of state.

Master Kung of the state of Lu taught no theology, no story of creation, Heaven or Hell, and if he himself was later deified, he was only so treated in the complimentary, courteous and largely poetic way which the Chinese have, says Dr Needham, 'of dealing with notable inventors, virtuous governors and particularly beneficent dragons'.

In his own time his admonitions went largely unheeded. The strife between the states intensified. In 479 BC, the year of his death, the state of Chen was annexed by its neighbour Chu. This heralded the beginning of the period known as the Warring States.

Warring States: 476 to 221 BC

By Confucius's time the Son of Heaven was no more than one prince among many. The king of Chou still used the celestial title, but local

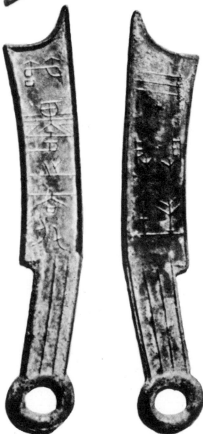

Spade and knife coins of the fourth century BC, excavated in Hsienyang on the north bank of the Wei river.

rulers no longer deferred to him; they sent no tribute, failed to pay homage and ignored the imperial rites. The Son of Heaven had lost his divine mandate. Ambitious local kingdoms, organised for war and aggrandisement, disregarded the ancient moral codes as well as the sufferings of their subjects.

The struggle resulted in the submersion of all the lesser by seven major states – Chi, Chu, Yen, Han, Chao, Wei and Chin. They were engaged in bitter internecine conflict during the Warring States period.

The use of iron became more widespread, to the benefit of agriculture. Ironsmiths using manual blast furnaces made many kinds of farm implements, including ploughshares, hoes, sickles and spades. They also made axes, chisels, saws, and knives, as well as swords, halberds and other weapons. More wasteland was cleared and brought under cultivation, while increased harvests arose from the land already under the plough.

There was a greater surplus of grain available for commerce, and to support urban populations of merchants and craftsmen. Cowrie shells, the earliest 'currency' had long been insufficient to meet the needs of increased trade; people therefore made replicas of them in bone, stone and bronze, in the time of the Western Chou. In the Warring States period the use of metal coinage became common and a money economy developed.

The metal tools which played such an important part in daily life were much sought after and were themselves used as items of barter. Later, small replicas of them were made as tokens of exchange. These developed into the 'spade' and 'knife' coins of which many examples have been discovered. The earliest ones were quite large, about four or five inches long. As they came into wider use smaller ones were made. Later on in the Warring States period round coins were introduced. They were made of cast bronze and had a hole in the middle, so that they might be strung together (usually in strings of a thousand). Chopsticks, another feature of Chinese everyday life, came into use by the end of this period.

Iron tools led not only to developments in agriculture but also to advances in water control. The legend of the Great Yu, who was the first to undertake water conservancy work on a large scale, has been supplemented by many stories of achievements during the Warring States period. The kingdom of Wei, for example, in the Yellow River basin, was troubled by flooding from the mountains after the summer rains. Priests told the people that the river god must be propitiated each year by the sacrifice of a beautiful girl: peasant families had to provide the sacrifice. The chosen girl was elaborately dressed and thrown into the river to drown. As time went on the region became depopulated, because families with adolescent daughters tended to move away. In the fourth century BC a local magistrate opposed this superstition. Instead he drowned the priests, and organised the construction of canals which drew off the surplus waters. This practical engineering proved more effective than maiden-drowning, and the state of Wei greatly benefited. The culture of the Middle Kingdom spread to the Yangtze during this period, bringing its language, its agricultural techniques and irrigation methods.

A similar story comes from the state of Chin, one of the most powerful of the Warring States. The turbulent Min river flooded during the seasonal rains and melting snows of summer. The flooding was attributed to the malevolence of a monster. Li Ping, governor of the locality, was a scientist with a considerable knowledge of astronomy and geography, as well as of hydraulic engineering. Together with his son he surveyed the river course and found that when the summer torrents from the mountains reached level ground, they slowed up and deposited silt brought down from the hills. This piled up and the banks overflowed. Li Ping explained that it was not a monster but the lie of the land which caused the flooding, and he organised the cutting of canals. His project for rechannelling the waters is said to be functioning to this day.

Irrigation helped to increase the harvest; surpluses were stored in granaries in the walled towns which sprang up to protect the neighbourhood. In earlier times armies had consisted mainly of nobles in war chariots. By this time the crossbow had been invented, which in the hands of archers on horseback meant the end of chariot fighting. Moreover increased grain production could now support troops of infantry, and these were drawn from the rising numbers of peasantry. The northern states of the Middle Kingdom, following the example of their nomadic neighbours, added cavalry to their forces, an advance significant mainly in the state of Chin in north-west China. The introduction of cavalry brought with it a change in Chinese dress, for the former long-skirted garb was not suitable for riding on horseback. Trousers became general.

Some time during the Chou period in China the inefficient throat and girth harness for horses, which half choked the animal, was replaced by a more efficient breast strap harness. This development, which enabled a greater peasant mobility, permitting him to live further from his fields in larger villages or small towns rather than in scattered hamlets, had minor repercussions in China where it first appeared; but in Europe, where it appeared later, it reinforced the tendency to a city-state culture. In China the horse throve only in the grasslands of the north, and was indeed at a disadvantage both for labour and for military purposes in the south, where the water buffalo became the essential plough animal, and where cavalry was impeded by irrigation channels.

Effigy of Li Ping in a temple in Szechuan province. In 250 BC Li Ping, governor of Shu and an outstanding hydraulic engineer, carried out a brilliant project for the control of the waters of the turbulent Min river.

The Hundred Schools of Thought

This period was one not only of constant struggle between the different states, the stronger ones absorbing their weaker neighbours, but was characterised by internal factions. The nobles within the states attempted to usurp the authority of their prince. Centuries of warfare and social upheaval made people ask questions and seek answers. We have seen that the rulers themselves felt the need to patronise scholars and advisers. After Confucius, other schools of philosophy arose; these became known as the 'Hundred Schools of Thought' ('hundred' like the Chinese thousand or ten thousand – is not to be taken literally; the meaning is 'many').

Taoists and others

Some of the schools of thought are associated with the names of individuals who may or may not have had an historic existence. Perhaps the most influential, after the Confucians, were the Taoists. The Taoist Classic – the *Book of Lao Tsu* – is a collection of ideas derived in fact from a number of people, but attributed to a sage Lao Tsu (Old Master) of the Spring and Autumn Period. The Taoists had a mystical view of life, which was the opposite approach to that of the Confucians. They found the man-made world bad, and advocated a renunciation of the world and a return to 'natural' simplicity, to the harmony of nature. Human institutions, human ambition and striving, were evils to be eliminated by passivity. Civilisation was the source of suffering; the 'Tao' – the 'Way' (of nature) – alone could lead man back to tranquillity. They held that those who strove for nothing, could not be disappointed. All things are relative, said the Taoists; it depends on the point of view. Water 'is life to the fish but death to man'. The individual can achieve tranquillity not through man-made society but by fitting into the pattern of nature with its

Lao Tsu and his disciples. Traditional picture by Huang Shao Ming.

mutually balancing forces. The Taoist ideal of harmonious interaction with nature is expressed in the dream of the philosopher Chuang Tsu:

Once I, Chuang Tsu, dreamt of being a butterfly; a butterfly that flitted hither and thither, enjoying itself as it wished. Nor did it know that it was Chuang Tsu. But suddenly, awakening, there, amazingly, it was Chuang Tsu. Now know I not: Is it really Chuang Tsu who was dreaming he was a butterfly? Or is the butterfly dreaming it is Chuang Tsu?

Taoists opposed the Confucian concepts of right and wrong, and the ritual embodying them. Their ideal was a primitive, uncontrolled existence. They taught compassion and humility, the ending of selfish endeavour, and their doctrine of quietism led to withdrawal from society and movements for social reform. Some Taoists became recluses and lived apart from other men, fishing or farming, in communion with nature.

As time went on Taoists became preoccupied with the question of death and the quest for longevity. The search for the elixir of life played a prominent part in their history; it led not only to the development of Taoist alchemy, but to important scientific discoveries.

In addition to the Confucians and the Taoists other schools of thought developed their views of society and the world. The school of Mo Tsu, the Mohists, was one of the oldest of these. Mo Tsu believed in universal love, irrespective of family tie and rank. Everyone should love every other person as much as he loves himself, so that the interests of all would be served. This was clearly opposed to the Confucian code of family priorities. He believed that there should be government by men of ability and virtue, rather than by hereditary rulers. He deplored everything that did not contribute directly to the general well being, and proposed measures to enrich the country in general. The Mohists thought it criminal for some to live in luxury so long as there was insufficient food and clothing for all. Mo Tsu was a practical and austere man, and had no time for ritual or art or any non-utilitarian pleasures.

Two Confucians in the third century BC who succeeded in securing a considerable following for their doctrines were Meng Tsu, known in the west by the Latin form of his name, Mencius, and Hsun Tsu. Mencius held that human nature was essentially good, and that it was evil circumstances that corrupted man's mind and actions. He believed that man's inborn virtue could be cultivated by conscious effort and education. He therefore thought highly of scholars. He held that rulers should attend to the needs of the people if they wished to remain in power, and that government should be in the hands of the men of virtue.

Mencius formulated a view of social hierarchy which dominated the outlook of the Chinese upper class until very recently; according to this view society was composed of two complementary groups – the

Pottery head of singer. Tomb figure from Warring States period.

Pottery horse, representative of the early tomb figures, Warring States period.

superior men, those of the ruling group, and the mean men, those meant to be ruled. He stated that

'some labour with their minds and govern others; some labour with their hands and are governed by others. Those governed by others feed them. Those who govern others, are fed by them. If there were no men of superior grade, there would be no one to rule the countrymen. If there were no countrymen there would be no one to support the men of superior grade.'

The contempt of intellectuals for manual labour increased with the centuries, and is only now being eradicated.

The commoners, the ruled, have since ancient times been divided into different status groups—farmers, artisans, and merchants, in that order. Although manual workers, the farmers were regarded as the foundation of society, and had the highest status amongst the ruled strata. The least respected were the merchants, a non-productive group, regarded as parasitic. Soldiers (in some societies an élite) were so little respected in traditional China that they were outside and below normal society.

Hsun Tsu held a contrary view of human nature to that of Mencius. He believed that man is naturally evil: human emotions and natural desires lead to conflict and are bad. He believed that the observance of ritual helped to curb evil human tendencies; for man is made good only by training; education too is important in helping man to overcome his evil nature.

The nature of man is evil—his goodness is only acquired by training. The original nature of man today is to seek for gain. If this desire is followed, strife and rapacity result and courtesy dies. Man originally is envious and naturally hates others . . . hence the civilising influence of teachers and laws, the guidance of the rites and justice, is absolutely necessary.

Hsun Tsu rejected the idea of supernatural beings; he was a rationalist. He said once of a contemporary superstition: 'Beating a drum to cure rheumatism will wear out the drum, but it will not cure the rheumatism.' He admired strong authoritarian government.

Legalists

The most immediately successful school of thought was that of the Legalists. They too believed that man's nature was essentially evil; they held that people had to be restrained by the powerful laws of society. They preached the need for a strong centralised state with absolute authority and control. They supported policies of repression. They believed in hereditary rulers dedicated to creating a militarily strong and prosperous state. Everyone, they held, should be obliged to do productive work. Merchants and scholars were out of favour with them as they were not producers of wealth. The teaching of music, history and philosophy they condemned as corrupting influences. The Legalists opposed the old nobility that was not based on military achievement. Han Fei Tsu, a prince of the Han state, was leader of this school of thought, and believed that military power and

Pottery roof decoration: dragon head. Warring States period.

productive agriculture were more important for the success of the state than benevolence. A historian a few centuries later wrote that he 'delighted in the study of punishments, names, laws and methods of governing'. (Han Fei Tsu was one of the several Legalists who were killed by the rulers they assisted to power.) In the long term Confucianism and Taoism were the only survivors amongst the rival schools of thought.

The debate between the many schools of thought continued alongside the struggles amongst the nobles and princes and between the different states. The stronger ones, having absorbed their weaker neighbours, declared their own prince supreme and stopped sending tribute to the king of Chou, who, towards the end of this period had no more prestige or authority than a prince of a small realm.

Of the seven states that emerged from this process of elimination and aggrandisement, the state of Chi early became pre-eminent; it was a rich country, on the east coast, with abundant resources of iron, silk, salt and fish.

Rise of Chin state

Another state to consolidate its power was the state of Chin, in the north-west, around the Wei river valley (which had in fact been the centre of the Chou state). Chin had early learned from her northern nomad neighbours how to use cavalry, and had also developed successful irrigation works in the Wei valley. The Chin state built particularly strong political and military power as a result of the measures introduced by Shang Yang, one of the Legalist leaders. In 361 BC, Shang Yang became chief minister to the ruler of Chin. He reduced the powers of the old aristocratic families and encouraged a new military aristocracy. In place of the granting of fiefs, government officials were appointed to administer the new lands won by the state. His measures stimulated agriculture and textile production, but discouraged trade. The whole population was militarised. He decreed that:

the people be organised into groups of families which should be mutually responsible for each other's good behaviour, and share each other's punishments. Anyone who did not denounce a culprit would be cut in two at the waist; anyone who denounced a culprit would receive the same reward as if he had cut off the head of an enemy soldier. . . . A family including two adult males would have to be divided, or pay double taxes.

Military prowess was to be rewarded by the ruler with titles of nobility according to a definite schedule. Members of the ruling family were to be excluded from it if they failed to show military merit. Those who fought each other because of private quarrels would be punished according to the severity of their offence. All, great and small, would be compelled to work in the basic occupations of farming and weaving; those who produced a large quantity of grain or silk would be exempted from forced labour. Those who sought gain from

Wooden figure of a serving-maid, from the tomb of a noble family of the Kingdom of Chu, one of the seven great states of the Warring States period. The huge tomb was airtight and its contents in excellent condition.

Bronze Hu vase, with lotus-petal lid topped with a crane. A food vessel of the Spring and Autumn period.

Chu Yuan, poet and patriotic statesman of Warring States period. A traditional representation by Chen Hung Shou, a Ming artist famous for his woodcuts and paintings of figures.

secondary occupations (trade and crafts), and the lazy and indigent, would be made slaves. Other measures, such as the legalisation of buying and selling of land, removed some of the curbs on economic growth.

After these reforms, the power of the old nobility diminished in favour of a military autocracy. Agricultural production increased; this was also favoured by the extension of irrigation works. Communications improved and revenues increased. Large-scale political as well as social organisation became possible.

The state of Chin increased in power, and its armies seriously threatened the existence of other states. Using diplomatic as well as military tactics, Chin sowed dissension amongst the six others, so that they continued to quarrel amongst themselves instead of allying against their common enemy.

Chu Yuan

One example was the state of Chu, east of Chin, which had long since broken away from the king of Chou, had stopped paying tribute to the court of the Chou king, and had declared its own sovereign supreme. Chin tried to persuade the king of Chu to sever relations with the state of Chi. Most of the Chu ministers, bribed, it is said, by Chin, supported this proposal. One alone stood out, advocating an alliance with Chi against Chin. He was a minister named Chu Yuan, one of China's most famous poets. The king of Chu followed the advice of the majority and sent Chu Yuan into exile. Chin attacked and defeated Chu and Chi severally.

During Chu Yuan's exile in the south, he found himself in a long stream of war refugees. He was tormented by the sufferings of his people and wrote many poems expressing his concern for his country. The 'Li Sao', the Lament, written during the last years of his exile, is a long lyrical poem which has been translated into many languages and ranks amongst the world's classics. It describes the searching of the poet's soul in distress, riding on dragons and serpents from heaven to earth. He reached the gate of paradise and called the gate keeper to open up, but the keeper simply leaned against the door looking at him. Finally the poet sighed and concluded: 'Even in Heaven there are no good people.'

Long did I sigh and wipe away my Tears
To see my people bowed by Griefs and Fears . . .
Swift jade-green dragons, Birds with Plumage gold,
I harnessed to the Whirlwind, and behold,
At daybreak from the Land of Plane-trees grey,
I came to Paradise ere close of Day . . .
The dragons quenched their thirst beside the Lake
Where bathed the Sun, whilst I upon the Brake
Fastened my Reins; a golden Bough I sought
To brush the Sun, and tarried there in sport.

The pale Moon's charioteer I then bade lead,
The master of the Winds swiftly succeed;
Before the Royal Blue Bird cleared the Way;
The Lord of Thunder urged me to delay.
I bade the Phoenix scan the Heaven wide;
But vainly Day and Night its Course it tried . . .

In this poem, Chu Yuan expressed the feeling, two thousand years gone by, that all things in nature possess life and can be harnessed to man's purpose. Wind, rain, thunder and lightning, clouds and the moon, become his attendants and charioteers. Phoenix and dragon draw his chariot. He gallops to the sky and reaches the gate of Heaven, then climbs up the roof of the world and wanders to the uttermost parts of the earth. But he finds no rest anywhere and finally takes his own life.

In the year 278 BC on the fifth day of the fifth lunar month, the soldiers of Chin seized the Chu capital. Chu Yuan, exhausted mentally and physically, drowned himself in the Milo River.

In commemoration of this event, Dragon-boat festivals are held in many provinces at this time of year, where there are suitable rivers, for tradition says that the local Chu people, fearing that Chu Yuan's body would be devoured by dragons in the water, decorated their boats in the form of counterdragons, and raced down the river beating drums and gongs to scare the monsters away.

The other five states were annexed by Chin in similar fashion, as a silkworm devours the mulberry leaf, said the historian Ssuma Chien. In 256 BC the Son of Heaven was dispossessed of his lands, and in 222 the last independent kingdom fell. By 221 BC the Middle Kingdom was united under one master—the overlord of Chin, who took the title of Chin Shih Huang Ti (First Emperor).

Dragon-boat race. Traditional representation from Ching period woodblock. Dragon-boat festivals are held in commemoration of the death of Chu Yuan. The craft, which are specially made for the occasion, have long narrow hulls with high sterns. The prow is decorated with multicoloured silk streamers, and shaped like a dragon's head with whiskers and a jaw that opens and shuts as the boat moves through the water. The stem of the craft is painted in colours to simulate dragons' scales. The boats are propelled by twenty or thirty oarsmen, seated, as the saying goes in China, 'as close as centipedes feet'.
The races take place to the rhythm of beating gongs and drums and the cheers of the crowds packing the banks. The festival is also celebrated by the eating of little packets of sticky rice, which have been wrapped in bamboo leaves and steamed. This too had its origin with Chu Yuan. They say that people filled bamboo tubes with rice and threw them into the water so that his spirit should not starve.
It is likely that the Dragon-boat festivals arose from celebrations held at the completion of seasonal rice transplanting in the southern regions, an occasion linked with many dragon legends; the association with Chu Yuan may too have developed later.

4. Chin

221–206 BC

The Chin empire was formed after nearly two centuries of warfare; it initiated four centuries of imperial unity. At Hsienyang an autocratic government was set up, with the emperor exercising absolute power. A Legalist prime minister, Li Ssu, introduced a series of measures designed to quell opposition, to bring all corners of the empire under centralised control, to promote agriculture and to increase the military strength of the empire. Important affairs were discussed by the ministers but the final decision rested with the emperor, whose decrees were obeyed unconditionally.

A centralised bureaucratic type of government replaced feudal authority. The empire was ruled by officials who were not titled aristocrats, and whose positions were not hereditary. The large feudal estates were expropriated. It was recorded that 120,000 families of hunting and fighting feudal aristocrats were transported from their former estates to live near the capital, where they could be prevented from making trouble. The country was divided into provinces, and these into counties. Both provinces and counties were under the

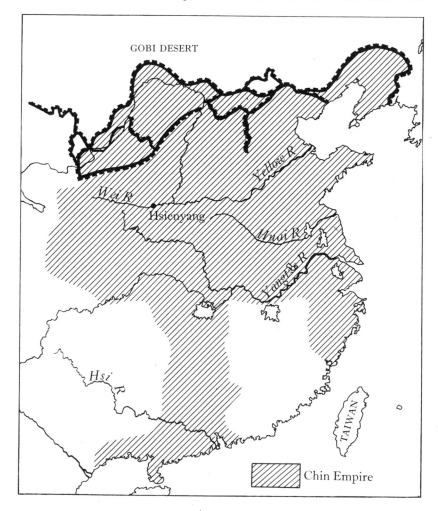

3. Chin Empire.

direct control of the central government, which appointed governors and other officials. The duty of the governors, besides enforcing the law and collecting revenue, was to conscript men for labour and military service. Army commanders and inspectors were also stationed in the provinces to watch over the conduct of the governors.

Many administrative measures were taken to reinforce centralised control. A detailed census of the whole country was taken, recording the number of households, the heads of families, the name, age and birthplace of individual citizens. (This was some twelve centuries before Domesday in England.) Such a measure was necessary for the effective imposition of poll taxes, corvée (forced labour) and military service. In the year AD 2 over 12 million households were registered in China, totalling some 59½ million individuals. The Middle Kingdom under Chin Shih Huang Ti (221–210 BC) stretched from the foothills of the Mongolian plateau to the Yangtze River basin, whence his armies pushed south to subjugate the northern regions of Vietnam and the coastal areas near Canton.

Other measures were taken to consolidate Chin rule. The written language was simplified and made uniform over the whole country. Weights, measures and coinage were standardised throughout the empire. The old spade and knife coinage was abolished, and a new round coin became the sole official means of exchange. This coin had a square hole in the middle and became the standard for the Middle Kingdom for the next two thousand years. A symbol of the Chin emperor's control over the empire has come down to us in the form of one of the 'tiger tallies'. This was a bronze symbol of authority, split longitudinally. One half was issued to a local military commander; the other was kept by the imperial government. Only when the commander received the half matching his own, did he have the right to move troops. As a further precaution, all war weapons not required by the Chin army itself were collected and melted down.

Chin Shih Huang Ti inaugurated a network of roads stretching from the capital to the extreme limits of the empire. These imperial highways were fifty paces broad, with a central alley reserved for imperial use. Standard dimensions were imposed for the axles of all chariots and carts. This common gauge made it possible to negotiate the wheel ruts, which were thus maintained at a uniform distance apart on all highways. It was no longer necessary to change carts going from one region to another, in order to accommodate wheels to different width of ruts.

The first Chin emperor encouraged land reclamation and tillage, as well as the weaving of textiles. Farmers were given more rights over their land than they had in earlier times, but they were subject to very heavy taxation. Chin Shih did not favour the merchants, but although measures were directed against them they found some of the new conditions advantageous.

Rubbing of bronze plate bearing the imperial decree of Emperor Shih Huang Ti of Chin, ordering the standardisation of weights and measures. Excavated at Hsienyang, capital of the Chin empire, together with knife and spade coins, arrow heads, harness bells, belt fittings, jars and seals.

Tiger tally of the Chin period. The words on it read: 'This is the army tally; the right half is with the Emperor, the left half is at Yangling.' Only when the two halves were presented together by a commander could an army be taken out on a campaign.

37

The Legalists wished to eliminate all opposition, including differing schools of thought. The Chin emperor feared that speculation and debate would disturb his rule. He therefore ordered the imperial inquisitors to hold an enquiry amongst the scholars; according to historical records, they tried to evade punishment by incriminating each other, and some 460 were punished by being buried alive. Moreover all books were ordered to be destroyed by burning, except those in the imperial archives and those dealing with technology, divination and medicine. For a time it seemed that the ancient literature of China had entirely vanished.

In the later part of the Chou period, when the use of iron tools had improved the techniques of production, commerce had increased and prosperous towns arose in the China plain. These towns and the plains of north China were frequently raided by the nomads living to the north of the Mongolian Plateau. Excellent horsemen and archers, they came out and went like the wind, charging and breaking the ranks of the foot soldiers resisting them. To protect themselves against these raids, the northern states of that time (Chao, Yen, Wei and Chin) had built walls along the mountain range.

Protection from attack by northern nomads became one of the preoccupations of Chinese governments for a score of centuries. Emperor Chin Shih Huang Ti, as soon as he came to power in 221 BC, ordered his general Meng Tien to lead a force of 300,000 soldiers and peasants to drive out the nomads and to build a continuous 'ten thousand li' wall to guard his dominions. The separate walls of the former northern states were connected together to form the Great Wall.

The extension of the Wall for six thousand kilometres across mountain peaks and ravines was an immense undertaking. Many legends grew up about the sacrifices of the people mobilised to build it. One of the most famous is the tale of the woman, Meng Chiang Nu, whose husband had been conscripted to work on the Wall. During the years of separation Meng Chiang Nu longed for her husband's return. Finally she set out in search of him. Coming at last to Shanhaikuan at the eastern end, she learned that her husband was dead and that

The Great Wall of China.

The 'ten-thousand li Wall' is 6,000 kilometres in length, a gigantic rampart standing 5–10 metres high, 7 metres wide. Separate walls were linked together during the Chin period, but sections have many times been reconstructed and repaired. The Wall as it stands today dates mainly from the Ming period. It is filled with earth, faced with brick and stone, and crowned with metre-high battlements. There are block houses at intervals and beacon towers. In addition to the two extremes, there are twelve important gates or passes through the Wall.

'Chin Shih Huang Ti is dead, but the Wall still stands': Chinese proverb.

his remains were buried beneath the Wall. She wept so long and so piteously that the Great Wall fell apart in compassion where she stood, and exposed the bones of her beloved. A temple was built to her memory and it still stands at Shanhaikuan.

The completion of the Wall, which separated the settled peoples from the pastoral nomads, was followed by a period of peace and quiet along the border. During the next two hundred years the Wall was repaired and extended. For three or four centuries after that many sections collapsed for lack of maintenance.

During the reign of the first Chin emperor hundreds of thousands of people were conscripted to build palaces and a mausoleum for him. According to Ssuma Chien, a historian of a subsequent dynasty, each time Chin Shih Huang Ti annexed a rival state he built a palace in the architectural style of the new dominion to stand as a reminder of his feat. A poet later describing the Chin palaces, wrote: 'They block out the skies for more than three hundred li.' Ssuma Chien said that even before he became emperor of China, Chin Shih Huang Ti planned to build a palace on the south bank of the Wei river. The building was to seat ten thousand men, but the project was so tremendous that it was not completed in the emperor's lifetime. Recent excavations of Hsienyang, the capital, confirm that the emperor was a builder on a grand scale. The foundations of this palace have been uncovered, as well as walls of rammed earth, drinking wells, a drainage system, and foundations of dwelling houses. Huge pots, which reflect the grandiose style in which the Son of Heaven lived and the lavish banquets which must have been held in the palace, have been recovered, as well as a wall painting (the oldest in China) consisting of geometric designs in red, yellow, blue and black. It is said that Chin Shih Huang Ti's palaces at Hsienyang were crowded with women from captured harems, and with the bells and drums of the defeated princes.

A satirical couplet given by Ssuma Chien describes the emperor as a 'man with a prominent nose, with large eyes, with the chest of a bird of prey, with the face of a jackal; without beneficence, and with the heart of a tiger or of a wolf'. The emperor, they say, was aloof and mysterious, living in carefully guarded secrecy obsessed by the fear of assassination. In his great palaces he moved from one apartment to another, and only a handful of eunuchs knew where he was to be found. But he worked indefatigably, handling daily 120 pounds of reports on bamboo strips, or wood. He also travelled about his realm a great deal, often incognito. He died in 210 BC while journeying in the eastern provinces, and the news was kept from all except a few ministers and eunuchs. As the cortège moved back across China the weather was hot and the body began to decompose. The ministers found it necessary to place a cartload of rancid fish behind the imperial chariot to prevent the soldiers and attendants from suspecting that the sovereign was dead.

Big pots, excavated at the Chin capital of Hsienyang, being measured. One wine jar, 72 cm tall, had a capacity of 400 kilograms.

Chin Shih Huang Ti (221–210 BC), first emperor of imperial China. Based on traditional representation.

Ssuma Chien tells us that

in the 9th moon the First Emperor was buried in Mount Li, which in the early days of his reign he had caused to be tunnelled and prepared with that in view. Then, when he had consolidated the empire, he employed his soldiery, to the number of 700,000, to bore down to the Three Springs and there a foundation of bronze was laid and the sarcophagus placed thereon. Rare objects and costly jewels were collected from the palaces and from the various officials, and were carried thither and stored in vast quantities. Artificers were ordered to construct mechanical crossbows, which if anyone were to enter, would immediately discharge their arrows. With the aid of quick silver, rivers were made . . . and a great ocean, the metal being poured from one into the other by machinery. On the roof were delineated the constellations of the sky, on the floor the geographical divisions of the earth. Candles were made from the fat of the walrus calculated to last for a very long time.

The Second Emperor said 'It is not fitting that the concubines of my late father who are without children should leave him now', and accordingly he ordered them to accompany the dead monarch to the next world, those who thus perished being many in number.

When the interment was completed, someone suggested that the workmen who had made the machinery and concealed the treasure knew the great value of the latter, and that the secret would leak out. Therefore, as soon as the ceremony was over, and the path giving access to the sarcophagus had been blocked up at the innermost end, the outside gate at the entrance to this path was let fall, and the mausoleum was effectively closed, so that not one of the workmen escaped. Trees and grass were then planted around, that the spot might look like the rest of the mountain.

The mound covering this collective graveyard was originally 166 metres high. After two thousand years of weathering and ravage, the mound is today only 34 metres in height.

Though progress had been made in many ways, the times were oppressive for the people of the Celestial Empire. The Chin government was geared for war, not for peace. The peasants were weighed down with heavy taxes and forced labour. Although they farmed hard and wove endlessly, they had neither enough to eat nor to wear. The law of the Chin state was strict, and people were liable to be punished at any moment by imprisonment or execution. The punishment of the individual frequently involved his family, and the conviction of a household could also involve the neighbours.

Chin Shih Huang Ti's eldest son was not a dedicated Legalist. He had, for example, opposed extreme measures such as the burning of the books. Prime Minister Li Ssu plotted with a palace eunuch to do away with this prince, who was caused by intrigue to commit suicide. The second son, the weak Er Shih Huang Ti, succeeded to the throne. Two years later the eunuch contrived to have Li Ssu executed.

The misery of the people increased under the second emperor. Male adults were sent by hundreds of thousands to guard the frontiers or to forced labour. The women were left to till the soil alone, or do the work of transport. The second emperor considered cruelty to be a good test of an official's loyalty. During his reign vast numbers of people were sentenced to hard labour, were punished by torture or death. The only escape was to flee to the mountains, forests or marshes, and to live as outlaws.

The first peasant rising

In the summer of 209 BC the second emperor ordered further conscription to garrison the frontiers. One group of peasants, some nine hundred strong, were held up by heavy rains which made the way impassable. According to the law failure to arrive on time meant execution. Two of them, Chen Sheng and Wu Kuang, killed the officer in charge and called on the rest to revolt. The peasants rallied and a rising started. They were joined by bands of men already living as outlaws. The call of the conscript Chen Sheng was heard far and wide and the empire answered him like an echo. This was the first of a succession of great peasant risings which have been a feature of Chinese history up to the twentieth century, and which have gained for the Chinese the notoriety of being the 'most rebellious but least revolutionary' of peoples. Throughout the centuries the peasants had no recourse for relief of their miseries other than rebellion. As often as they overthrew the sovereign, he was replaced by another: they did not change their social order.

Confucians and Mohists who hated the Legalist state, as well as dispossessed feudal lords, joined the rebels, who elected Chen Sheng king and set up a government. Chen Sheng sent out generals to attack in different directions. One advanced on the capital, absorbing smaller risings as he went until he had amassed a huge peasant army. Marching at the double they reached the capital. Meanwhile members of the

First Peasant Rising, which overthrew the Chin dynasty (206 BC).
Contemporary painting by Liu Tan Chai.

royal clans of the former rival states of Chin had set up their own governments, not only refusing to acknowledge Chen Sheng but denying him reinforcements. Within a few months the peasant army was defeated. Wu Kuang was killed by subordinates; a treacherous carriage driver murdered Chen Sheng.

The struggle continued under the leadership of Liu Pang, a petty official of peasant origin, and Hsiang Yu, a noble. Liu Pang occupied the capital Hsienyang and the Chin dynasty fell in 206. Hsiang Yu meanwhile defeated the main Chin army, and the two leaders fought each other for years for the ultimate position of emperor. It was said of Hsiang Yu the aristocrat, that 'as befitted one so highly bred, he had a very low regard for humanity in general, and enjoyed nothing so much as to boil or burn a captured enemy alive'. Although he gained victory after victory, his armies melted away; finally, when he realised that there was no hope of a comeback, he committed suicide.

Ssuma Chien gave an account of the last struggle between Hsiang Yu and Liu Pang, described to him by an eyewitness:

At night Hsiang Yu heard men singing from the enemy camp the song of his own people. He was greatly alarmed and exclaimed 'Have all my men gone over to Liu?' He then rose and spent the night drinking in his tent. He had a beautiful wife named Yu, and a superb horse called Dapple which he always rode. He sang of his sorrows:

My strength uprooted the mountains,
My force dominated the world.
But fortune has forsaken me:
Dapple can gallop no more.
If Dapple can gallop no longer,
What can I achieve?
And Yu, Yu, what will be your fate?

He and queen Yu sang many stanzas together . . . the king was weeping, and their attendants could not bear to lift up their eyes and look on them. . . .

5. Han

206 BC—AD 220

Former, or Western Han, 206 BC to AD 24

The Chin dynasty lasted only fifteen years but the empire that had been established survived.

Liu Pang, founder of the new Han dynasty, was of peasant origin. Before the revolt he had been an official in charge of a group of convicts. The convicts had escaped, and this had made him liable to the death penalty. Like many others, Liu Pang deserted, and became the leader of one of the groups of rebels. He gained his first title of king of the Han in 206 BC, the year in which he captured the capital and put an end to the Chin dynasty. Since those times, the people of China, other than the national minorities, have tended to call themselves the Han people. It was not until 202 BC, however, that Liu Pang overcame his rival, a victory due to the cruelty of his opponent as well as to his own popular measures and powers of leadership. Liu Pang took the title of Emperor Kao Tsu when he gained control of the whole Middle Kingdom, and set up his capital at Changan, close to the old capital in the west. One of his early proclamations says:

Fellow countrymen!
You have long groaned under the despotic sway of the Chins. To complain openly was to incur the penalty of extermination. Even casual words of objection were punished by decapitation.

Now, it was agreed between myself and the other nobles that whosoever first entered the territory of Chin should rule over it. Therefore I am come to rule over you. With you, I further agree upon three laws, viz:

For murder, death.
For injury to the person, proportionate punishment
For theft, proportionate punishment.

The remainder of the Chin laws to be abrogated.
The officials and people will continue to attend to their respective duties as heretofore. My sole object in coming here is to eradicate wrong. I desire to do violence to no one. Fear not.

The details of these times have been handed down to us vividly and fully by contemporary historians, who were also court officials, and disposed therefore to write favourably of the dynasty. According to Ssuma Chien the most famous of the Han historians, Liu Pang, although talented, was not an altogether lovable man. When hard pressed by his rival Hsiang Yu, on one occasion, Liu Pang escaped in the following circumstances:

The king of Han (Liu Pang) was totally surrounded; but then a storm arose, tearing up trees, overthrowing houses, raising clouds of dust and sand, so that the sky darkened and it was night in broad daytime. Liu Pang was able to flee under cover of this darkness with a handful of horsemen. On the way he met his

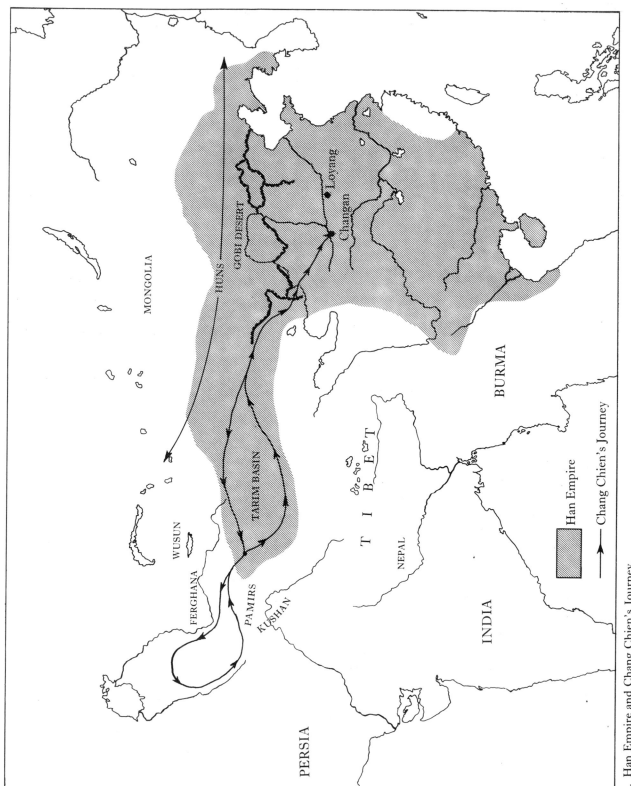

4. Han Empire and Chang Chien's Journey.

son and daughter and took them into his chariot to escape with him. Then when the horsemen of the enemy were hard on their heels, he threw the prince and the princess out of the chariot. One of his officers, the governor of Teng, dismounted and put them back in the chariot. This scene was repeated three times, until the governor of Teng said, 'Although we are closely pursued, we cannot go any faster. What then is the use of abandoning them?' and so they all were able to escape.

The centralised political system of the Chin was preserved by Emperor Han Kao Tsu (206–195 BC), except that a certain number of feudal kingdoms were restored as rewards to generals whose support he wished to acknowledge. The power of the vassal kingdoms was curbed, however, especially by later rulers.

In the first half century of Han rule effective measures were taken to rehabilitate the economy, to encourage agriculture and to aid the peasants. Such measures were urgently needed, for, as Ssuma Chien wrote,

When the House of Han arose, the evils of their predecessors had not passed away. Husbands still went off to the wars. The old and the young were employed in transporting food. Production was almost at a standstill, and money had become scarce . . . so much so, that even the Son of Heaven had not carriage horses of the same colour; the highest civil and military authorities rode in bullock carts; and the people at large knew not where to lay their heads.

Soldiers were encouraged to return to farm work, and those who did so were exempted from corvée for periods of six to twelve years. Those who had previously sold themselves into slavery on account of poverty, had their liberty restored. Land and poll taxes were reduced. Many of the harsh laws and punishments of the Chin were rescinded with a consequent reduction in the level of crime. To encourage population increase, Emperor Kao Tsu decreed that families with newborn babies should be exempted from corvée for two years. For the same reason a later Han emperor decreed that families having unmarried daughters over the age of fifteen should pay a supplementary poll tax.

As a result of these measures, the improvement in farming techniques, and of progress in water control, agriculture began to prosper. During the reign of the fifth Han emperor, Wu Ti (141–87 BC), when the Celestial Empire reached its zenith, important programmes of canal construction were undertaken, one of which connected the capital Changan with the Yellow River, facilitating the transport of tax grain to the capital region. It took three years to cut this canal, which served also for irrigation. In 132 BC when the Yellow River dyke broke and the river overflowed its banks, it is said that the emperor came out in person to supervise the construction of the dam. In the Shansi region a canal was dug to irrigate lands covered with salt. New land was brought into cultivation; the production of grain and fabrics increased; so did the population. Ssuma Chien wrote of these times:

'The public granaries were well stocked, the government treasuries were full.'

During this half century of economic consolidation the Chinese empire reached a high point of development, rivalling in brilliance the contemporary Roman empire in the West.

While the first Han emperor encouraged agriculture, he held the traditional low regard for commerce, and tried to restrict the amassing and display of fortunes by traders. Ssuma Chien commented:

By and by when the empire was settling down to tranquillity, His Majesty Kao Tsu gave orders that no trader should wear silk nor ride in a carriage; besides which the imposts levied upon this class were greatly increased, in order to keep them down. Some years later these restrictions were withdrawn; still however the descendants of traders were disqualified from holding any office connected with the State.

By the reign of the energetic Emperor Han Wu Ti increased production had so greatly stimulated commercial activity, that the supply of currency proved inadequate. To overcome this the right to mint coins privately had been granted to wealthy families. This led to abuses such as the debasement of the currency, which together with the speculations of merchants and the creation of monopolies, drove prices up very high. During the time of Han Wu Ti a number of fiscal and economic experiments were carried out, some of them with a very modern sound, to solve these problems. As a check on private monopolies created by speculators, Wu Ti set up state monopolies: the salt and iron industries were taken over, forges and salt pans were nationalised. Later he introduced licensing for the liquor trade.

A state transport system was instituted to control the distribution of produce. State workmen made carts, and officials controlled all forms of land and water transport. These measures brought in money dues for the treasury, and helped prevent wild fluctuations of price through sudden releases of stocks on to the market. Another measure aimed at stabilising prices was the 'levelling system': the state purchased grain when it was abundant and cheap, and released it for sale when alternative supplies were scarce and dear. This helped also to maintain supplies in state granaries, and for military purposes. Wu Ti placed the minting of coin under state control, and introduced the first experiment in proto 'paper' money. The skin of a rare white deer, found only in the emperor's hunting reserves, was used as token for a high denomination. It was issued to nobles coming to court, in exchange for 400,000 copper coins. Nobles were obliged to pay their respects by buying one of these 'white stag notes', and to present their gifts to the emperor on it.

This was an inflationary measure but the imperial treasury benefited for a time, as it did from the duties levied at the rate of one-twentieth on the large fortunes still being made in commerce.

The needs of the exchequer overruled the dislike for merchants, who were for the first time granted permission to purchase titles and gain positions as officials. The sale of ranks, a practice beneficial for the treasury, was often undertaken in later days, combined with the extortion of great gifts from the wealthy.

Strongly centralised control, reminiscent of Chin rule, was a feature of Wu Ti's reign. To lessen the danger of a resurgence of great vassal kingdoms, which had been introduced by the first Han emperor, Kao Tsu, and his successors, it was decreed that estates should not be inherited by the eldest son but be divided between all sons. Wu Ti controlled the activities of the vassals by appointing advisers, government officials who were in reality watchdogs, to be resident at the court of each vassal prince.

Liu Pang–Han Kao Tsu–First Han emperor (202–194 BC). Contemporary presentation.

Confucian revival

During the Chin period the burning of books had been ordained, to stifle discussion and to prevent the growth of opposition to the Legalist state. In the first century of Han rule, the ban on philosophical and historical writings was lifted. The classics were reassembled. Some of the old scholars were able to reconstitute the texts that they had learned by heart in their youth. One old man of ninety came forward, able to recite most of the *Book of Songs* and the *Book of History*. Copies of books which had been hidden away instead of being burned, were recovered from recesses in old walls. Veneration of the classics was revived and many scholars dedicated themselves to the work of restoring and interpreting the classical Confucian literature. Commentaries were produced in explanation of the ancient books, some of which are known to us only through the work of the Han scholars. These naturally interpreted the classical literature in terms of the thought of their own times.

Confucian tradition began to replace the Legalist school of thought, and by the time of Emperor Han Wu Ti students of Legalist philosophy were barred from state positions. Confucian teaching was declared official state doctrine.

Rule by the able

The first Han emperor, Kao Tsu, the former peasant, did not hold scholars in high regard, but he recognised the need for educated men in the government if only to curb the feudal aristocracy, and he sent out a call for the services of men of talent. His successors did likewise, including Emperor Wu Ti, who issued a proclamation in the following terms:

Exceptional work demands exceptional men. A bolting or a kicking horse may eventually become a most valuable animal. A man who is the object of the world's detestation may live to accomplish great things. As with the intractable horse, so with the infatuated man; it is simply a question of training.

We therefore command the various district officials to search for men of brilliant and exceptional talents, to be Our generals, Our ministers, and Our envoys to distant states.

A reply has come down to us from the second century BC. It was sent to the emperor by a wag called Tung Fang So: 'I am now twenty-two years of age. I am nine feet three inches in height. My eyes are like swinging pearls, my teeth like a row of shells. I am as brave as Meng Fen, as prompt as Chin Chi, as pure as Pao Shu, and as devoted as Wei Sheng. I consider myself fit to be a high officer of State; and with my life in my hands, I await your Majesty's reply.' This joker became the friend and adviser of the emperor, continuing in his favour until his death. He once drank off some elixir of immortality prepared for the Emperor, who, enraged, ordered Tung Fang So's death. The wag responded, 'If the elixir was genuine, then I can come to no harm. If it was not, what harm have I done?' Such joking was not without its dangers. For Wu Ti, competent and clearsighted in many matters, was swayed by the Taoist elixir seekers when it came to his own mortality. In fact he married his eldest daughter to a magician who promised to obtain for him the elixir of immortality. When the man failed to deliver, Wu Ti had him cut in two at the waist.

Since Han Kao Tsu's day the Chinese empire has been governed by a body of officials selected, in theory at least, not on the basis of blood, wealth, or the sword, but on merit, in fulfilment of the injunction: 'Employ the able; promote the worthy.' This search, a hundred years before Christ, for men of virtue and ability to run the state, has perhaps only one parallel in England, occurring at the time of Cromwell's Commonwealth in the seventeenth-century, when Parliament was in the hands of a picked body of 'saints'. The congregational churches in each county were asked to submit suitable names from which a gross or so of righteous men were selected by Cromwell. The Parliament of Saints (named Barebones after its leader Praise-God Barebones) endured four months. The Chinese bureaucratic system lasted two thousand years. During the Han period the social structure of imperial China achieved its permanent form.

Scholar officials

Through the deliberate suppression of the feudal aristocracy in favour of government by officials, bureaucrats, the emperor gained greater despotic power. The officials owed their position, at first through recommendation and later through the examination system, directly to the throne, rather than to their own social group.

In 124 BC, during the reign of Wu Ti, an imperial university was set up for the study of Confucian classics; its students were destined for government service. Fifty of the scholars of this college were supported by the state. The number of students grew rapidly and by the end of the dynasty had reached some 30,000. Provincial schools were also established. The principle came to be accepted that the administrators of the empire, the officers of state, should be not merely virtuous, but educated men. The emperor introduced examinations to test the competence of his officials in the Confucian classics. Confucian orthodoxy was reinforced by conferences held under imperial auspices to determine an acceptable interpretation of the classics. The government subsequently had the approved version of the works carved on large stone tablets which were erected in the capital. The descendants of Confucius were enobled, and sacrifices to him were ordained in all government schools. From the time of Emperor Han Wu Ti, Confucian philosophy retained its position as official doctrine until the twentieth century. Through its hold on the state, Confucian thought permeated and helped to unify Chinese society. An élite class of bureaucrats, educated in the Confucian classics, became a dominant feature of Chinese social structure. The bureaucrats formed the ruling group, cultivated, privileged, superior; the others were the ruled, those who laboured, unlettered and unprivileged.

Cultural advances

The cultural developments in China during the Han period were of great consequence. In early times the Chinese had begun to write with brushes instead of with the pointed instruments which had been used to inscribe strips of smooth bamboo. Ink replaced mixtures of brick dust and water, and during the early Han, people began to use silk and hemp to produce a kind of writing material like paper. Later on paper was made from bark, hemp, rags and old fishnets. The production of paper from cheap materials led to the replacement of the cumbersome wooden and bamboo slips formerly used for books; the use of silk as a writing base was also reduced. In the following centuries paper was introduced into a number of foreign countries – Korea, Japan, India and Arabia, but it took more than a thousand years for the knowledge of paper-making to spread from China through central Asia to Europe.

These developments promoted the dissemination of books, and the whole body of Chinese classical literature and history became standardised. In place of the local traditions of numerous states or provinces, a culture common to all parts of China took deep root. Despite the political disruption and long periods of partition which followed, the cultural unity of China has never been destroyed.

Ssuma Chien and the histories

The Han was the period which produced not only the definitive texts of the classics, but also the first dictionaries and the first general

Left: Ssuma Chien, 145–86 BC.
Grand Historian; his Shih Chi, or
Historial Records, chronicles nearly
3,000 years, from the time of the
legendary emperors, to his own
period.

Right: tomb of Ssuma Chien, Grand
Historian, in Shensi province.
'I can hope for justification only
after my death', Ssuma Chien wrote
to a friend, after losing the favour
of the emperor.

history of China. Ssuma Chien (c. 145–86 BC) lived during the reign
of the Emperor Han Wu Ti. He inherited his father's position of court
recorder and astrologer. In his youth, his father sent him on a long
tour to broaden his education. He visited the home of Confucius, and
studied the chariots, costumes, and ceremonial vessels in use in the
sage's day. On the banks of the Milo River he mused on the fate of
Chu Yuan. He visited the villages of men who had been associates of
the Han emperor Kao Tsu, and got many firsthand accounts of the
events leading to the establishment of the Han dynasty. As an official
of Wu Ti, he accompanied him on many voyages, noting the geography, customs and history of the different places, and visiting the
local elders and scholars. His position also gave him access to the
imperial library of bamboo books, and he embarked on the task of
writing a complete history of China. This masterpiece, *Records of the
Grand Historian* took ten years to write. It is a vivid and illuminating
work incorporating many first hand testimonies.

Ssuma Chien was a man of courage and conviction as well as a great
scholar. His work was interrupted and endangered when he incurred
the emperor's wrath by defending the action of one of the generals.
This general had been stationed in the border regions and had surrendered to the nomad hordes after facing overwhelming odds and
awaiting reinforcements that never came. Ssuma Chien maintained
his view against the general opinion of the court. The enraged emperor ordered Ssuma Chien to be mutilated and thrown into prison.
He was released three years later during a general amnesty. Thirty
volumes of his work were devoted to the family histories of the feudal
princes, and seventy volumes were written on the lives of eminent
men. Previous historical works, like the *Spring and Autumn Annals*,

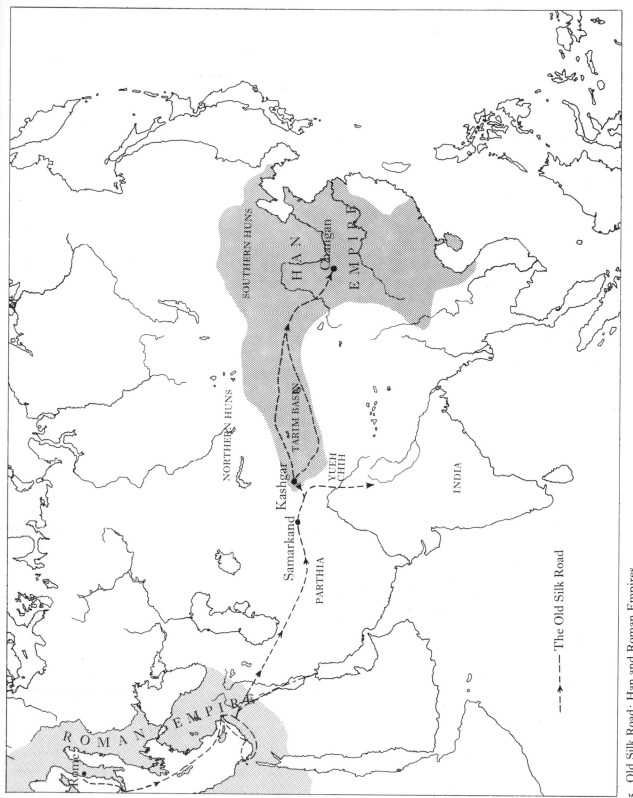

5. Old Silk Road; Han and Roman Empires.

Instructress at court.
Detail from scroll painting by Ku Kai Chi (c. AD 345–406), the first great painter of China. The inscription runs: 'Thus has the instructress, charged with the duty of admonition, thought good to speak to the ladies of the Harem.' This scroll is one of the most precious in the collection of the British Museum.

had been simply court chronicles. Subsequent histories followed the pattern introduced by the Grand Historian.

After Ssuma Chien's death the historical tradition was continued by the Pan family, who wrote during the Later Han period. Pan Piao the father started to bring the Ssuma Chien *Records* up to date. The work was continued after his death by his son Pan Ku, and was completed by his daughter Pan Chao, China's earliest and most famous woman scholar. The Pan family limited their task to the preceding dynasty, the early Han. This was the first single dynastic history written in China; after that, every dynasty had its history recorded by official historians.

Pan Chao was an outstanding woman. She married young, like many women of her time, at the age of fourteen. She continued writing after the completion of the history, producing treatises and poems. When she was over fifty years old she wrote a work on the education of women. In her *Lessons for Women* she recommended the traditional feminine 'virtues' of her time:

Let a woman retire late to bed, but rise early to duties: let her not dread tasks by day or by night. Let a woman be correct in manner and upright in character in order to serve her husband. Let her live in purity and quietness. Let her love not gossip and silly laughter. Let her cleanse and purify and arrange in order the wine and the food for the offerings to the ancestors . . .

But added a plea for the extension of education to women:

Only to teach men and not to teach women – is that not ignoring the essential relation between them? According to the 'rites' it is the rule to begin to teach children to read at the age of eight years and by the age of fifteen years they ought to be ready for cultural training. Only why should it not be that girls' education as well as boys' be according to this principle?

It seems that Pan Chao was not the only woman of her day to seek learning. The Empress Teng was her contemporary, and as a child had received the family nickname of 'the student'. At the age of six, according to the annals, she was able to read a book of history; at twelve she recited the *Book of Songs* and the *Analects*. Her interest was in ancient books and records, and she never paid any attention to home duties. Her mother often scolded her saying 'You do not learn needlework with which you may make garments; instead you set your heart on studies. Is it proper that you should be raised to a doctorate?' But the studious princess was a kindhearted little girl full of proper respect for age. The annals also say that when she was five years old her grandmother, who was fond of her, cut the child's hair. The grandmother was old, with failing eyesight, and cut the forehead of the princess, who suffered the stab without a word. The child afterwards explained: 'It was not that it did not hurt. But Grandmother loves to cut my hair. It is hard to wound an old person's feeling, so I put up with the pain.'

In the Han period there was a systematic recording of medical,

Chang Heng's seismograph (Reconstruction). Each of the eight dragons on this bronze vase holds a ball in its mouth. An earthquake at any point of the compass causes the dragon facing that direction to spew its ball into the open mouth of the toad below.

Chang Heng (AD 78–139) was the court astronomer. He opposed the current idea that the earth was flat, covered by the dome of the sky. He believed the earth to be at the centre of the universe, suspended in it like the yoke of an egg.

Man riding horse. Pottery figure of Han period.

Tomb figures, usually of pottery, wood, stone or metal have been found in large numbers in Han tombs. Models of servants, dancers, musicians, domestic animals, as well as of houses, barns, pavilions, were buried with the dead so that the spirit might enjoy the comforts known in life.

mathematical and other knowledge. The physician Chang Chi wrote a *Treatise on Fevers* which became one of the classics of Chinese medical literature. About the same time a surgeon Hua To developed the use of anaesthetics called *ma fei san*. When drunk with wine the patient lost consciousness and could undergo operations without pain. He also initiated setting-up exercises known as 'Five Animals Play' which consisted of imitating the movements of a tiger, deer, bear, monkey and bird. Such exercises are regularly performed by many men in China to this day. Great scientific and technical advances were made. Chang Heng, astronomer, mathematician and poet, made an armillary sphere which showed the movements of the stars. He invented a seismograph, an instrument which indicated the region of an earthquake.

The production began at this time of the fine porcelain which gained the admiration of the rest of the world. This signified a major advance in health as well as in craft, for the smooth surfaces of the glaze were much more sanitary for eating utensils than the rough ware of former days. The quality of Han textiles also was in advance of the rest of the world. Han towns, constructed largely of wood, have mostly disappeared. But the ceramic figurines excavated from the ruins and from Han tombs reflect the achievements of the times. The Shang custom of burying people and objects with the dead for their comfort in the next world had given way to the thriftier habit of burying pottery replicas of the objects which had delighted on earth. Excavated Han tombs have yielded countless funerary objects which give an intimate view of the life at least of the wealthy. They include terra cotta models of houses, pavilions, farms, stoves, pet dogs, dancers, female attendants, musicians, as well as personal chattels, such as dishes, bowls and trays, jewellery, belts, boxes for cosmetics, hairpins and mirrors; they also include writing brushes, hats, shoes, and silk and woollen clothing.

The Han forts strung across central Asia were rubbish dumps whose contents have been preserved by the dry desert atmosphere. From them have been recovered lists of weapons, military orders, other scraps of writing, and many articles of daily life. These forts were a relic of the expansion of the Celestial Empire especially during the reign of the martial emperor Han Wu Ti, who came to the throne when he was sixteen years of age, and ruled for over half a century (141–87 BC).

One of the major developments of this period was the defeat of the Hsiung Nu hordes (Huns), the penetration of central Asia, and the opening of the caravan route known as the Old Silk Road to the west.

Han and the Hun Nomads

Since earliest times the Middle Kingdom had been subject to attack by her northern neighbours, the nomad tribal societies of the steppe, whose mobility as mounted archers using strong reflex bows had enabled them to outmanoeuvre the fighting chariots and foot soldiers of the Chinese.

When the Middle Kingdom was becoming an empire under the Chin, a process of unification had been taking place in Mongolia. A tribal federation was formed of the Hsiung Nu (Huns), the most powerful of the nomad hordes, which by the third century BC stretched from western Manchuria across Mongolia as far west as the Pamirs. It was said that at this time the Hun emperor had more than a quarter of a million horse archers under his command. They raided and looted the border regions, especially in times when their own grazing lands failed, or when the Middle Kingdom was in difficulty; at these times Chinese rebels were inclined to join the nomads, taking with them useful information. The Great Wall had restrained but had not removed the menace from the north. It has indeed been suggested that the function of the Wall was as much to contain dissident elements within the Celestial Empire as it was to impede nomad advance.

The first Han emperor, Kao Tsu (206–195 BC) found himself hard pressed by the Hsiung Nu during his early struggles, for they had streamed south of the Wall and established themselves in the Ordos region, north of Changan. Kao Tsu once led a direct military attack. The nomad emperor simulated defeat and withdrew his hordes. Kao Tsu fell into the trap and pushed on in pursuit with a small body of men. He was captured. Thus silently might Liu Pang have slipped out of history. However the peasant emperor, turned courtier in captivity, made a considerable impression on the chief wife of the Hun ruler; the lady it seems was susceptible to rich Chinese presents. She in turn worked on the superstitions of her spouse; Kao Tsu and his entourage were allowed to escape and to return to China.

Turning again from martial to marital devices, Emperor Kao Tsu then attempted to buy off the Huns with the offer of a Chinese princess in marriage with their emperor. This routine of marriage alliances became a regular part of Chinese–barbarian policies, with varying degrees of success. On this occasion, Kao Tsu had intended to send his own daughter as the bride, but his consort, the Empress Lu, a tough woman who had seen hard times with him as a peasant girl, put her foot down. The Hun ruler Mao Tun received one of the most beautiful ladies from the Celestial harem. It is possible that Mao Tun did not notice any difference.

Kao Tsu died in 195 BC leaving affairs of state in the hands of Empress Lu, who kept control for fifteen years, a capable but cruel ruler. (The annals record of her, as they tend to do of all female rulers, a number of villainies. In this case they say that she seized her husband's favourite, after his death, had her hands and feet cut off and her eyes put out, finished her off with poison and cast her into a pit.)

Pleasure pavilion. Han pottery tomb figure.

Drummer. Earthenware tomb figure of Eastern Han period.

55

It is also said that Mao Tun sent the Celestial widow a message admitting that he was lonely, and hinting at the advantages of a marriage alliance between them. Empress Lu expressed gratitude for the honour of his interest, but pointed out that age and physical condition made her unequal to the task of receiving his affections. 'I have become short of breath, my hair and teeth are falling out, my gait has become halting, but I possess two imperial carriages and two four-horse teams, and these I send you that you may always ride therein.'

In addition to the supply of Chinese princesses, whose marriages were accompanied by sumptuous dowries, the conciliation policy introduced by the Han included the annual despatch of gifts of grain and silk, of wine and other delicacies, to the royal Hun kinsmen. The nomads were not restrained by niceties of gratitude from periodic attacks on their kin, however, and even came galloping across the wheat field within sight of the celestial capital.

An elegant letter survives, addressed by Emperor Wen Ti (son of Kao Tsu) to the chief of the Huns (whom he calls Captain), complaining of breaches in the peaceful relations:

We respectfully trust that the great Captain is well. We have respectfully received the two horses which the great Captain forwarded to us.

The first emperor of this dynasty adopted the following policy: All to the north of the Long Wall, comprising the nations of the bow and arrow, to be subject to the great Captain: All within the Long Wall – namely the families of the hat and girdle, to be subject to the House of Han. Thus, these peoples would each pursue their own avocations: Ours, agriculture and manufacture of cloth: Yours, archery and hunting, in the acquisition of food and raiment. Father and son would not suffer separation; suzerain and vassal would rest in peace; and neither side would do violence to the other. . . . The Hans and the Huns are border nations. Your northern climate is early locked in deadly cold. Therefore we have annually sent large presents of food and clothing and other useful things; and now the empire is at peace and the people are prosperous. Of those people, We and You are, as it were, the father and mother; and for trivial causes, such as an Envoy's error, we should not lightly sever the bonds of brotherly love. Heaven it is said covers no one in particular; and earth is the common resting place of all men. . . . Let us now forget bygone troubles in a sincere desire to cement an enduring friendship, that our people may live like the children of a single family, while the blessings of peace and immunity from evil extend to the fishes of the sea, to the fowls of the air, and to all creeping things . . . and when peace shall prevail once more, rest assured that its first breach will not proceed from the House of Han.

This policy of conciliation with the Hun alternated, between periods of military attack, with a policy of alliances with other barbarians against the Hun enemy. Instead of undertaking costly military expeditions which were usually indecisive because of the extreme mobility of the enemy, the Chinese preferred to secure the services of tribes which were also harassed by the Huns, to attack the common enemy from the flank. The arrangement had the advantage that the barbarians were provided with legitimate means of securing those products they desired from the Chinese, without resorting to raids. Instead the barbarians sent 'embassies' to the Chinese capital, bearing gifts such as horses, and gold dust, which the Chinese diplomatically termed 'tribute'. In return the envoys received thousands of bolts of silks and other valued presents. In due course the Chinese came to regard this tribute system as a symbol of vassalage, a system whereby the grateful barbarian acknowledged his allegiance to his superior, the Son of Heaven.

Emperor Han Wu Ti felt strong enough to launch a full military attack on the Huns, and shortly after ascending the throne he prepared for attack. He sent one expedition after another, numbering tens of thousands of cavalry supported by infantry and supply trains. The northern deserts as well as the enemy took their toll of them in prodigious numbers. Wu Ti decided to seek allies amongst other nomad tribes in the northern steppe lands.

Chang Chien

Ssuma Chien wrote: 'At that time the Son of Heaven made enquiries among those Huns who had surrendered and they all reported that the Huns had overcome the king of the Yueh Chih and had made a drinking vessel out of his skull. The Yueh Chih decamped.' From this the Son of Heaven concluded that the Yueh Chih were likely allies for his offensive against the Huns. The Yueh Chih had been driven westward towards Central Asia. Han Wu Ti called for volunteers to seek out the Yueh Chih in the heart of Asia and to secure an alliance with them against the common foe. Chang Chien, an officer 'of strong physique, magnanimous and trustful, and popular with the foreign tribes in the south and the west', volunteered to start out with a retinue of a hundred, across the deserts and mountain ranges, for the unknown regions of the west (138–126 BC).

On reaching the borderlands Chang Chien was captured almost immediately by the Huns. He remained captive for ten years, after which, being guarded less closely, he managed to escape with some of his followers and the Hun wife who had consoled him in captivity.

He continued on his mission, eventually catching up with the Yueh Chih who had moved to the region of Bactria south of the Oxus River; (they subsequently invaded Afghanistan and founded the Kushan dynasty). He stayed with them a year, but found that they were unwilling to rejoin issue with the Huns.

The dogged traveller started back for China; and was once more captured by the Huns. After a year, profiting from dissensions among his captors, he again escaped, and returned, accompanied by one survivor from his original band, and his Hun wife.

Emperor Wu Ti loaded the persistent envoy with honours and conferred on him the title of Marquis. Chang Chien had brought back with him extensive information about the lands to the west and the riches that might be secured by trade with such countries as India, Persia and beyond; in fact he 'discovered' Europe for China a thousand years or so before Europe discovered China; he also brought back a variety of plants and natural products. Particularly attractive were his accounts of Kokand in the abundant land of Ferghana, an oasis valley in central Asia famous for its thoroughbred horses:

Ferghana is to the south-west of the Huns and due west of China. The people are permanent dwellers and given to agriculture, and in their fields they grow rice and wheat. They have wine made of grapes and many good horses. The horses sweat blood and come from the stock of heavenly horses. They have walled cities and houses. Their arms consist of bows and halberds and they shoot arrows while on horseback.

China was not a horse-breeding country, and the Son of Heaven was naturally strongly inclined to secure a supply of the celestial mounts. Han Wu Ti sent a number of missions to secure them. The early ones were unsuccessful, many were attacked en route and failed to reach their destination; others were refused their request, and the Son of Heaven had to send strong forces to back up his demands. Eventually Ferghana was defeated (101 BC).

Chang Chien himself commanded an expedition against the Huns which was defeated, and for this he was condemned to death. He managed to buy back his life but lost all titles and honours.

Wu Ti renewed his efforts to secure allies in the west, and Chang Chien was again entrusted with a mission to the Wu Sun, another central Asian people, to propose alliance against the Huns. He found his way there and returned with some envoys from the Wu Sun and with a few dozen fine steeds as a gift for the emperor. In the quest of alliances, the Son of Heaven spared no effort, even to the extent of personal sacrifice. He despatched one of the ladies of the imperial harem to be the bride of Kun Mo, king of the Wu Sun. Unhappily Kun Mo was in his dotage, quite senile. He saw his new wife once or twice a year, when they drank a cup of wine together. They had no common language and the couple could not even converse. The sorrows of the forlorn lady, who expressed herself in poetry, entered the folklore of the Celestial Empire:

My people have married me
In a far corner of Earth;
Sent me away to a strange land,
To the king of the Wu Sun.
A tent is my house,
Of felt are my walls;
Raw flesh is my food
With mare's milk to drink.
Always thinking of my own country,
My heart is sad within.
Would I were a yellow stork
And could fly to my old home!

The decrepit Kun Mo eventually made the lady over to his grandson and heir. The princess was horrified at this turn in her affairs and sent a messenger asking advice of the Son of Heaven. Wu Ti ordered her to overcome her scruples in the interest of imperial policies and the importance of an alliance in the event of a war against the Huns. The princess obeyed; she died giving birth to her first child. A replacement princess, less squeamish, proved more resilient. She married the reigning Wu Sun king and several of his successors, and lived to a ripe age after producing numerous progeny.

The Han Empire and the Old Silk Road

Until these times there had been no contact between China and the western regions. Central and eastern Asia, including India and Persia, had constituted separate worlds. After Chang Chien the Emperor Wu Ti sent several missions annually to the west, developing cultural exchanges, as well as numerous military expeditions which pushed the bounds of the Celestial Empire westward across the Tarim Basin to include a great part of central Asia. The conquest of Ferghana marked the limit of Chinese domination over numerous oasis states across high Asia. A route to the west was opened up—the Old Silk Road. Grapes and clover were introduced to China, Chinese silks flowed through Parthia and Asia Minor into Europe. The route followed the chain of oases skirting the foothills of the Tarim basin. From these hills came streams that watered the oases before vanishing into the desert sand. The routes reached the Pamirs and joined at oases such as Samarkand on the way to Parthia and the Mediterranean. This route to the west was defended by a series of military posts which were maintained by prisoners and exiles. Wu Ti made strenuous efforts to colonise the region in the north of the Yellow River bend. Hundreds of thousands of migrants were sent to Kansu, to dig canals, to irrigate, to raise stock and to make the region habitable, as well as to guard the main oasis outposts. The Great Wall was extended westward to Yemen, the Jade Gate.

After the opening of the Silk Road there were references in western literature to China and to Chinese products. Chinese silk eventually reached the Roman empire where it was so highly prized by Roman ladies that the demand for it was said to have caused a drain of gold and silver from the Roman imperial exchequer. Moreover China started sending ambassadors as far afield as Persia. Chinese records note that Persia was a great nation, whose people wrote on parchment with characters going across the page: 'They paint rows of characters running sideways on stiff leather to serve as records.' (The Chinese write from top to bottom.) Ssuma Chien related that 'more embassies were sent to Parthia, Syria, Chaldea and India, and as the Son of Heaven had such a fancy for the horses of Ferghana, ambassadors followed upon one another's heels all along the route . . . more than ten such missions in a year . . . those sent to distant countries would return home after eight or nine years.'

Amongst other things, the Parthians were reported to have ostriches in their land. Indeed Wu Ti's first embassy returned with a present of an ostrich egg from the Persian sovereign, and a number of conjurors.

At this time [says the historian] the emperor often made tours of inspection to the seaside, when he was generally accompanied by numbers of foreign guests, upon whom he would bestow abundant provisions in order to impress them with the wealth of China. On such occasions crowds of onlookers were attracted by the performance of wrestlers, mummers, and all such wonderful entertainments, and by lavish feasts of wine and meat, by which the foreign guests were made to realise China's astounding greatness. They were also made to inspect the several granaries, stores, and treasures, with a view to showing them the greatness of China, and to inspiring them with awe. Later on the skill of these jugglers, wrestlers, mummers and similar performers was further developed, and their efficiency was increased from year to year. It was from this period that the coming and going of ambassadors of the foreign countries of the northwest became more and more frequent. The countries west of Ferghana which, being of the opinion that they were too far away from China, had as yet calmly stood on their national pride, could not be won over by our polite civilisation into a state of vassalage.

However, despite this 'national pride' and the intransigent deserts of high Asia, the Han empire had a greater range by the first century BC than its contemporary the empire of Rome. Chinese silk softened the existence of denizens of the Middle Kingdom and of barbarians across the Eurasian continent. Pieces of Han silk found their way throughout the known world, and specimens have been recovered from central Asia, the Roman empire, and Siberia. Though China began to receive from the outer barbarians luxury items such as precious stones, perfumes, ivory and horses, the barbarian demand for silk was stronger than the Chinese need for barbarian products, with the exception of horses. Silk, so much prized abroad, was an item of exchange in China. It is recorded that in Han times silk was used to pay the troops. When Emperor Wu Ti inspected the troops along the Wall, he distributed, according to Ssuma Chien, a million bolts of silk in bounty.

The great camel caravans of the Old Silk Road did not make a through journey across the whole of the Eurasian continent. The merchandise was carried from stage to stage by different caravans. Thriving market centres grew up along the route, at the different stages and oases where the caravans halted. The route was kept open and relatively safe from attack not only by the chain of Han fortresses which stretched out from the Middle Kingdom, but also by the blows struck against the Huns by the Han.

Three massive expeditions by Wu Ti against the Huns succeeded in driving them out of the Ordos country back beyond the Wall and the Gobi desert. The wars continued under later Han rulers and the nomads were forced on the defensive, weakened by warfare and attacked also by natural calamities. Large numbers were lost through violent winter snow storms; a series of droughts and plagues of locusts reduced vegetation over huge areas. The nomads and their stocks perished. Internal dissensions took further toll, and eventually the Hsiung Nu separated into two groups, the northern and the southern Huns. The southern Huns submitted to the Han in 51 BC, and the ruler came himself to Changan to pay homage to the Dragon Throne. The northern Huns from their grazing grounds on the Mongolian Plateau continued to harass communications with the west. They were several times beaten by the Han army, and gradually moved to the north-west. When the Huns moved, other nomad hordes rode in and occupied the vacated pastures. The northern Huns started on the western migrations which eventually brought them to the grazing lands of central Europe. These outer barbarians became the grave-diggers of the Roman rather than the Celestial Empire. Their descendants sacked not Changan, but Rome.

The Han empire expanded eastwards and to the south, as well as through the heart of Asia. In the days of the first Chin emperor, an expedition had been sent over the eastern sea to Japan to make contact with the celestial beings who were supposed to dwell in the islands of the Pacific. Han Wu Ti sent a military expedition east and extended Han domination to north Korea and southern Manchuria. From Korea, Chinese influence, especially cultural, reached Japan. Direct contact also was made with Japan in the first century AD.

In the south, the weak states were soon mastered by the warlike Son of Heaven; Han population spread southward; Kwangsi and north Vietnam were brought under Chinese suzerainty.

Through its contact with south-east Asia tea was introduced into China, at first as a medicinal beverage, but later it became a general drink. It was often boiled with rice, or ginger salt, or with onion, orange peel or milk. Then the practice of drinking tea by itself developed, a practice which became ritualised in the Middle Kingdom and elsewhere.

Communications from the west were noted in the Later Han. The sea-route (known as the Spice Route), opened up between China and the Roman west. It was recorded that a group of merchants in AD 166 reached the southern borders of the Celestial Empire from Tongking; they claimed to be envoys from An Tun the emperor of Ta Chin (Rome)—in other words they claimed to come from Mark Antony.

During the reign of Wu Ti the Celestial Empire had trebled in size. The rising prosperity, which had enabled the early Han rulers to relax some of the harsher measures of the Chin empire, could not survive the demands of the Wu Ti period. The long wars, especially against the Hsiung Nu, had depleted the imperial treasury and emptied the granaries. Peasants had been pressed into the armies in vast numbers, and much land was left uncultivated. In times of drought and flood the peasants died of famine. The songs of the day record the misery of those taken from their villages to fight in the north:

They fought south of the ramparts,
They died north of the wall
They died in the moors and were not buried.
Their flesh was the food of crows. . . .
I think of you faithful soldiers
Your service shall not be forgotten.
For in the morning you went out to battle
And at night you did not return.

Ssuma Chien summed up the times:

'Nothing in fact but wars and rumours of wars, from day to day.'

At length under lax laws, the wealthy began to use their riches for evil purposes of pride and self-aggrandisement and oppression of the weak. Members of the imperial family received grants of land, while from the highest to the lowest, everyone vied with his neighbour in lavishing money on houses, and appointments and apparel, altogether beyond the limit of his means. Such is the everlasting law of the consequence of prosperity and decay.

There followed extensive military preparations in various parts of the empire . . . the establishment of a trade route with the barbarians of the south-west, for which purposes mountains were hewn through for many miles. The object was to open up the resources of those remote districts; but the result was to swamp the inhabitants with hopeless ruin. Then again there was the subjugation of Korea; its transformation into an imperial dependency: with other troubles nearer home. The Huns violated their treaty and broke in upon our northern frontier, with great injury to the empire. Nothing in fact but wars and rumours of wars from day to day . . .

Meanwhile certain levies were made on a scale calculated to meet the exigencies of public expenditure; while the land tax and customs' revenue were regarded by all officials, from the Emperor downwards, as their own personal emoluments, and such revenue was not entered in the ordinary expense of the empire. Grain was forwarded by water to the capital for the use of the officials there. Soldiers massed on northern frontier against the Huns; food so scarce that the authorities offered certain rank and titles of honour to those who would supply a given quantity of grain. Later on drought ensued in the west, and official rank was again made a marketable commodity while those who broke the law were allowed to commute their penalties by money payments . . .

By the end of the first century BC the number of peasants whose lands had been appropriated by landlords had risen steeply. Individual plots were too small to produce sufficient for their current needs and reserves for times of natural calamity. To meet the demands of tax collectors they borrowed money at extortionate rates of interest, often in excess of 20 per cent. To meet his debts the peasant was forced to sell his land to the landlord, who in turn was anxious to extend his domain. Children of peasants were frequently sold; in the town houses of the wealthy they became slaves, singing girls or eunuchs. Thereafter the landless peasant became a hired labourer on the estate of the landlord, or a tenant, paying half of the produce as rent; some took to the wilds and lived as outlaws.

The officials, who were often themselves landlords or related to landlords, exempted their own estates from taxation. Their rank entitled them to other privileges such as reduced sentences for crimes. The officials who were responsible for tax collection, shifted the burden more and more on to the shoulders of those 'free' peasants still on the tax registers, outside the big estates. The problem of the accumulation of land in the hands of a limited class of landowners recurred in each dynasty. Measures resulting in temporary amelioration were sometimes devised, but no dynasty provided a long-term solution.

While the condition of the peasant in the Han period became more and more intolerable, the life of the privileged became overtly parasitic. The scholar Chung Chang Tung described such life in his biography:

Let the place where one lives have good fields and a large house set upon a hillside and looking over a river, surrounded by canals and bamboo pools. In front are laid out the threshing floor and the vegetable garden, and behind is planted an orchard of fruit trees. There are enough carriages and boats to ensure that one shall not have the trouble of walking or wading; there are enough servants to ensure that one shall not exhaust oneself with menial tasks. For nourishing one's family, the finest viands are at hand: wife and children do not have to bear the burden of doing any hard work . . .

In the last years of Wu Ti there was a series of large revolts, among both peasants and among the slaves of the government works.

Wang Mang

In the early days of the Han, factional quarrels throughout the country had been avoided through curbs on the power of the feudal princes. Factions later grew up at court itself, however, around the kin of the imperial consort. In AD 8 for example a successor of Wu Ti was overthrown by the nephew of one of the empresses. This nephew Wang Mang assumed the title of emperor.

He is notable for the reforms which he attempted to introduce to meet the agrarian and fiscal crises.

He restored the 'levelling system' whereby the government bought and stored grain when prices were low, and released stock on to the market when prices rose. He built up government monopolies again. He tried to deal with the lack of state revenues by calling in gold currency in exchange for copper coins.

Uncultivated fields were to be taxed, and he attempted a redistribution of large estates amongst peasants by taking over the land and distributing it amongst the peasants on the tax registers. He decreed the end of private slavery; but, as this could not be enforced, he instituted a heavy tax on slave owners.

These measures were resisted by the wealthy landowners, and Wang Mang had no means of enforcing them. The higher officials, who entered government service as a result of their education, were the kin of the wealthy land-owning families who alone could support the expense of education. This monopoly of education enabled them to retain political power for many generations. They were more inclined to increase the taxes of the peasants than to involve their own families in sacrifices. The fiscal reforms also provided the officials with opportunities to enrich themselves—at the cost of the success of the reforms.

Natural calamities aggravated the general distress. There were breaks in the dykes of the Yellow River; large areas were devastated near the capital.

Red Eyebrow and Green Woodsmen risings

Secret societies, which were a characteristic expression of agrarian distress, arose. A new series of rebellions ensued.

In the Hupei region the rebels were known as the Green Woodsmen after the forests in which the peasants took refuge; in Shantung there were the Red Eyebrows, from the distinguishing mark they adopted. Men of these societies had strong Taoist affinities; they led simple disciplined lives.

Wang Mang's army was defeated, and the capital Changan fell to the rebels. Wang Mang was killed. Amongst the rebel forces were a number of landlords and nobles, including a descendant of the Han imperial house, Kuang Wu; he turned the rebellion to his own advantage, and in AD 25 re-established Han rule, with his capital at Loyang. Han rule survived two more centuries.

Later, or Eastern Han, AD 25–220

Han Kuang Wu suppressed the Red Eyebrows and other rebels and restored a strong centralised administration. In the fighting many of the great landowners had been wiped out; more peasants were added

to the tax registers, thus improving the tax returns to the state.

The northern nomads had once again profited by the conflict within the Middle Kingdom to raid the borderlands and interrupt communications with central Asia and the Old Silk Road. Although the southern section of the Huns made their peace with the Son of Heaven, fighting continued with the others throughout the first century of the Later Han. Central Asia was reconquered by General Pan Ch'ao (brother of the woman historian mentioned above). He was made governor general of central Asia, and subsequently led his army across the Pamirs to conquer the whole area as far as the Caspian. At this point in history only Parthia separated the outposts of the Han and the Roman empires from each other. Some Chinese control of this area lasted until the middle of the second century AD, by which time the Later Han was in decline.

Emperor Kuang Wu, who re-established the Han dynasty, took steps, like Kao Tsu, to increase production and relieve the plight of the peasant. Soldiers returned to their native places to help with agriculture. Taxation and corvée demands were reduced; water control works were undertaken. The use of improved iron implements on the land also helped to increase production. A century of comparative peace ensued. However the same problems faced the Later Han that faced their predecessors, and they were no more successful in the long run in dealing with them.

The power of the great landowners increased; indeed it was their support which had enabled Kuang Wu to seize the throne. It was they who benefited most from the increase in agricultural production, the population growth and the bringing of scrubland into arable cultivation. While they paid to the government in taxes about one-thirtieth of the yield of their estates, they claimed in rent from their tenants some half of the peasant crop. In addition many of them used their official positions to secure total exemption from taxation.

Again impoverished peasants gave themselves into the service of the great landowners, with the status more or less of serfs; or they joined the private armies of the landlords, who also built themselves fortified manors. Or they took flight and joined bands of rebels.

The dynasty began to face a double danger: the threat to the throne from powerful families with their own armies, forts and estates, and the revolt of peasant bands.

At the same time, at court, the conflict between factions increased, inflamed by the fact that in the second century AD many of the successors to the Dragon throne were minors.

Court factions

The Son of Heaven had many wives, but the mother of the heir elect was usually accepted as empress, and the family of the consort scrambled for and generally secured positions of power. When Kao

Dancer: pottery funary figure. Early Han.

Tsu the first Han emperor died, leaving the throne to a child, the dowager Empress Lu became regent; it seems she aimed at usurping power for her own kin. On her death the whole Lu clan was massacred.

The Han emperor, Wu Ti, made a drastic attempt to solve this problem – by the destruction of all the relatives of the woman whose son was declared heir apparent.

Later on, in the second century AD the family of the empress Liang dominated the government, to the extent of numbering in its ranks seven princes, three empresses, six imperial concubines and three grand generals of the army. Fifty-seven other members of the clan were appointed ministers of state.

The problem of the empresses' kin was aggravated by the intervention of the court eunuchs, who guarded the imperial harem. These were the only people with whom the empresses and the imperial children were in contact, and they came to exercise a great influence. The eunuchs were frequently men of lowly origin, and could rely only on their own machinations for advancement; they found plenty of scope in the environs of the Dragon Throne, and they frequently received high positions and huge estates. These upstarts of little education threatened the power of the court officials, and the two factions became deadly rivals. The dynastic histories contain many records of the infamy and greed of the court eunuchs; the histories were however written by scholar officials who were their mortal enemies.

The scholar officials and students formed an association to defend their interests, and at one stage over two hundred students of the imperial college were arrested as anti-government rebels.

Palace revolts became the order of the day; in the sixties and seventies of the first century AD open conflict broke out between the eunuchs and the officials. The eunuchs gained the upper hand, and the mortality amongst the mandarins was considerable.

Yellow Turban revolt

The condition of the Middle Kingdom degenerated further. In the last quarter of the century revolts gathered force, bands of peasants arose against officials and landlords. In east China the 'Way of the Great Peace' (Tai Ping Tao) – called the Yellow Turbans because of the yellow kerchiefs they wore on their heads, rose under the leadership of a wandering Taoist magician who was believed to have curative powers. The Yellow Turbans were also influenced by the secret sect of astrologers who used their 'knowledge' to predict the downfall of dynasties. In the west, the rebels were led by the 'Five Pecks of Rice Band', so called because of the dues paid to the leaders.

The Han court assembled large armies to deal with the revolts. Instead the army generals used the forces under their command to

establish their own power. The palace eunuchs revolted in turn. Capital and palace were sacked and destroyed. The Chinese empire broke up in disorder.

The dynastic cycle

The features of this collapse were to be repeated in many later periods. The central problem, as Ssuma Chien recorded, and most other commentators noted, was the ruin of the peasantry. Peasant holdings were insufficient to provide a livelihood. In the best of seasons peasants were unable to meet the rent demands of their landlords and the tax demands of officials, to feed their families, and to keep seed for the spring sowing. The peasant accumulated debts to the landlord and moneylender: as these and the government official were frequently members of the same family, if not the same individual, the peasant was without recourse, his plight without remedy.

On the other hand, the landlord-officials, the gentry, were also money-lenders as well as the speculators who profited from seasonal variations in crop prices; they paid little for the crops received at harvest time, and sold at high rates in spring and times of shortage. The peasant was forced to make over his holding to the landlord and the great estates became greater.

Lu Chih, writing in the eighth century, described the process which was repeated into the twentieth century:

When the peasant is ruined, he has to sell his field and his hut. If it happens to be a good year, he may just be able to pay his debts. But no sooner has the harvest been brought in than the grain bins are empty again, and contract in hand and sack on back, he has to go off and start borrowing again. He has heavier and heavier interest to pay, and soon has not got enough to eat. If there is a famine he falls into utter ruin. Families disperse, parents separate, they seek to become slaves, and no one will buy them . . . the rich seize several times ten thousand mou of land, the poor have no land left, and attach themselves to the big powerful families and become their private retainers. They borrow seed and food, and lease land as tenants. All the year round they work themselves to death without a day's rest, and when they have paid all their debts they live in constant anxiety whether they will be able to make both ends meet. The large landowners however live on the rents from their land, and are trouble free and carefree. Wealth and poverty are clearly separated . . . .

A couple of centuries later Su Hsun commented:

Those who till the fields do not own them, and those who own the fields do not till them . . . the men at work are urged on with whip and cudgel, and the master treats them like slaves. He, on the other hand, sits at his ease and sees that his orders are carried out. . . . Of the produce of the fields, he takes half, although there is but one owner and ten labourers. Hence the owner, his half daily accumulating, attains wealth and power, while the labourer, his half merely providing his daily fare, falls into poverty and starvation.

The only escape from the burden of rent, tax and interest demands, and summonses for corvées, was through flight to the wilds; num-

bers of peasants became vagabonds and were officially treated as bandits; they lived as outlaws, eventually, perhaps, joining with others in secret societies and periodic peasant revolts. The peasants who remained in the villages had to shoulder the tax and corvée burdens due from those who fled or those who had left to work for the landlord. When drought, flooding and inadequacy of water control measures resulted in crop failures, when wars or court extravagances produced government deficits and demands for increased corvée and taxes, or when population growth outpaced the productivity of the peasant holdings, agrarian crises reached a new pitch of intensity. Secret societies took root; the peasant bands increased, and revolts swept the land. At this stage conflicts at court, and attacks by barbarians profiting from the troubled times, further weakened the dynasties, which collapsed and were replaced by others founded by peasant leaders, by adventurers from gentry or aristocratic families, or by military usurpers.

The new rulers were content to leave society basically as it was. In particular they turned to the same group of gentry officials to restore order. Power fell again into the hands of the literate; so that even in those cases where attempts were made, as they were early in the life of a dynasty, to relieve peasant distress, the measures were indifferently applied and quickly relaxed; the pattern of dynastic decay recurred.

A seventeenth century philosopher, Huang Tsung Hsi observed, 'Whether there is peace or disorder does not depend on the rise and fall of dynasties but upon the happiness or distress of the people.'

The first four centuries of Chinese imperial unity ended with widespread revolt and the political division of the Middle Kingdom.

6. Disunity

AD 220–581

The period of Disunity which followed the overthrow of the Later Han and the breakup of the first Chinese empire, lasted some three and a half centuries, during which time the kingdom reverted to smaller political units. It was the first of several interludes of division and struggle in the history of the empire.

Three Kingdoms

The generals became independent warlords, and three rival kingdoms were established. In the north the Wei state occupied the China plain; it was set up by a brilliant poet, General Tsao Tsao, the adopted son of a eunuch, and his sons, also poets. The other two states, of Shu and Wu, covered the upper and lower Yangtze basins respectively. Each of the three kingdoms was based on a natural geographic region. The warlords and their supporters fought out their rival claims in incessant conflicts, with disastrous loss of life and to the ruin of agriculture. The times were reminiscent of the period of the Warring States before the founding of the First Empire by the Chin. The stories of these centuries are filled with accounts of massive disasters: of warlords who massacred hundreds of thousands of victims, so that rivers were blocked with the bodies of the dead. Even the troops were short of food. In one province, they were reported to be living on a diet of mulberries; in another, the only food available was river snails and oysters.

The period was made famous by a cycle of stories, known as *The Romance of the Three Kingdoms* written by the Ming novelist, Lo Kuan Chung and based on the history of these kingdoms. In this book the period was glamorised as an age of chivalry; many episodes of a heroic and extravagant nature, have since been dramatised. The work is known throughout the Middle Kingdom. According to one episode General Tsao Tsao, after many losses, secured the services of Kuan Yu, a daredevil whose exploits became legendary; he was subsequently deified, and temples honouring him as the God of War appeared in many parts of the Kingdom. He was adopted as municipal god, as guardian angel of many Chinese cities:

Suddenly it was announced that the enemy, under General Yen, was preparing an attack; and Tsao Tsao took Kuan Yu to the top of a hill to reconnoitre. They sat down, and the other generals stood around them, while Tsao Tsao pointed out the position of the enemy, the fresh-looking splendour of his standards, the dense mass of his spears and swords, all drawn up in formidable array . . . 'You see this powerful force of men and horses . . .' 'I do,' answered Kuan Yu. 'They remind me of a lot of earthen cocks and pottery dogs.' Again Tsao Tsao

Pottery tomb guards. These figures probably represent magicians holding in their hands weapons directed against evil spirits.

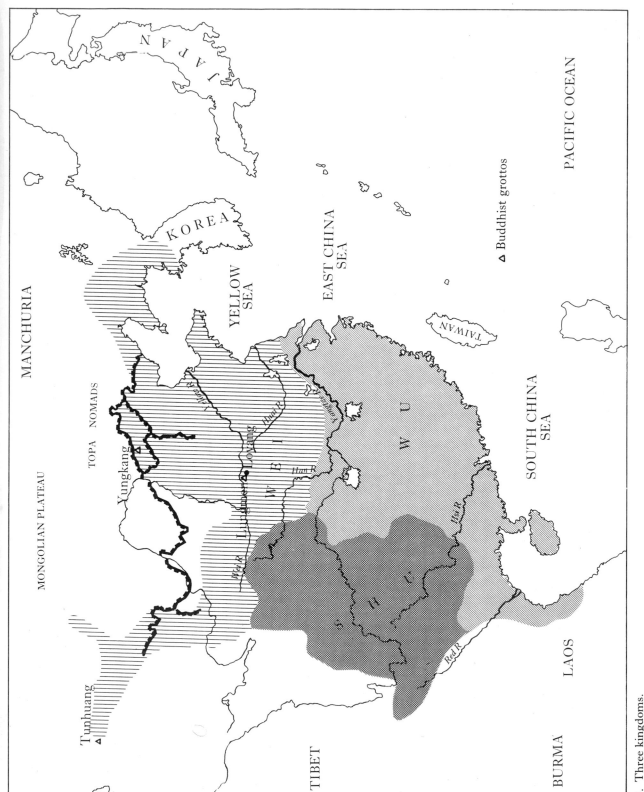

6. Three kingdoms.

Map labels (reading as positioned on the map):

MANCHURIA

JAPAN

MONGOLIAN PLATEAU

TOPA NOMADS

KOREA

YELLOW SEA

Tunhuang △

Yungkang △

WEI

Loyang
Ch'angan

Wei R
Han R
Yellow R

Han R

EAST CHINA SEA

Buddhist grottos △

PACIFIC OCEAN

TAIWAN

W U

SOUTH CHINA SEA

TIBET

Hsi R

Red R

BURMA

LAOS

pointed and said, 'There under the standard, with the embroidered robe and the golden coat of mail, holding a sword and standing still on his horse–is General Yen.' Kuan Yu raised his eyes and looked over in the direction indicated; then he said, 'To me General Yen looks as if he had stuck up an advertisement for the sale of his head.' 'Ah,' cried Tsao Tsao, 'you must not under rate him.' . . . Kuan Yu rushed off at once, and jumping on his horse, with his sword reversed, galloped downhill. With round, glaring phoenix-like eyes, and his silkworm-moth eyebrows raised straight up, he dashed right among the enemy whose ranks opened like parting waves, until he reached General Yen himself. General Yen had no time to lay his hand on his sword before he was knocked off his horse. . . . Kuan Yu jumped down, cut off the general's head, hung it round his horse's neck, remounted in a moment, and with sword drawn made his way through the enemy's ranks as though no one was there to stop him. Officers and men were all terrified and a perfect panic ensued. Tsao Tsao's troops seized the opportunity for attack and slaughtered the enemy in great numbers, besides capturing many horses and quantities of munitions of war. Kuan Yu rode his horse up the hill, to receive congratulations from the various commanders as he presented the head to Tsao Tsao who exclaimed 'General, you are indeed no mortal man!'

Tsao Tsao is depicted in most of the popular stories as a talented but treacherous villain. His help for the Han poetess, Tsai Wen Chi, shows him in a different light. Tsai Wen Chi experienced many vicissitudes together with her father, a scholar, whose fortunes alternated between official favour and disgrace. On her return with her family from exile, she was captured by the Huns, who were making one of their last incursions south of the Wall. She was given to a tribal chief, and lived with him for twelve years, bearing him two sons. When Tsao Tsao came to power he sent messengers with gifts to the Huns, asking for her return. Tsai Wen Chi was sent back, but was not allowed to bring her two children with her. In China, she married an official who also fell from favour, but whose life was saved through his wife's intervention with Tsao Tsao.

The lady wrote 'The Eighteen Laments', a poem for music, describing her unhappy existence as a captive, and her longing for the silky ripple of young rice in her homeland. Her story became the subject of several paintings. Her poetry, now much admired, was not at first acclaimed, possibly because, according to the ethic of the day, Tsai Wen Chi should have killed herself rather than become the wife of an enemy chieftain.

During these times, the big landlords became even more powerful, amassing huge estates, and evading taxation. They fortified their houses against predatory neighbours, and used them as bases of attack, threatening to usurp the authority of the rulers. The Middle Kingdom became an arena for countless wealthy soldiers of fortune to try out their strength.

The degeneration of the scholar officials, the mandarins, into an effete and parasitic caste, who worked generation after generation only on behalf of their landlord kin, did not help matters. They were

Pottery dog monster. Northern Wei (Topa) period.

The captivity of Tsai Wen Chi.
Part of an unsigned painting,
probably Ming period illustrating
the captivity of Tsai Wen Chi with
the Huns, and her return to China.

In her poem, 'The Eighteen
Laments', Tsai Wen Chi says:
I would not have thought
That growing older I would have
Been able to return to Han again;
I hugged my Hun children,
Tears drenching my clothing;
The Han ambassador coming for me
Had a cart with four horses,
And I inside it yet weeping . . .

Wondering how I could
Give these sons of mine each a pair
Of wings so that they could fly back
With me . . .'

Lament XIII.

coming to regard even indirect contact with physical labour as degrading; they cultivated manners which indicated how remote they
were from such activity. One scholar poet and military official for
example was famous for 'his small waist, joined eyebrows, long finger-
nails, as well as for the speed at which he could write'. The incredibly
long nails of the mandarins became the sign that they did not undertake any manual labour.

Another description says that the mandarins were clean-shaven,
rouged, powdered and perfumed. They rode in long covered chariots.
When sitting, they rested their arms on embroidered cushions. When
they walked, attendants supported them. They knew nothing about
farming. They had never seen people working in the fields, since they
spent all their time in the capital. The story goes that one of these
officials, Wang Hi Chih, was asked by a superior officer, what office he
held: Wang replied that he thought it might be master of the Horse,
for he often saw men about the place leading horses. When asked how
many horses were under his charge, he replied that since he knew
nothing about the animal he could not tell how many there were.
Had many died recently? He replied that as he did not know the
condition of the living, surely he could not be expected to speak of
those that were dead.

When the capital was besieged, these individuals lacked the energy
even to mount and to flee for safety. It is said that the mandarins remained in the doomed city and starved. When the capital fell, they
put on their finest clothes, collected their gold and jade; and lay on
their beds, waiting for death.

As in the Warring States period before the First Empire, so too the turmoil of the third and fourth centuries AD gave rise to speculation, philosophy and different forms of religious attachment. Confucian orthodoxy was challenged on the one hand by a revival of a degenerate form of Taoism, and on the other by the introduction of Buddhism.

A number of the Han rulers had patronised the Taoists and had taken a special interest in the efforts of their alchemists to find an elixir of longevity, perhaps even of immortality. Kuang Wu, the first emperor of the Later Han, was reported to have been a regular Methuselah; he lived most of his six score and two years as a recluse on a mountain studying alchemy. His search for the drug of immortality appears to have been moderately successful, for he was last heard of ascending to heaven on a dragon.

In the second half of the third century there was a famous group of Taoist scholars who called themselves the Seven Sages of the Bamboo Grove. They fortified themselves against the troubled times with drink. One was notorious for riding about the capital in a small cart drawn by a deer. A servant followed bearing a large pot of wine, in case of need. Another servant carried a spade, with orders to bury his master wherever he might happen to drop dead in his cups. A later Taoist sage wrote a treatise on the drug of immortality. He argued that if animals could attain a long life, then man with the aid of knowledge could certainly surpass the brutes. The recipes he recommended were intended to rejuvenate as well as to prolong life.

Many of the scholars and recluses, however, were content with forming groups to cast off worldly troubles and to commune with nature; they engaged in philosophical discussion, composed poetry, played on the lute; and they drank.

Preoccupation with elixirs and alchemy resulted in the production of the earliest book on alchemy in the second century AD; a monumental encyclopaedia on the art of achieving immortality was produced at the beginning of the fourth. Another result was the untimely demise of a number of Sons of Heaven, through overdoses of cinnabar (mercuric sulphide), lead, gold, and other toxic substances held to be antidotes to mortality.

Humbler folk were attracted to the different Taoist sects whose creeds incorporated local superstitions and magical practices, and a multiplicity of traditional deities and guardian spirits, in a celestial hierarchy of immortals. Many sects became attached to various ideas of inner hygiene and nature cure: they denied themselves meat, grain foods and wine, for these were thought to nourish the three 'worms' of disease, senility and death. Some believed their own breath and saliva to be the purest forms of nourishment. They opened up their inner channels by special exercises, and purified their bodies generally by holding their breath for very long periods.

Buddhism

Buddhism spread from India to China towards the end of the third century AD. The prevailing disorders, aggravated by barbarian invasions and the flight of Confucian scholars to the south, gave Buddhism scope and a wide appeal in China, despite the fact that it had little in common with the rational humanistic traditions of Chinese classical thought. Historical Buddha, known as Sakyamuni, the teacher of the Sakya sect, was a contemporary of Confucius; he had been prince of a northern state in India near Nepal, around 500 BC. During a time of spiritual crisis in his life, a moment of enlightment came to him one day sitting in meditation under the Bo tree (the tree of knowledge). He discovered the path to personal tranquillity through moderation, the middle way between the extremes of self-indulgence and self-mortification. He taught that as desires are the source of pain in life, the pain of existence can be eliminated only by eliminating desires. To this end he advocated right living, in order to overcome personal craving. The rules for right living prohibited the killing of any living creature (Buddhism recognises no distinction between humans and animals), speaking falsehood, unchastity, and strong drink. His disciples practised confessionals; they lived a simple and ascetic life. The objective was Nirvana, the condition of complete serenity of spirit, when all cravings, strife and pain have been overcome, giving way to a peaceful merging of the spirit with eternal harmony.

This non-existence, this serenity, could not be achieved in one existence but only in the course of a series of rebirths, by which a pious person could rise in the hierarchy of beings and be ready for final deliverance. The pious person was reincarnated as a human being, the sinner was degraded and might become a dog, a pig or a demon. Intercession for the dead, whereby those with a full set of virtues (for example some monks) might increase the stock of merit of those in need, became an acceptable transaction. Contributions to Buddhist communities served the same humane end.

For many centuries the disciples were ascetic mendicants, and Buddhism developed through oral tradition. Before long they settled in monasteries and, by the first century BC, had committed much of the doctrine to writing. A voluminous sacred Buddhist literature grew up in India, where the faith spread under royal patronage, and also in Ceylon. At the end of the first century AD, Buddhism reached north into central Asia through the Kushan empire of the Yueh Chih, an empire stretching from north India to the Tarim Basin, whose emperor Kanishka was an ardent patron of Buddhism. From central Asia, the faith spread into north China. The earliest to bring Buddhism to China may well, however, have been the Indian traders sailing to China across the southern ocean. A later development of Buddhism, theocratic lamaism, spread subsequently into China

Kuan Yin, the Buddhist Goddess of Mercy, guiding a soul.
This painting was found at Tunhuang, and is probably a copy of an earlier Tang original. Kuan Yin originated in India as a male god and in early pictures is shown, as here, wearing a moustache; in the course of time the Chinese came to think of Kuan Yin as a goddess. On the right is a lady in the dress of the Tang period.

through Tibet and Mongolia.

At the time of the Emperor Ming Ti of the Later Han (AD 57–75) there was a Buddhist group at court. During the period of Disunity, the appeal of Buddhism became widespread. The form which was brought to China included popular elements, such as faith in the efficacy of repetitive prayers before bodhisattvas (images of Buddhist saints who dispense virtue; they have postponed their own salvation in order to help others), a handy all-purposes routine for times of stress. Although the alien religion in its denial of the significance of the social order ran counter to the Confucian trend, it nevertheless offered a possibility of individual relief and personal salvation in times which seemed to afford little prospect of general deliverance.

Zealous missionaries soon came to China to consolidate the early casual conversions. It is recorded in the annals that a Parthian prince, known by his Chinese name of An Shih Kao, was translating Buddhist scriptures and winning converts in Loyang towards the end of the second century AD. More famous was Kumarajiva, born in central Asia of an Indian father; he was captured towards the end of the fourth century by a Chinese expedition. In China he translated nearly a hundred Buddhist texts.

From the third century onwards there were a great many contacts between Chinese and foreign Buddhists. Buddhist monks came into China from India, Ceylon and central Asia. On the other hand Chinese converts became active in seeking the sources of their faith. A series of great journeys were undertaken by Buddhists from China during the next few centuries.

Above: marble Head of Kuan Yin, the Buddhist Goddess of Mercy, the most popular boddhisattva, a saintly being who has postponed her own elevation to Nirvana in order to help mankind. Tang period.

Fa Hsien

Fa Hsien (AD 319–414) walked from central China, across the Gobi desert, over the Hindu Kush mountains, through India south to the Hooghly River, where he took ship and returned to China by way of Ceylon and the straits of Malacca, arriving home after fifteen years,

Above left: Mi Lo Fu, the Laughing Buddha – a boddhisattva. This 'Laughing Buddha' is carved on the hillside of the 'Peak that Flew Over', the name of a mountain near Hangchow.

with a collection of scriptures which he settled down to translate at Nanking. He left a record of his journey from which we see that the intrepid travellers of those days faced not only physical hazards but extraordinary supernatural perils. Of the Gobi desert he said: 'In this desert there are a great many evil spirits and also hot winds; those who encounter them perish to a man. There are neither birds above nor beasts below. Gazing on all sides as far as the eye can reach in order to mark the track, no guidance is to be obtained save from the rotting bones of dead men, which point the way.' Further westward the pilgrim crossed the Bolor Tagh range: 'On these mountains there is snow in winter and summer alike. There are also venomous dragons, which if provoked, spit forth poisonous winds, rain, snow, sand and stones. Of those who encounter these dangers not one in ten thousand escapes. The people of that part are called men of the Snow Mountains.'

Fa Hsien spent six years in travelling from Changan to central India; he stayed there six years, and it took him three more to return home. He wrote down on bamboo tablets and on silk an account of his experiences.

Imperial patrons supported Buddhism in a number of the states of China that were established during the period of Disunity. In the sixth century the ruler in Nanking was an adherent. So intense was his conviction that he thrice renounced the world and his throne for holy orders, and each time he had to be redeemed by his ministers. Buddhism in China coexisted with other faiths and doctrines; indeed some Taoists tolerated Buddhism as an alien form of Taoism, discovered by a barbarian who might nevertheless at some time join the hierarchy of Taoist immortals, albeit in a lowly rank. Chinese deities have never shown the exclusivity of their western colleagues, and have set an example of good neighbourliness for long periods. Rivalry between Buddhism and Taoism came at a later stage, as did the conflict between the Confucian state and Buddhism.

Buddhism continued to flourish in China from the middle of the fourth century until the eighth. This was a period of contructive and artistic energy, especially in the north, where many dynasties of the Disunity period had their capitals. Much of the energy was directed to hewing and decorating great cave temples in the cliffs. Numbers of artists and craftsmen were employed throughout the centuries carving the shrines and hillside grottoes, decorating them with frescoes and stone reliefs by the thousand. Some of these 'Thousand Buddha Grottoes' have only recently been explored.

A famous set of grottoes is at Yunkang, in the sandstone cliffs of north Shansi. In one cave was erected a stone image of Buddha, seated in Indian fashion, measuring fifty feet in height. At Lungmen near Loyang, the limestone caves in the cliffs facing the I river (connected with the legendary water control exploits of the Great Yu of

the Hsia), there is a profusion of richly decorated, well preserved grottoes. Perhaps the most outstanding are the shrines at Tunhuang, an important station on the Old Silk Road, where merchant caravans and pilgrims halted before setting out across the desert.

The Three Kingdoms survived for most of the third century, but precariously. One of the rulers of the Kingdom of Wei, in the north, faced with civil war in his state, made the mistake of inviting some of the nomad tribes to come to his aid. (The nomads had become active again along the Wall, during the period of Disunity.) His rival called in another tribe. The nomads streamed over the Wall and reached the Yangtze. The barbarian hosts were defeated in the battle of the Fei River in AD 383, and so prevented from crossing into southern China.

Northern and Southern Dynasties

The two following centuries of division and buccaneering were known as the period of the Northern and Southern Dynasties, owing to the consolidation of power based on the two main areas: the former consisted of the Yellow River basin northwards to the Wall; the latter of the Yangtze basin and lands south to the Red River.

One tribe of nomads, the Topa, which had moved in from Mongolia, founded their own dynasty, known as the Northern Wei. They grew slowly more powerful and in the first half of the fifth century eliminated their last rivals in north China, and established their capital at Loyang. They drove back other barbarians and repaired the Wall. Their armies spread north-west through the Tarim basin into central Asia. Their state incorporated areas which had benefited from water conservancy measures, between the Yellow and the Yangtze rivers, the granary of the kingdom. Like other nomad conquerors in

Yunkang Grottoes, Shansi province. Large image of Buddha in Grotto.

The Buddha is about 50 feet tall. These Grottoes, among the largest and most ancient in China, were carved in the fifth and sixth centuries, during the Northern Wei period, and are a treasury of Buddhist culture. They stretch for a kilometre along the cliff face.

77

Archer—from the Murals at the Tunhuang Grottoes, Kansu province. Tunhuang was a station on the Old Silk Road, the caravan route through central Asia.

A celestial from the Tunhuang Grottoes.

the centuries that followed, the Topa settled and became thoroughly sinicised. They called on scholar officials to rule and directed their energies to rehabilitating agriculture and increasing their revenue. A land equalisation measure distributed government lands to peasants according to family size; much waste land was reclaimed, and productivity increased. Chinese was made the official language at court; Topa aristocrats were required to adopt Chinese dress, customs, and surnames. They were also encouraged to intermarry.

This period of nomad attack in the north, like others subsequently, resulted in tens of thousands of people fleeing south, bringing across the Yangtze the cultural and economic standards of the Yellow River area. When Loyang fell to the Topa many of the less supine scholars had also fled southwards. Economic development in southern China which had tended to lag behind that of the Yellow River valley, now began to advance with the application of greater agricultural knowledge. Water control projects were extended, especially in the Yangtze valley, waste land was brought under cultivation, and in some areas good management produced two crops of wheat and rice a year. The south began to rival the northern region in terms of economic, cultural, and political importance.

Four dynasties ruled in the south in the fifth and sixth centuries; although agriculture advanced during this time, and silk and porcelain enterprises began to flourish in these regions, the people in general benefited little owing to the heavy demands of landlords for rents, and the state for taxes and corvée. Again the extravagance of the rich was contrasted with the oppression of the poor.

Describing the aristocrats, a contemporary said that with their perfumed clothes, raised shoes, silks and other decorations 'such was their grace as they came in and went out that they looked like fairies'.

In the north, the Topa rulers had assimilated the bureaucratic mode of life. Landlords and officials assisted each other to riches. It is said of one noble, that he 'used silver for the feeding troughs in his stables and gold for his horses' bits. At his sumptuous banquets, guests drank wine from crystal vessels, from cups of agate and ruby; they were entertained to exhibitions of his riches. These included 'a hundred gold vases and silver jars, and store houses where countless silk and other articles from all parts of the country were hoarded'.

Rebellions by different tribes of nomads, together with peasant risings against rulers who had become increasingly oppressive, increased in the middle of the sixth century, and culminated in a *coup d'état* in 581 when the Northern Wei throne was seized by a royal relative, who became know as Wen Ti, first emperor of a new dynasty, the Sui.

Wen Ti reduced the scale of taxation and the conscription periods, and added to the tax registers large numbers of peasants concealed by the landlords. After a few years he was able to send an expeditionary force across the Yangtze to conquer the south. Over three centuries of division were ended. The reunification under the Sui proved to be the prelude to the rise of the Second Chinese Empire, under the Tang.

The three centuries of political division had not disrupted the cultural homogeneity of the Middle Kingdom, nor lessened its vitality. The Dark Ages in Europe which followed the collapse of the Roman empire—a period roughly contemporary with the age of Disunity in China—were followed by an epoch in Europe when society was basically different from that of the Roman empire. The civilisation of China was not transformed during the disturbances. The barbarians who overran the north, were assimilated into Chinese culture. Chinese intensive agriculture, technology, and social organisation were adopted by the invaders. The Topa tribes had been assimilated; the southern regions integrated more fully than erstwhile into the Middle Kingdom.

In the field of science and mathematics there were even many advances. Ma Chun, a mechanical engineer of the Three Kingdoms period, invented a loom for weaving silk gauze which worked five or six times faster than the old models. He also invented a wheel to raise water for irrigation. Water mills became widespread at this time. Tsu Chung Shih, a mathematician of the fifth century, was the first to establish the value of the mathematical expression pi (π) to eight decimal places. Apparently the ratio of the circumference to the diameter of a circle had long been a preoccupation of Chinese mathematicians. An important agricultural encyclopaedia was produced during the Three Kingdoms period, as well as a geography of all the waterways of China, dealing with rivers, canals, salt wells and springs. It also included mines and volcanoes.

The wheelbarrow was developed in these times, a device not used in Europe until ten centuries later, where 'it may be among the humbler machines of the Renaissance, and it undoubtedly aided the industries then developing'.

Water-Lift, known as dragon's-backbone, invented by Ma Chun, a third century mechanical engineer. The lift, working like a modern ladder dredge, moves a series of flat pieces of wood which raise water from river to fields. Woodcut from a Sung Book of Agriculture.

Water-lifts can be seen, worked by peasants, to this day.

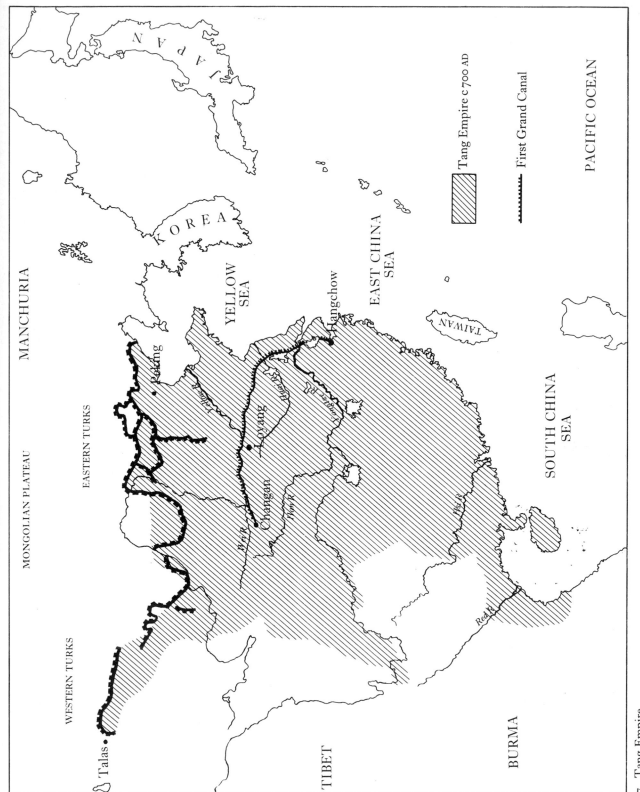

MANCHURIA

MONGOLIAN PLATEAU

EASTERN TURKS

WESTERN TURKS

Talas

TIBET

BURMA

KOREA

JAPAN

Peking

Loyang

Changan

Hangchow

YELLOW
SEA

EAST CHINA
SEA

TAIWAN

SOUTH CHINA
SEA

PACIFIC OCEAN

Yellow R.

Wei R.

Han R.

Yangtze R.

Min R.

Red R.

Tang Empire c 700 AD

First Grand Canal

7. Tang Empire.

7. Sui and Tang

AD 581–907

The ultimate victory the Sui and the reunification of the Empire may be ascribed to the irrigation works in the territories under their control, which provided substantial grain reserves; to the economic development of the southern regions of the empire, which led to a mutually beneficial and more stable integration of the two divisions of the Middle Kingdom; and to the military tactic of starving out opponents in preference to meeting them in pitched battle. A second great period of imperial unity was inaugurated.

The first Sui emperor, Wen Ti, introduced a series of economic reforms. Taxes and labour requirements from the peasants were reduced. Instead of young men being called up at the age of eighteen to serve one month annually, they were now liable at twenty-one, and for twenty days each year. A careful census placed many on the tax registers who had previously escaped through the connivance of the landlords they served; general tax requirements were reduced. Soldiers were given farm work. The penal code was reformed; the practice of displaying the head of a decapitated person on a pole was abolished, and the number of punishments reduced to: flogging with heavy or light sticks, imprisonment, exile, and death.

A constructive development was the continuation of the land equalisation system, which had been tried earlier by the Northern Wei. Waste land and public lands were distributed among the peasants so that each male adult would have as his own property an area of some 20 mou (called the mulberry field), and another 80 mou of land for arable farming, which returned to the state when the peasant was too old to work it, or on his death. Women were entitled to 40 mou of arable land. The tax rates required each couple to pay annually three piculs of grain, one bolt of silk, three ounces of silk floss or fifty feet of hemp cloth. Single men paid half the amount levied on couples.

Such measures helped to bring more land under cultivation and encouraged agricultural production. Other measures stimulated handicrafts and commerce. Up to the turn of the seventh century the population rose considerably; imperial granaries were full, and millions of bolts of silk packed the state depositories.

The second Sui emperor, Yang Ti, was inspired with grandiose ideas, some productive, others tyrannous and extravagant. Among the former was the construction of canals, especially the Grand Canal based on ancient canal works, which linked up the Yellow, Huai and Yangtze rivers. Many natural obstacles had to be overcome in the course of construction, for which two million people were conscripted; if there were not enough men they called up the women as well.

Emperor Yang Ti's trip on the Grand Canal. A traditional woodcut.

It was a wide canal, with tree-lined boulevards along the banks. The Son of Heaven celebrated the opening of the waterway with a pleasure cruise along it, on a magnificent dragon boat with four decks towering fifteen metres above the water. It was escorted by a retinue of thousands of other craft carrying officials and eunuchs, the empress and concubines. The line of boats is said to have stretched for a hundred kilometres, needing 80,000 labourers to tow them. Food for the junketing was requisitioned from the locality; huge surpluses were thrown away.

The Canal was more than gigantic folly. In a country where the main water routes flow west to east, the Canal formed a south to north artery of major significance. It linked the rich southern provinces, the ricelands of the Yangtze delta, to the northern provinces. Supplies were made available not only for the capital but also for the armies defending the northern frontiers. It was an important factor in the integration, political, economic and cultural, of the northern and southern regions of the Celestial Empire; it contributed to the growing economic significance of the Yangtze valley.

The construction of the palaces and pleasure parks of Loyang, for which further hosts of men were conscripted, was another matter. The tree trunks for the palace pillars came from the south, borne on the backs of peasants half of whom died on the journey; carts coming into the capital were filled with corpses. It was said that in the winter, when flowers died, the trees in the imperial park were adorned with artificial blossoms of silk, to please an imperial whim; the birds of the imperial park were almost exterminated to provide down for the Emperor's cushions.

Great extravagances depleted the treasury. The people of China, or, to use the official expression 'all under Heaven', were ordered to pay ten years' taxes in advance. Added to this was the burden of a series of wars launched against neighbouring states. Conscription and the requisitioning of supplies were intensified. Chariots and warships were built at breakneck speed; craftsmen building them were urged on till they died of exhaustion; thus nearly half the labour force was lost.

Particularly disastrous were the wars against Korea. A Chinese army of over a million was put to flight by the Koreans, with the loss of provisions and weapons. Peasant troubles recurred, especially in those provinces most hard pressed for recruits and supplies; peasants seized the grain in the granaries and distributed it to the hungry.

Despite the Korean defeat Emperor Yang Ti continued his extravagances. In AD 618 he was assassinated in an army coup; one of the successful rebel officers, Li Shih Min, installed his own father as emperor, founding the Tang dynasty. It took him a decade to eliminate rivals, after which, having secured his father's abdication, Li Shih Min took the throne himself as the emperor Tai Tsung.

Tang, AD 618 to 907

The empire consolidated by the Tang was the largest and probably
the most populous state in the world at that time. This was the age of
Charlemagne in Europe and Alfred the Great in England. Li Shih
Min was the first of several outstanding Tang rulers during whose
reigns the Celestial Empire prospered and reached the high points
of economic and cultural achievement for which the period is famed.
The second was a woman, the Empress Wu (683–705), China's first
and only female 'Son of Heaven'.

Li Shih Min was an able general, a scholar and a successful admini-
strator. Learning one lesson from the downfall of earlier dynasties,
he said: 'The emperor likes to have a palace built, but the people do
not like building it. The emperor craves the flesh pots, but the people
hate doing labour service. It is dangerous to burden the people with
excessive labour service.' Also: 'An emperor collecting too heavy
taxes is like a man eating his own flesh. When the flesh is all gone, the
man dies.'

The reunification of China and the rise of the Second Empire were
not primarily questions of military successes or personal achievement,
but were based on the developments of earlier decades. Canal and
other communications helped to reinforce the political and economic
unity of the empire, and to make centralised government effective.

Emperor Tang Tai Tsung (Li Shih
Min), AD 626–649, founder of the
Tang dynasty. From an engraving
on a stele in Shensi.

83

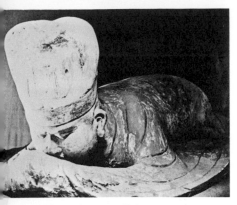

'If you bow at all, bow low.'
Chinese proverb.

The early Tang rulers not only restored the equal field system but applied it more thoroughly than before. Every three years, a full census of the population, by province and district, was taken, including names and ages of all members of peasant households. Annual tax rates were reduced and concessions granted. A man could contract out of the silk tax by contributing an extra fifteen days corvée, and thirty days extra labour service could secure exemption from the grain tax as well. On the other hand corvée labour could be commuted into textile or money taxes. This flexibility enabled peasants to avoid interruptions at critical times in their farm work. Indeed in times of natural calamity the corvée was excused completely. Remissions of taxes and services were also granted to those bringing new land under cultivation.

The system of commutation led to the development of units of uniform value in the principal commodities. A string of a thousand cash, an 'ounce' of silver, a 'bushel' of grain, a bolt of silk or a weight of silk floss came to be standardised and roughly equivalent in value.

The measures worked satisfactorily for a time. The interests of the state as well as those of the peasants were served by keeping as many peasants as possible solvent and 'free' from slavery or serfdom on the great estates where the landowners were exempted from taxation. The 'free' peasant was the tax-paying peasant on the state tax registers. Later, during the Tang, taxation shifted away from the poll-tax to a land based tax. More irrigation canals were dug. Successful campaigns were launched against locust scourges. Agricultural production revived and livestock increased.

The scale of punishments in the penal code was further modified. The lightest category was flogging, divided into two grades, the more severe of which often proved fatal. Next in severity were two categories of banishment, the lighter, for periods up to three years, within the offender's native province; the heavier for life, to some distant province, as soldiers to man the Long Wall, to the garrisons of central Asia, or to the unhealthy southern provinces of the empire. The fifth penalty was death, by various means. Li Shih Min enacted that each death sentence should be reviewed on three separate days, and that the magistrate concerned should abstain from meat, music and entertainment during this period, so that he would be conscious of the serious nature of his responsibility all this time. The laws against rebellion, as in all periods, were very severe, involving the family of the convict in proportion to the degree of kinship, for it was held that the individual was inseparable from his family.

Examinations and the bureaucracy

The early Han system of selecting officials for government service on the basis of merit had disappeared in the centuries of Disunity. Powerful local families had tended to recommend their own nominees

Kneeling official. Pottery figure, Tang period.

for office. Men were appointed through favour or nepotism regardless of merit.

The first Sui emperor had revived the Han system of examinations based on the Confucian classics, and the Tang systematised and expanded it. Li Shih Min enlarged the imperial college at Changan. Over three thousand scholars were in residence there. Provincial colleges were also maintained.

Examinations for the highest degree of *chin-shih* included the whole field of literature; candidates were required to write essays and poems according to traditional canons of style, and to write about political and administrative problems. Several thousand students assembled in their regional capitals for these trials. The successful candidates were summoned to the capital for another series of examinations, both written and oral, before any political office was granted. Appearance as well as oral ability were taken into account at this stage. A further series of examinations was used for the grading of selected candidates.

The Chinese system of a civil service based on examinations (which preceded by more than a millennium the British recruitment of civil servants by examination) reached its full development during the Tang period. It helped to produce the administrators who could meet the demands of an immense empire under centralised control, where tax and corvée registration and organisation, the conduct of public works like water conservancy, as well as the state enterprises, demanded a level of bureaucratic competence.

From the Tang dynasty onwards the imperial examination system remained, until the twentieth century, the principal avenue to official position. Education became tied to these examinations and as such became a system for the selection rather than the education of the Chinese ruling élite. Success in the examination was for the scholar like being touched by divinity:

He had a black gauze cap and green silk gown,
A jaspar ring on his cap and a purple belt;
His socks were white as snow,
His shoes like rosy clouds;
He's a lordly look and a natural dignity.
A man like that, if not a god,
Must be at least a high official or ruler of men.

To achieve such blessings the scholar might well sacrifice his youth:

Shadows of pairing sparrows cross his book,
  of poplar catkins, dropping overhead . . .
The weary student from his window-nook
  Looks up to find that spring has long since fled.

Once official appointment had been secured, promotion was achieved through seniority and through the recommendation of superiors, by a complex system of merit ratings. The sponsors of an official shared the downfall if their protégé fell from grace. The function of the government was not so much to administer the laws, but to collect revenue and to promote agriculture on which the revenues depended. Supreme power was exercised by the Emperor, aided by a small council of ministers. The empire was divided into prefectures which were again subdivided into districts, each in the charge of magistrates (officials) who combined all functions and exercised complete control over the area in their charge; they were responsible for the collection of revenue, the supervision of public works, and the maintenance of the peace, which included the administration of the penal laws.

In Tang times the 'three chiefs system' helped ensure the collection of taxes. The people were divided into groups mutually responsible for each other's conduct and for tax payments. Five families were grouped into a neighbourhood; five neighbourhoods constituted a village, and five villages an association. At each level a chief was appointed. This was an elaboration of the system of collective responsibility.

Tang emperors were supported by competent ministers. The central government machinery as well as the examination system became models for posterity. The emperor himself took an interest in the examinations, making or confirming the final selections.

The examinations were open to all ranks except, generally speaking, merchants, and the 'mean' or outcast groups; these were actors, beggars, bondsmen, prostitutes, the boatmen of the south coast, and others who had no social rights. Apart from these, all who could afford the education, were eligible. State service gave rise to self perpetuating privilege; the power and wealth acquired became the hereditary asset of an élite with the monopoly, through wealth, of education. These state officials were exempted, according to their grades, from taxation, from the corvée and usually from military service. They had immunity before the law, which they themselves administered as magistrates. They had every opportunity of enriching themselves and securing privileges for their families, backed by the comfortable Confucian conviction that this was after all no less than their filial duty.

Local appointments were made by members of the central bureaucracy who were also influenced by Confucian considerations as well as by the merits of the candidate. High officials had the privilege of recommending their protégés for office, thereby bypassing the examination system.

Education moreover came to be regarded primarily as a prerequisite for state service. Attention was concentrated on literary agility, on absorbing the Confucian canon. There was pedantic attention to textual quotation, analysis and precedent, and an insistence on orthodoxy in scholarship. The outlook of those who survived the regimen and reached the highest levels was narrow and inflexible. Many officials were too scholastic or antiquarian to be effective administrators, and ill-adapted to cope with social or political change.

But it would be wrong to underestimate the contribution of the scholar officials, the mandarins, to the revival of the Chinese empire or to the consolidation of Chinese culture. In Tang times, the bureaucracy of scholars was the most advanced administrative organisation which had evolved anywhere. The officials chosen by examination and appointed by the throne, were sent out from the capital to rule all provinces of the empire. Despite the privileged backgrounds of the scholars, it was a system which attached overwhelming prestige to scholarship, as opposed to the barbarian standards of military power, birth, or riches. The Tang, like other dynasties, had a hierarchy of hereditary nobility, but the possession of a title though it provided wealth, did not of itself confer power.

The mandarin system also contributed to cultural unity at a time when the empire was assimilating many peoples from the north, the north-west, and the south. It promoted concepts of loyalty to existing authority, of the priority of family interests, and a strong sense of decorum. Despite recurring periods of civil strife and political division, Chinese cultural unity persisted. The system served the Tang dynasty for centuries, and survived as an institution into the twentieth.

There is a tale dating from the end of the eighth century which bears witness to the private dreams of scholarly success of centuries of Chinese in all ranks of society. It is known as the 'Yellow Millet Dream': An old peasant met a Taoist at an inn. While the innkeeper was preparing a bowl of millet porridge for their supper, the peasant dozed off to sleep. In the land of his dream he passed with distinction the state examination; he was given important posts, had his own house, married a lady from one of the best families, and ended up as governor of the capital and victor over a barbarian army. He survived official disgrace brought about by a rival faction, and was restored to office; his sons not only secured high positions themselves but provided the family with ample progeny. He was contemplating happy retirement and a resting place with his ancestors, when he woke to find himself once more in the squalid inn where the pot of porridge was still heating. 'All human affairs are like this,' said the Taoist.

Agrarian surpluses combined with administrative efficacy, contributed to the great expansion which took place during the Tang. The contrast remained between the poor peasant struggling to exist, and the privileged landowner, exempted from taxation and other obligations. But during the first century of the Tang at least, the empire benefited from a period of peace, the more thorough application of the land equalisation system, the irrigation works, and the relief from corvée.

Agrarian surpluses also made possible the growing prosperity of the handicraft industries, the increase in commerce and in urban development. Towns expanded and became thriving cosmopolitan centres. With the transport system from south to north provided by the Grand Canal, the problem of provisioning the capital, which included the extensive bureaucracy as well as the court, was to some extent solved. The capital Changan could be supported by the grain producing regions in the eastern and central provinces—the Great Plain and the Yangtze valley. Changan was in fact situated on the plateau above the dangerous San Men rapids of the Yellow River, and losses by shipwreck in this region were severe. At one time the rapids were bypassed by transferring the grain to carts on land, involving the use of some 1,800 carts; the system was abandoned as uneconomic. Most of the towns which thrived in Tang times were situated on the great waterways or lines of communication from distant provinces. From Changan, roads radiated to all parts of the empire.

A Japanese Buddhist pilgrim, named Ennin, travelling through the Middle Kingdom later during the Tang period, commented on the well established thoroughfares of the empire. He and his companions were never in danger from bandits; they never lost their way. He described the lookouts set up every five *li* along the road, square mounds of earth, pointed at the top and broader beneath. Inns and refreshments were available everywhere. Ennin mentioned that there were post stations along the waterways as well as on the roads, where boats instead of horses were changed.

Changan

Changan had been the capital of such ancient dynasties as the Chou, the Chin and the Han. Wen Ti, founder of the Sui, rebuilt the city as his capital and in Tang times it became the most splendid metropolis in Asia. The population of the city and suburbs at the height of its prosperity rose to nearly two million people. It was a cosmopolitan city, the eastern terminus of the great trans-Asian caravan route.

Changan covered a rectangular area some five miles by six (Sian, the town on the same site today, covers an area of two miles by three). Like most ancient capitals of the Middle Kingdom, Changan comprised three parts—the palace, the imperial city and the outer city, separated from each other by walls of rammed earth.

In the outer city, divided up like a chessboard by streets crossing at right angles, lived the ordinary people. This part of the city had an eastern and a western market, with a great central thoroughfare leading to the imperial city and beyond that to the palace city. Rows of elms and locust trees lined the ditches beside the main highway, providing shade for the vermilion horsedrawn carriages of the great officials and nobles.

Alleys divided the two markets each into nine squares, or wards,

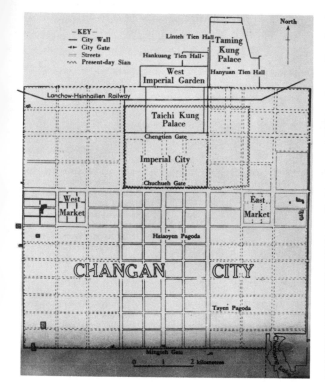

the central one of which was the administrative centre, with managers, supervisors, secretaries and scribes. Each section of the market contained booths and warehouses of merchants and artisans engaged in the same trade. The wards were surrounded by moats and ramparts, and they could be entered only from the main streets. No one except a high official was permitted to have a gate opening directly onto the street. Drums were beaten to signal the curfew, for the wards were closed at night.

At sunset the drums were beaten eight hundred times and the gates were closed. From the second night watch, mounted soldiers employed by the officers in charge of policing the streets made the rounds and shouted out the watches, while the military patrols made their rounds in silence. At the fifth watch, the drums within the palace were also beaten, and then the drums in all the streets were beaten so as to let the noise be heard everywhere; then all the gates of the wards and the markets were opened.

As time went on, the growth of commerce caused the strict ward system to decline, together with the curfew. In fact in the eighth century the markets were continued far into the night.

Stores, workshops and booths of more than two hundred trades lined the streets; they provided silks and garments, saddles and harnesses, ornaments, fruits and provisions. Excavations have unearthed a great variety of articles as well as many coins: carved bone articles such as hairpins, combs, brush handles, and dice, glass beads, pearls, and ornaments of agate and crystal. According to the records mer-

Above left: city plan of Changan, Tang dynasty capital, as revealed by excavations. The city was several times sacked and burned.

Above right: palace of Changan. Traditional picture after Li Ssu Hsun. Tang period.

chants from central and western Asia owned wine and jewellery shops in the western market. Here were Persian merchants, experts in assessing the value of gems, and other merchants who ran wine shops where foreign girls served the customers. Some of these were men of letters like the poet Li Po, who dropped into one of these agreeable places one day:

Like a flower, the foreign maid, sitting behind the stove,
smiles at the spring breeze, then comes forward to dance,
shaking the sleeve of her gown.
How can you go home without getting drunk?

Sassanian coins from Persia, and gold coins from the Eastern Roman empire have been found in Tang tombs; inscriptions on the tombs of foreigners also indicate the brisk international trade carried on in those days.

The palace city, where the emperor lived, was an area of about two square miles, beyond which lay the imperial park, sloping down to the Wei river. This park, with its lakes, pavilions, gardens and small palaces, was laid out for the pleasure of the court. In the seventh century a new palace was built in the imperial park on higher ground, as the former palace was found to be too hot in summer. In one of the halls of the new palace, paved with marble flagstones, the emperor held banquets; records mention one occasion when two hundred high military officers were feasted here. A stone tablet recovered by excavation tells of the construction of a polo ground near the palace in the ninth century. Other records indicate that in the eighth century, the emperor watched a polo match between some of his own officials and members of the suite of Tibetans who came to escort Princess Wen Cheng to the Tibetan king she was to marry.

Traditional Chinese buildings have few walls. Screens of carved wood or bamboo separate the different areas. The roof beams and other supporting woodwork were lacquered or painted with intricate designs in rich colours and gold leaf. The tiled roofs were beginning to be tilted up at the edge like wings, allowing the maximum winter sun, and providing shade during the summer time. The end tiles at the eaves were splendidly decorated.

The imperial city, where nobles and officials resided, was also surrounded by a wall. For ordinary people this area was taboo. The Tang penal code included a punishment of seventy blows of the rod for an ordinary inhabitant found trespassing on the ramparts, in the enclosures surrounding office buildings, or even on the walls of the wards and markets.

Tang economic development involved a large measure of state control. State control of mining was a long established principle, especially for the copper and silver mines, which provided metals for the mints, for weapons and for tools. Large numbers of miners and foundry workers were employed by the state, and were usually exempted from other forms of corvée and from military service. Salt production was a state monopoly and most of the transport system was a state enterprise. Staple goods, cereals and cloth, reached the capital through a series of complicated stages most of which were controlled by public authorities; river transport, canals and granaries were state enterprises. Following earlier practices, contracts were required for all purchases of slaves, horses, oxen, land or houses. A 4 per cent tax was paid on every sale, 3 per cent contributed by the buyer and 1 per cent by the seller; the tax went to the treasury.

At each of the fords to the east and to the west of the capital cities a Master of the Ford was set up, with a police station and five sailors, who were responsible for controlling contraband goods and smugglers. Goods like reeds, charcoal, fish and firewood, paid a ford tax of 10 per cent to the treasury.

Every prefecture and subprefecture with a minimum population of 3,000 families (about 15,000 people) had the right to establish a regular market under the supervision of a manager. Thus, north of the river Huai, there were over a hundred large markets and many small ones. Each market was supervised by state officials exacting heavy taxes.

Moneylenders thrived in these centres of commerce. The interest rates were 6 per cent per month; the state had its own stake in usury, charging 7 per cent on government funds. Despite the high taxation and interest rates, commerce flourished from the fourth century on. Many merchants came from overseas. In Canton, Arabs and Persians established a sizeable trading colony.

The great market at Loyang had been a thriving commercial centre from the time of the northern Wei in the fourth century. Round the city were grouped communes or villages which were the quarters of artisans and merchants, each trade having its own base. Two quarters in the east were known as 'Commercial Relations' and 'Circulation of Goods'. In the southern market were places of amusement, taverns, inns and brothels. On the west side alcoholic drinks were sold. The wards known as 'Maternal Love and Filial Piety' and 'Final Resignation' contained the establishments of the undertakers and coffin makers.

During the Tang period there was a great expansion of silk production. In one centre, engaged mainly on the weaving of tissues to be presented as tribute silk at court, as many as five hundred looms were in operation. The production of fine quality porcelain also increased in the Tang period.

The evident benefits of commerce did not reduce the traditional stigma attached to trade which was still regarded as parasitical and unproductive. Merchants suffered not only the lowest social prestige but also bore the heavy burden of tolls and taxes, which were devised both to support the exchequer and to control the growth of merchant

Chung Kuei, the Guardian Deity. It is said that Chung Kuei was an accomplished scholar of the Tang period, a good-hearted man in spite of his appearance. After his death he was deified as a protector against ghosts and demons. Pictures of Guardian Deities have been placed at the side of gates since the time of the first Tang emperor. Chinese gates also have walls in front of them, which were likewise supposed to protect the residents from baleful influences. Woodblock, traditional.

activity. Whereas in Europe the towns of the late Middle Ages were the base on which bourgeois enterprise effected a capitalist revolution. in Tang China the towns were also the seat of provincial government and of a dominant hierarchy of officials hostile to merchants, who were for long periods totally excluded from office. The guilds or corporations of merchants which were formed to safeguard their commercial interests helped to reinforce bureaucratic control over them, for the corporations became responsible for the supply of consignments of their products to the government.

Li Shih Min, the greatest of the Tang emperors ruled a mere score or so of years (AD 626–649). When he first succeeded to the throne he was taken ill, and it is said that his sleep was disturbed by a devil who kept banging on the door of the imperial bed chamber. The empress took counsel among the leading ministers to deal with this dangerous intrusion. Two generals offered to guard the doors, clad in full war panoply. This did the trick; the devil was intimidated and Li Shih Min slept in peace. However after several nights the emperor grew concerned for the health of his generals, who continued guarding his tranquillity at the expense of their own rest. He suggested that pictures of the generals placed outside his door would probably serve the same purpose. The silly devils, as expected, mistook the images for the reality. The generals rested, and the emperor recovered. Similar devices were successful at the back door, to which the devils transferred their attention when they had recovered their wits. Since that time pictures of generals in war regalia have hung protectively beside the doors of homes throughout the Middle Kingdom.

In less than the fulness of time the malignant devil returned, and this time broke through. Li Shih Min, knowing that his end was near, in the summer of 649 retired to his favourite summer residence, the Kingfisher Blue Palace in the Nan Shan mountains south of the capital, where he died aged forty-nine.

Amongst the monuments to his interest in culture and the arts, four stone tablets have survived from Changan, on which books of the classics were engraved, copied from the emperor's own brush. The approaches to his tomb at Chaoling, in Shensi, were decorated with the famous bas reliefs of horses, which were executed in the Emperor's own lifetime.

China's first and only woman to rule as sovereign in her own right continued the capable rule with which the epoch opened. For centuries Empress Wu (AD 683–705) was condemned as a vicious woman and ruthless ruler. It is likely that this view had its origins in the poisoned brushes of the court historians who were supporters of rival factions, and upholders of traditional standards which denied women a role in public life, and expected them to remain subservient to the men. It is not possible to say how much of the traditional story of her rise to power is based on fact, but even if only a small portion were

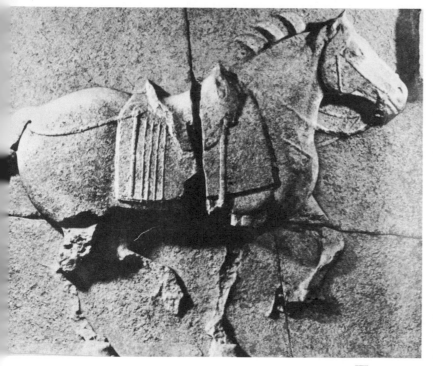

true, then the empress showed herself to be possessed of infinite political skill as well as of an iron nerve and a level head.

Wu Chao, a beautiful girl of thirteen, was summoned to the court of Li Shih Min, where she joined the imperial harem, with the rank of concubine of the fifth grade and the title of 'Elegant'. (The Inner Palace contained no fewer than 122 ladies holding official grades, concubines of various degrees. The first lady was, of course, the Empress, whose sons alone were entitled to the succession.) Above Wu in rank were the 'Beauties' and the 'Accomplished Ones'.

When the emperor died, Wu was twenty-four years old, with enough energy and ambition to outpace any number of Sons of Heaven. By that time she had succeeded in attracting the attention of the Crown prince. Wu Chao was sent away from the Palace, together with the other concubines as was customary, to a Buddhist convent, where the redundant ladies shaved their heads and were expected to live out the rest of their lives in decent seclusion. After a visit to the convent by the new Emperor Tang Kao Tsung, Wu was brought back to court. This move has been attributed to the childless Empress Wang, who thought to provide the emperor with a counter-attraction to the concubine with whom he was currently infatuated. The plan was over fulfilled; Wu bore the emperor a son. As a result of the intrigue which followed, the Empress Wang was demoted and imprisoned, together with the erstwhile favourite, and Wu Chao was promoted to Empress.

One version of the story relates that the Emperor relented when he later contemplated the unhappy fate of Empress Wang and his

Left: Shih Fa Chih, one of Emperor Tai Tsung's six famous battle chargers. They were carved by order of the emperor.

Right: the Empress Wu, 'Son of Heaven' (AD 690–705), the only woman to rule China as sovereign in her own right. Traditional representation.

93

Lady of Tang Dynasty. Pottery tomb figure, engraved and painted.

favourite; Wu, fearful of the possible return of her rivals to influence, ordered their hands and feet to be cut off, after which they were done to death in a brewing vat. It is related that the dying concubine prayed that in a future life she would return as a cat, to torment Empress Wu as a cat torments a mouse. Henceforth Wu ordered that no cats be kept in any of her palaces.

Emperor Kao Tsung, well-meaning, weak and lazy, allowed the control of affairs to pass into the hands of his talented empress. It was she who wielded power for the thirty-four years of his reign, helped by the fact that the emperor suffered a stroke which impaired his sight and his remaining faculties.

Wu Chao gained the support of the scholar officials from whom she commissioned works. She encouraged agriculture and silk production, reducing taxes and corvée demands from those engaged in this work. She announced a foreign policy of peace, and disbanded a large number of troops.

She moved her capital eastward to Loyang (Changan they say was haunted by the curses of her victims, and cats).

Tang Kao Tsung died in 683, and power remained in the hands of Wu, who was then fifty-five years old. Her son remained the puppet emperor until he was deposed in 690; then Wu assumed the imperial title herself, the only Chinese woman to be sovereign in name as well as in fact.

During her rule administration was well ordered and the Middle Kingdom was tranquil. Intrigue continued at court, however, and stories circulated about the unseemly behaviour of the empress. One of the measures that provoked bureaucratic resentment was the establishment of examinations for women, to select some for posts in state service. Wu survived all effort against her until 705, when a palace coup forced the old lady to abdicate. She spent the last few months of her life in retirement, dying at the age of eighty-one.

Her son, the deposed puppet, was restored to the Dragon throne, surviving intense court intrigue for five years; then he was poisoned by his spouse. The throne was seized by the late emperor's nephew, grandson of Wu, who inherited some of the talent of his ancestors, and secured another half century of stable and prosperous government. This was the emperor Tang Hsuan Tsung (712–756), whose reign marked a brilliant period of Chinese art.

Hsuan Tsang, Buddhist pilgrim

Buddhist influence increased during the early Tang, and probably reached its peak in the seventh century, under the Empress Wu, who was an ardent patron of Buddhism. Buddhist monasteries flourished in these times, receiving endowments of land and treasure from rulers and other prosperous devotees. These monasteries became important landowners and rich agricultural communities. They exploited and extended their wealth through usury.

In early Tang days missionary fervour still inspired Buddhist endeavours. At this time the 'prince of pilgrims', Hsuan Tsang, made the round trip to India by way of central Asia, to gather Buddhist texts from their source. He left the Celestial Empire in the early days of Li Shih Min, without imperial permission, when the havoc of civil war had not yet abated. His biographer tells us that:

The imperial capital had become a nest of bandits and the region between the Yellow River and the Lo River, a place occupied by cruel and evil men. Civilisation in the region collapsed and the Buddhist public dispersed. Skeletons everywhere whitened the fields and roads. . . . At that time the imperial government was newly established, and the boundaries of empire were not extensive, the common people were prohibited by imperial decree from going to the Western Regions.

Hsuan Tsang travelled across the deserts and mountain ranges of central Asia two centuries after Fa Hsien, but the way was still infested by dragons and demons with irritable if not positively cantankerous natures:

Frequently fierce dragons impede and molest travellers with their inflictions. Those who travel this road should not wear red garments nor carry loud sounding calabashes . . . the least neglect of these precautions could cause the monster to raise a storm of violent winds and flying sand which would flay the traveller to exhaustion. . . . Now alone and deserted, he traversed the sandy waste, his only means of observing the way being the heaps of bones and the horse dung; thus slowly and cautiously advancing, he suddenly saw a body of troops, amounting to several hundreds, covering the sandy plain; sometimes they advanced and sometimes they halted. The soldiers were clad in fur and felt. And now the appearance of camels and horses, and the glittering of standards and lances met his view; then suddenly fresh forms and figures changing into a thousand shapes appeared, sometimes at an immense distance and then close at hand, and then they dissolved into nothing.

At first he thought them to be robbers, but then he realised they were demons . . .

From the demon-haunted desert his route traversed the frozen waste of the Pamirs and the Ice mountain which was 'precipitous and seemed as high as the sky. Since the creation of the world, it has been covered with snow which has accumulated and turned into ice that never melted whether in winter or summer. Cold mists mingle with cloud, and when one looked up one could see only white snow without end.' Hsuan Tsang stayed in India over ten years. He brought back to China many Buddhist scriptures and spent twenty years translating them. On his return to the celestial capital in AD 645, he was given an imperial welcome:

On that day the authorities instructed all the monasteries to bring out all their banners, tapestries, and other ceremonial appliances to assemble at the Red Bird Street in the morning of the following day, to receive the newly arrived

scriptures and images of the Buddha. The people vied with each other in making stately arrangements with great enthusiasm and prepared their best banners, tapestries, umbrellas, precious tables and carriages. When the different monasteries had sent out their ceremonial processions by different ways, the monks and nuns, properly dressed in their religious garments, followed. The court and monastic musicians played in front, while the people holding incense-burners in their hands followed them . . . carrying the scriptures and images of Buddha, they marched forward with pearls and jades tinkling in the air and golden flowers scattered over the road. For a distance of several tens of li, beginning from the Red Bird Street and ending at the main gate of the Hung Fu Monastery, the people of the capital, scholars and imperial and local officials, stood by the sides of the road and looked on the procession with respect . . . As the street was overcrowded, the authorities, fearing that the people might tread upon one another, ordered that they should not move, and that they should burn incense and scatter flowers only at the places where they were standing.

The emperor invited Hsuan Tsang to become an imperial adviser, but the pilgrim refused to return to secular life.

Because he feared that the scriptures might be lost in the time to come, or that they might be destroyed in case of fire, the Master decided to construct a stone pagoda at the southern side of the main gate of the monastery to store the scriptures and the Buddha's images which he had brought back from the western countries. The Pagoda was designed as 300 feet in height, to show the magnificence of a great country, and to be a monument for the Sakyumuni Buddha. Before he started to build it, he made a report to the emperor, who ordered an imperial secretary to inform the Master: 'As the pagoda you intend to construct is so tall, it will perhaps be difficult to build with stone. It should be constructed with bricks. I do not wish the Master to worry about it.' . . . Thus the Pagoda was constructed with bricks in the west court of the Monastery . . . The Master participated in the construction of the pagoda by carrying bricks and stones for it, and it took two years to complete.

Above: return of the Buddhist pilgrim Hsuan Tsang to the capital, and the imperial welcome. Based on traditional representation.

Above right: Tayen Pagoda in the southern outskirts of Sian, as it is today. Built in AD 652 by Hsuan Tsang, for preserving the relics and texts he had brought from India, and where he translated the Buddhist scriptures from Sanskrit.

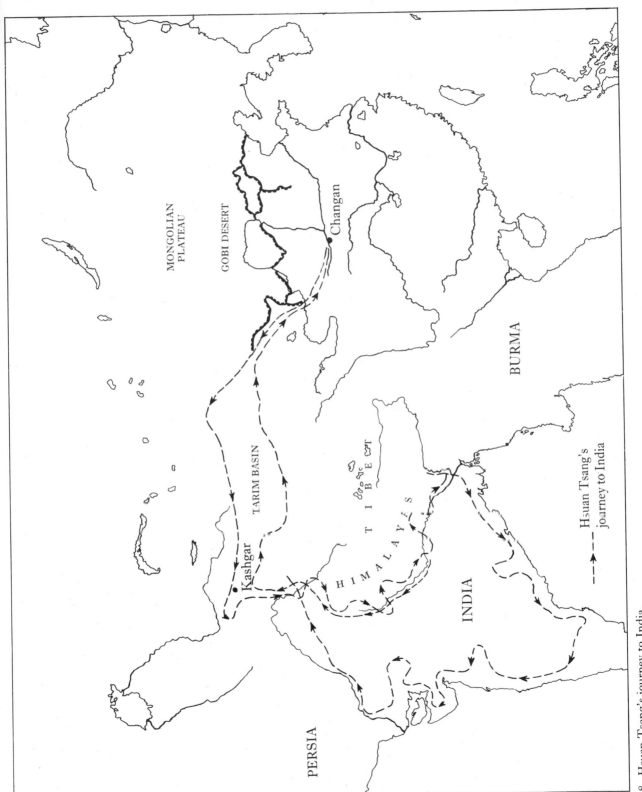

8. Hsuan Tsang's journey to India.

During its advance Buddhism developed a number of sects. In China they polarised into two main ones: the Pure Land Sect, or Western Paradise of Amida, a sect which stressed the efficacy of simple expression of faith through repeating the name of Buddha; and Chan (Japanese Zen), which emphasised the importance of meditation and intuitive insight.

The Buddhist monasteries acquired, as time went on, many temporal functions; they acted as sanctuaries, as inns for travellers, as hospitals, as public baths and more. They came to represent a challenge to the state and to orthodox opinion. It was not congenial to the Confucian tradition that men should withdraw from their familial role to the celibacy of monastic life; the monasteries in addition withdrew men in large numbers from productive activity on the land; the tax registers were to an equal extent depleted. The state was deprived of progenitors and tillers. At the same time the wealth of the monasteries attracted the attention of avaricious officials. Many of the communities tended in time to relax their standards and become centres of indulgence, encouraging the activities of charlatans.

During the Tang period therefore the view developed that monasteries should be restricted in number, and that their personnel and their wealth should be limited. The state did not hesitate to introduce controls in this respect as in other social spheres. The monastic limit for each prefecture was one establishment with thirty monks. Surplus celibates were defrocked by the government. In fact a clerical census was taken in 729, to keep the numbers under control. Two decades later the Government began to issue permits to limit the ordination of new monks, and all monks were required to carry a state permit.

Direct persecution also occurred from time to time, inflamed sometimes by Taoist priests who competed with the Buddhists for imperial patronage, and sometimes on account of the alien origin and doctrine of the religion. The targets were fiscal rather than doctrinal. Monasteries were deplored as parasitic institutions; property rather than persons bore the brunt of the attack. The most strenuous anti-Buddhist challenge occurred in the 840s, under a Tang emperor who had become a fanatical seeker after Taoist immortality. Official accounts mention the destruction of over 4,000 monasteries and 40,000 shrines. A quarter of a million monks and nuns were defrocked, and these, together with the 150,000 slaves on their estates, were restored to the tax registers.

It was during this period that the Japanese Buddhist pilgrim, Ennin, crossed the sea to China (AD 838) and travelled through the Tang empire for a decade before returning to Japan. He kept a diary of his travels, which is the earliest known record of life in China made by a foreign visitor. Ennin, like Marco Polo many centuries later, noted that the Chinese used coal for heating: ' On the rocky mountain called Chin Shan there is coal all over the mountain and all the people from the prefectures near and far come and get it to burn. For cooking meals it has a great amount of heat.'

He reported crossing the Yellow River with 'ferry boats on both banks, each with walled enclosures' and many boats costing five cash for each person and fifteen for a donkey. Ennin and his colleagues made a pilgrimage to one of the holy sanctuaries on the sacred Wu Tai mountain, just south of the Long Wall. A perilous journey indeed, for

approaching Mount Wu Ti from the east one goes among the mountains and valleys for five hundred li up to the summits of precipices, crags, and down to the floors of deep valleys; five hundred poisonous dragons hide themselves in the mountains and spew forth wind and clouds . . . When the heavens suddenly clear . . . one sees on the five terraces a pale yellow light and then one sees on the terraces a speck of cloud arise and all of a sudden heavy clouds cover the mountains.

Tang Empire

The Tang was a period of great imperial expansion which reached its apogee in the first half of the eighth century, when the peoples of Tibet and central Asia in the west as far as the Pamirs, of Mongolia, Manchuria and Korea in the north, and of Annam in the south, recognised Chinese suzerainty.

Turkish nomads

During the time of the Han, the Hun nomads had started on their western migration, and hordes of other nomads moved onto the Mongolian plateau. Some, like the Topa, overran north China, established dynasties, and settled. Some became vassals of the Middle Kingdom; they furnished contingents of cavalry to the Chinese for use against rival nomad hordes; in return they received favourable trading conditions with China, and Chinese princesses were sent as wives for nomad rulers. Still others resisted these approaches and made periodic attacks south of the Wall. Amongst the intransigent new tribes, in the middle of the sixth century, were a powerful people whose language and culture was Turkic. These Turks had consolidated their domination over an empire which extended from the mountains of Mongolia west across central Asia to the Caspian. By the time of the Sui, they had divided into eastern and western Turks. The eastern Turks impeded the unification of the Tang empire by harassing the borderlands, kidnapping the celestials and selling them as slaves, and by encouraging other tribes to attack the Middle Kingdom.

Li Shi Min prepared for war. He collected and studied information about the Turks and personally took part in the training of the troops. In AD 630, at a time when the Turks were troubled by civil strife owing to the oppression of their khan, Li Shih Min made a surprise attack on the headquarters of the eastern khan in the Yin Shan mountains. The Turks were defeated and driven back. In later campaigns, the Tang

emperor, aided by other nomad hordes, defeated the western Turks and restored Chinese control over the Tarim basin. The fame of the campaigns spread through central Asia, and Tang suzerainty spread to the Oxus valley. The route to the west was cleared. Caravans renewed their journeys, carrying their transcontinental burdens between Changan, Samarkand and Constantinople.

Communications by sea also developed. Cargo ships plied between Yangchow, Canton, and harbours in the Persian Gulf. Within a decade of the Hegira (AD 622, Muhammed's flight from Mecca to Medina), some Muslims reached Chinese shores. Li Shih Min, tolerant in matters of religion, permitted the Arabs to build the first mosque in China at Canton, and a Muslim community settled there. Chinese silks, porcelain and paper went to the West, and to China came perfumes, medicines, gems and pearls, elephant tusks and rhinoceros' horns.

During the Tang period Chinese ironsmiths, gold and silver smiths and paper makers, went to central Asia, enriching the handicraft industries of that region. The art of paper making came from China to central Asia in the middle of the eighth century.

Tibet

The Tibetans, living on the plateau to the west of China, were amongst the barbarians who for many centuries had harassed the borderlands of the Middle Kingdom. In the Tang period the Tibetans were partly nomadic, partly farming people, growing highland barley and wheat. Their principal herds were yaks and dromedaries. They made their clothes of felt and smeared their faces with red paint for decoration. They lived in felt tents. The tents of the nobles were joined together and could house hundreds of people. The Tibetans were Buddhists.

Above left: warrior in action. From Tunhuang Grotto, Tang period.

Above right: fighting horse. Tang period. Pottery, pink clay painted in red, orange and rose.

Early in the seventh century the Tibetan tribes became unified under Srongtsan Gampo, a ruler who established his capital at Lhasa. A Tibetan embassy came to the Tang court at Changan on behalf of their prince for the hand of Li Shih Min's daughter, the Princess Wen Cheng, famed for her beauty and talents. Princess Wen Cheng went to Lhasa with a dowry that included seeds of grain, farm tools, silkworm eggs, and books on agricultural and handicraft techniques as well as the Chinese classics; amongst her entourage were craftsmen, technicians, and an orchestra. Thus many new crafts came to Tibet. Srongtsan Gampo sent the children of Tibetan nobles to study in China, and invited Tang scholars to Tibet. He not only built a palace after the Tang model for his princess, but in deference to her wishes built a monastery in the centre of Lhasa. One day the princess came to inspect the work. The stone carvers were so disturbed at the sight of her that one of them absent-mindedly chipped off the nose of the stone lion he was carving. So that the lions should look alike, they were all carved without noses. That is why there are noseless lions in the Jokhan Monastery of Lhasa, to this day.

Gradually King Gampo and many of his people exchanged their clothes of coarse woollen felt or fur for silks and satin. The Tang arts of raising silkworms and making wine, the use of paper and ink, and building houses, became established, while Tibetan products such as horses and vessels of gold and agate were sent to the Tang empire.

In the days of the Sui, there had been disastrous campaigns against Korea; Li Chih Min's armies were also defeated in North Korea, but under his successors the peninsula, which became unified in the seventh century, came under the nominal suzerainty of China. As in the case of Tibet, there was considerable cultural and economic exchange.

Tang cultural influence spread beyond the eastern sea to Japan. During the eighth century Japan sent many envoys and students to China. They came to study the Chinese political system, philosophy and history, and Chinese crafts. Buddhist missionaries, like Ennin, came to establish contact with their colleagues and to learn more of their faith from sources nearer to the original. The missions, which often numbered hundreds, brought back to their own islands much of the advanced experience of the Tang which was adopted in government and culture generally. The Japanese capital was modelled upon Changan; the influence of the Tang upon Japan survived until modern times.

The extent of Tang influence throughout Asia may be judged by the clash between the Celestial Empire and the Islamic world in the middle of the eighth century. Muhammed, the founder of Islam, once said, 'Seek learning though it be as far away as China', and in 713 an embassy from the Caliph, the successor of Muhammed, was

Figure of Tang Princess Wen Cheng (AD 621–680). Princess Wen Cheng married Srongtsan Gampo, king of Tibet.

Musical instruments used by the orchestra brought to Tibet by Princess Wen Cheng, preserved in the Jokhan Monastery built by King Srongtsan Gampo in deference to the wishes of his princess.

received in Changan. The Arab armies of Islam brought their faith westwards through the Mediterranean lands, and eastward through Persia to central Asia. They brought their swords and their faith to Samarkand and Bukhara, where the populations turned from Buddha to Allah. Buddhist temples were converted into mosques. A Chinese army in the Pamirs clashed with the Arab forces, and were decisively defeated at the battle of Talas (AD 751), north of Ferghana. This marked the limit of Chinese expansion to the west. Chinese power in central Asia declined and was replaced by that of Islam.

A century before this clash Persia had been defeated by the Muslim armies at the battle of Nahawand (AD 642). The Persian monarch Yazdagard III, beaten back to Merv, appealed to the Chinese for help against the Arabs. He received no help, but in 674, Firuz, the son of Yazdagard, arrived as a refugee in Changan. He was given the title of general in the imperial guard, and stayed in China until his death some years later. The Persian refugees were allowed to build temples and practise their Zoroastrian faith in China. Friendly relations were restored also with the Arabs, to whom a later Tang emperor appealed when he was faced with rebellion at home. Arab mercenaries were actually sent to China by the Caliph, in support of the Son of Heaven. They settled in China, and established further Muslim communities which survived the attacks against the Buddhists and other alien creeds towards the end of the Tang.

Tang poets

The reign of the Empress Wu was followed after a brief interregnum by the reign of Tang Hsuan Tsung her grandson, the third of the outstanding Tang rulers (AD 712–756). The period was marked by great cultural achievements, especially in the field of poetry, which enjoyed the patronage of the Son of Heaven.

Meditating under the pines. This picture by the Tang painter Han Huang shows several poets and scholars meditating and humming poetry.

The great Tang poets were nearly all officials, disappointed in their bureaucratic hopes, disillusioned with government practice and life at court. Many consoled themselves with drink. Their work is of international stature and has been translated into many languages. Although we cannot enjoy the full quality of their poetry in translation, we can appreciate from the content what they saw and wrote of the world around them.

Li Po (AD 701–762) was one of the greatest of these poets, and one of the few that did not aspire to, or gain, official position. He was a member of a literary group of drunkards known as the 'Six Idlers of the Bamboo Grove', and of another called 'The Eight Immortals of the Wine Cup'.

After a gay and dissipated spell at court, he became the victim of intrigue and was exiled, at one stage being sentenced to death. He was reprieved but banished. According to tradition he met his death by drowning through hanging over the gunwale of a boat trying to embrace the reflection of the moon on the water.

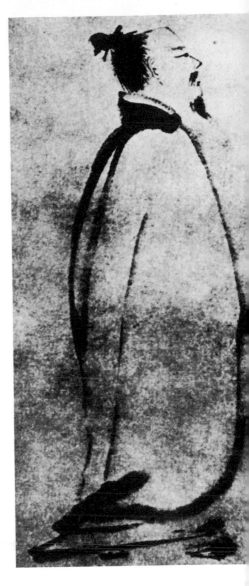

> . . . When I wake and look out on the lawn
>   I hear midst the flowers a bird sing;
> I ask, 'Is it evening or dawn?'
>   The mango-bird whistles, 'Tis spring'.
>
>   Over powered by the beautiful sight
> Another full goblet I pour
>   And would sing till the moon rises bright—
> But soon I'm as drunk as before.

Li Po was on the whole a cheerful poet, whose verses are filled with the traditional themes of Chinese poetry, nature, wine, friendship, death and immortality.

Tu Fu (AD 712–770) was his contemporary and friend. He made no progress in the government examinations, but later received minor posts in the capital and in the provinces. His political hopes faded and he had barely the means to support himself and his family. Some of his children died, it is said, of undernourishment.

> At dawn I knock on the doors of wealthy youths
> At twilight follow the dust their stout horses raise,
> Accepting the dregs of wine and cold scraps from feasts,
> And hiding all the grief of an aching heart.

During the turmoil at the end of the reign he was captured by rebels, and at great risk escaped. He gave up a minor post he had been granted and went to live in a 'thatched cottage' (a euphemism for a modest dwelling) he built at Chengtu in Szechuan. This home was wrecked in a storm. He too died in a boat, during his wanderings through Szechuan.

Like other poets of his day, but perhaps more bitterly, his work

Poet Li Po. Detail from Sung painting by Liang Kai.

Poet Tu Fu: stone engraving, Ching period. Traditional presentation.

The poet Po Chu I. Traditional presentation.

reflected disgust at the corruption and extravagance of court life, and sympathy with the sufferings of the poor. In the poem 'Pretty Ladies' he satirised the court, and the emperor's favourite Lady Yang Kue Fei. Another poem, 'Army Carts', described the scene as conscripts were rounded up for service on the frontiers. Of court life he wrote:

The silk shared out in the Vermilion Hall
Was woven by the hands of poor women
Women whose men were whipped in their own homes
By tax collectors who took the silk to court.

So many courtiers now throng around the court
That honest men must tremble;
And it's said that the gold plate from the treasury
Has gone to the kinsmen of the Lady Yang.

In their houses dance girls like fairies
With garments light as mist on jadelike limbs
While the guests sit warm in sables,
And shrill lutes accompany clear lyres.
Rare dainties are served — the pads of camels' feet
Winter oranges piled on fragrant tangerines,
Behind those vermilion gates meat and wine go to waste
While out on the road lie the bones of men frozen to death . . .

One of his most beautiful and famous verses is about 'Welcome Rain One Spring Night':

A good rain knows its season
And comes when spring is here;
On the heels of the wind it slips secretly into the night;
Silent and soft it moistens everything.

In his last poem, written on the boat before dying, his mind was on the thought that

Blood is still flowing as of old in battles
And the alarms of war can still be heard.

It is also said that he died through the effects of starvation followed by over-indulgence in roast beef and white wine.

Po Chu I (AD 772–846), another poet official, was of a later generation; unlike the others, his official career was relatively successful. He was at one time magistrate of Hangchow, where to this day a causeway and a dam at West Lake are named in honour of the water control work he sponsored. He ended up as governor of the province of Honan. He too wrote about the plight of the people. When he was leaving Hangchow in 824 and saying goodbye, he wrote:

What is the reason your tears fall so fast?
My taxes were heavy, though many of the people were poor;
The farmers were hungry, for often their fields were dry.
All I did was to dam the waters of the Lake
And help a little when times were bad.

His poem 'The Old Man with the Broken Arm' tells the story of a peasant who broke his own arm rather than be taken for the army, and who lived for sixty years in pain from the disjointed limb. The 'Red Cockatoo' is also a characteristic comment:

Sent as a present from Annam—
A red cockatoo.
Coloured like the peach-tree blossom,
Speaking with the speech of men.
And they did to it what is always done
To the learned and eloquent
They took a cage with stout bars
And shut it up inside.

These were but a few of the many poets who were the glory of the Tang period.

An Lu Shan and peasant risings

The reign of Emperor Hsuan Tsung ended in ruin. The frontiers of the empire were long and vulnerable to attack, and the provincial governors cared less for defence than for building up their own power. The central government could not effectively control the provincial armies. The break-up of the Turkic hordes which followed their defeat by Li Shih Min, left the way open for attack by other tribes; even those who had previously been loyal allies were ready to seize any opportunity for attack on the empire. In the second half of the eighth century the Tang suffered a series of defeats at barbarian hands, which marked the beginning of the collapse. In the same years as the defeat at Talas in central Asia (AD 751) the Tang armies were defeated in the southwest.

Once again military expenditure imposed intolerable strain on the exchequer. Once more the great landlords evaded taxation and appropriated to themselves the lands of peasants who quit because they could not meet their tax obligations. Despite efforts to restore it, the land equalisation system was in decline by the middle of the eighth century. Peasants, through either expropriation or population expansion, inherited less than the quota of 100 mou of land. Imperial grants to court favourites also diminished the amount of land available to the tax-paying peasants. Provincial commanders and officials made off with the taxes due to the central government.

Although the taxation system permitted the remission of corvée on payment of extra silk, at this stage the government often insisted on labour service. Some peasants spent their entire lives on military service in remote regions. The burden of military service was particularly crushing in North China. The wealthy could pay for substitutes to do labour and military service for them, but the poor were rendered destitute by corvée and they frequently deserted. The military service system began to be replaced by the recruitment of

Poet Li Po in his cups. Traditional painting, Ching period.

mercenaries, secured frequently from barbarian tribes whose loyalty could not be assured.

During the reign of Emperor Hsuan Tsung the life of the court and of the officials became particularly extravagant. The government was weakened by factional struggles. The bureaucracy had grown very strong, especially since the time of Empress Wu who had relied heavily on it. The most serious threat however came from the regional commanders.

The Tang stationed large garrisons in the frontier regions to cope with aggression from neighbours. The commanders of these troops, known as viceroys, were very powerful men, responsible for all civil government in their regions, as well as for military affairs.

In the middle of the eighth century An Lu Shan was a viceroy over three border commands. In AD 755, he rose in revolt. The unsavoury circumstances of the rebellion have become legendary in the Middle Kingdom.

The ageing emperor, Hsuan Tsung fell victim to the charms of his son's wife, Yang Kuei Fei. The son divorced the lady, who entered the emperor's harem and acquired great influence over the old Son of Heaven. This lady took under her patronage a Turk of obscure origin, born beyond the Wall, who had been captured and sold as a slave to a Chinese officer in a northern garrison. The Turk, An Lu Shan, was a man of some talent; he gained promotion to the rank of officer and later became a general. He also became uncouthly fat and adopted a devil-may-care clowning act which amused the court and in particular the Lady Yang Kuei Fei, who adopted him as her son. Promotion for An Lu Shan was thereafter rapid. He was made governor of a frontier province, and eventually received the title of second-class prince. He recruited large numbers of nomads into his forces. The emperor was warned that this charlatan was planning revolt, but the Son of Heaven would hear none of it. Lady Yang's brother meanwhile was appointed First Minister to the Emperor.

The revolt when it came, was overwhelming. The Tang government was ill-prepared. An Lu Shan routed such imperial forces as could be mustered and pushed on to the capital. Emperor Hsuan Tsung and the court took flight. The rebels occupied Changan and sacked the palace. The imperial party fled with a troop of ill-provisioned and demoralised soldiers, who in turn broke into revolt, accusing the First Minister of treachery. He was set upon and murdered. The emperor tried to pacify the troops, who demanded also the head of the Lady Yang Kuei Fei. The Son of Heaven, persuaded by his terrified court and fearing for his own life, eventually consented. Lady Yang was taken away by the chief eunuch and strangled in the village pagoda. This story was made famous in a poem by Po Chu I and by many tales and dramas based on the theme. The emperor (then aged seventy-two) abdicated the throne to his son.

The new emperor raised a force of Chinese and allies, including also Arabs sent by the Caliph. An Lu Shan was assassinated, but other rebel leaders took his place. The war dragged on for a decade, but the government could not bring the provinces under full control. Although the rebellion ended in 763, the Chinese empire had again virtually disintegrated.

The taxes collected in some regions never went to the government. Military expenses were defrayed by the introduction of new taxes, which began to be levied twice annually. Peasants who could not meet the demands once more took to the wilds; the big landlords appropriated their lands. More than half of the land on the outskirts of Changan, for example, fell into the hands of the eunuchs and their friends at court.

The waves of peasant risings which took place in the 870s continued for a further decade despite the opposition of the viceroys who sank their differences and joined together for a time to defeat the peasant armies. After the defeat of the peasants, the generals fought amongst themselves for three-quarters of a century. This second period of rift and conflict reopened the division between north and south.

Five Dynasties, 907 to 960

In the Yellow River valley in the north there was a succession of five Dynasties (907–960) whose rulers were military adventurers often of barbarian (Tartar) stock:

Long years the dragons and tigers fought,
In the Five Dynasties: Liang, Tang, Tsin, Han and Chou;
States rose and fell as candles gutter out in the wind, . . .

The south became divided amongst ten states.

During this period of struggle between the warlords, a new nation of nomads, known as the Khitan, gathered strength in the north-east. They became united under an elected khan towards the end of the ninth century. From the many Han refugees the Khitan learned the arts of farming, weaving and iron smelting; they developed a mixed pastoral/agricultural economy. With the aid of the Khitan, one of the warlords, Shih Ching Tang, won the throne in the north. As a reward for their aid the new ruler paid off the Khitan with sixteen provinces (from Peking to the Wall) and substantial annual tribute. The Khitan made Peking their capital. (From Khitan comes the word Khitai—Cathay—the name by which north China was known to medieval Europe, and Kitai, the Russian word for China.)

When Shih Ching Tang's successor stopped his tribute to the Khitan, they destroyed the dynasty, capturing Kaifeng, the capital, and claiming the dragon throne for themselves, under the dynastic name of Liao. They were, however, beaten back, and a further succession of military coups placed one ruler after another on the throne,

Lady Yang Kuei Fei, favourite of Tang emperor Hsuan Tsung. Traditional representation.

The Tang poet Po Chu I described the grief of the old emperor after her death:

On his return the garden was unaltered
With its Lotus and its willows;
The lotus recalled her face
The willows her eyebrows,
And at the sight of these
he could not hold back his tears.

until 960, when an army general, Chao Kuang Yin, seized power from an empress-regent and infant ruler; Chao Kuang Yin established a stable government and founded the Sung dynasty which endured some three centuries. The almost universal desire for peace and unity brought the remaining southern states to submission, and within two decades the Celestial Empire was reunited.

Changan under a new moon, and I in the evening
Listen to the sound of many women beating clothes
By the water.
An autumn wind blows and I know well
That many a woman feels its chill, and is anxious for
Her husband, fighting in the far north-west—
Then she thinks 'I wonder when the war
Will end, so that he will not longer need
To fight.'

Thus wrote Li Po, in the eighth century. But the dreaded problem of attack from the northern barbarian persisted. Another poet wrote in the tenth century:

They swore the Huns would perish
  They would die if needs they must. . . .
And now five thousand, sable-clad,
  Have bit the Tartar dust.
Along the river bank their bones
  Lie scattered where they may,
But still their forms in dreams arise
  To fair ones far away.'

During the following centuries of the Sung dynasty, the policy of compromise with the invader was preferred to that of resistance.

Hunters, a mural from a Tunhuang Grotto. Tang period.

8. Northern Sung
960–1127

It is said that General Chao Kuang Yin, founder of the Sung dynasty, which reunited war-weary China after three-quarters of a century of divided rule, came reluctantly to power. As commander of the crack troops of Chou, the last of the Five Dynasties, he had been sent north to repel the Khitan during troubles on the frontier. The army officers mutinied after a few days out, and came to Chao Kuang Yin who was asleep in his tent. At sword-point they insisted that he don the yellow robe, a symbol of imperial authority, and lead the army back to take possession of the capital.

When this had been achieved, the reluctant emperor, known as Sung Tai Tsu, called together the army chiefs and

invited them all to a banquet, and when the company had drunk deeply and were in cheerful mood, he said 'I do not sleep peacefully at night.' 'For what reason?' enquired the generals. 'It is not hard to understand,' replied the emperor, 'Which of you does not covet my throne?' The generals made deep bows and all protested, 'Why does you Majesty speak thus? The mandate of Heaven is now established. Who still has treacherous aims?' The Emperor replied, 'I do not doubt your loyalty, but if one day one of you is roused at dawn and forced to don a yellow robe, even if unwilling, how should he avoid being obliged to overthrow the Sung, just as I against my will was forced to overthrow the Chou?' All protested that none of them was sufficiently talented for such a thing to be thought of, and asked for his counsel. The Emperor said, 'The life of man is short. Happiness is to have the wealth and means to enjoy life, and then to be able to leave the same prosperity to one's descendants. If you, my officers, will renounce your military authority, retire to the provinces, and choose there the best lands and most delightful dwelling places, there to pass the rest of your lives in pleasure and peace until you die of old age, would this not be better than to live a life of peril and uncertainty? So that no shadow of suspicion shall remain between prince and ministers, we will ally our families with marriages, and thus ruler and subject linked in friendship and amity, we will enjoy tranquillity . . . The following day, the army commanders all offered their resignations, reporting (imaginary) maladies, and withdrew to country districts, where the emperor, giving them splendid gifts, appointed them to high official positions.

Thus the first Sung emperor trimmed the claws of the viceroys and generals, and reduced the danger of the local military commanders. The army became a national army under his immediate control.

Examination system
Tai Tsu built a strong central government. Administration had disintegrated during the struggles. The examination system for the selection of state officials was restored and further elaborated. The examinations themselves, which had previously been held sporadically, came to be held every three years at the district level, and

Reluctant emperor: First Sung emperor, Tai Tsu (AD 960–76).

thousands of candidates presented themselves. Of these candidates eventually some two hundred per annum gained appointments in the government service between the tenth and twelfth centuries. They were a competitive élite, obedient to the emperor's orders, in a non-competitive society.

The examinations became a physical as well as a mental *tour de force*. Candidates were closeted in small cubicles for several days and nights, cut off from the outside world, sustained only by previously prepared victuals and their ambition. Some are said to have lost their reason or died of exhaustion in the process. An attempt was made to eliminate fraud or favouritism by the system of anonymity of the candidate and the use of several examiners. Bribery of examiners, and various forms of fraud, were nevertheless possible. A candidate could sometimes secure a better examinee than himself as a substitute. On one occasion a tunnel was discovered running underneath the examination cells, through which to smuggle good answers.

Unsuccessful candidates could take the examination again and again, and some continued to do so until old age.

What agony it was thirty years ago
At the capital, waiting for the lists to appear . . .!

wrote one poet reminiscing about the examinations he had endured.

I met someone who told me I had passed;
I was bowled over by this thunderclap of joy and surprise,
I thought it was a mistake, thought it was only a dream;
I was in a sorry state of doubt and dread . . .
Parents, however much they love a child,
Have not the power to place him among the chosen few.
Only the examiner can bring the youth to notice,
And out of darkness carry them up to heaven.

Although the examination system provided the main avenue to official position, nepotism and wealth also gave access to office. Obscure officials could gain rapid promotion through recommendation by their superiors; this benefited in particular the protégés of the great families. The sale of office was a measure to which needy exchequers had frequent recourse, and which permitted wealthy merchants to buy their way into the bureaucracy. In Sung times, efforts were made to prevent commercial dealing between officials who were related to each other, and to prevent the relatives of the imperial consorts from gaining high office. Officials during this period were recruited from a wider range of social classes than before, but even so approximately half of them came from families with a bureaucratic tradition. Many leading officials of the Sung administration were famous scholars who had distinguished themselves in the examinations.

In the eleventh century, colleges were opened in the provinces on the initiative of the reforming minister Wang An Shih, who also sought to include more practical subjects in the curriculum. By and large, however, all instruction beyond the elementary stage was directed towards producing candidates for the official examinations, which demanded a knowledge by heart of the principal classics and a capacity to compose verse according to a formula. In the twelfth century, the National University was founded at Kaifeng, where students received free board, and lived under a very strict regime of monthly tests, with full examinations each spring and autumn.

Khitan and Hsia nomads

The first Sung emperor had attempted to remove the source of internal military conflict; external dangers remained. Sung dominion extended only partially over the territories previously united in the Celestial Empire. The north-eastern provinces were still ruled by the Khitan nomads who were also in control north of the Wall and in Manchuria. The Kansu corridor in the north-west, commanding the route to central Asia and the Old Silk Road, was dominated by the Hsia tribes. Twice the Sung attacked the Khitan to regain the sixteen provinces ceded to them, and were twice defeated. When, in 1004, the Khitan attacked and appeared to be advancing on the capital, the Sung ministers took fright, despite the fact that their forces had secured several successes in the field. The emperor made peace with the Khitan, accepted the existing borders with them and agreed to pay them an annual indemnity of 100,000 taels of silver and 200,000 bolts of silk; this was substantially increased three decades later under further pressure from the Khitan.

At the same time, in the north-west, the Hsia had grown strong and had launched several attacks against the Sung, who suffered heavy losses. A peace treaty was concluded between the Sung and the Hsia in 1044, whereby the Sung agreed to an annual indemnity of 70,000 taels of silver, 150,000 bolts of silk and 30,000 catties of tea. These peace terms, characteristic of Sung policy, gave rise to conflict at court and in the country, between partisans of the policy of appeasing the enemy through surrender of territory and annual tribute, and those who were in favour of continued military struggle against the barbarians.

The three centuries of the Sung dynasty (roughly contemporary with the period of Norman domination of Britain) were characterised by these appeasement policies and by a general subordination of military to civil interests. The Sung emperors remained hostile to the powers of the military, and among the common people the standing of the soldier was low. Since the eighth century, when the army was no longer composed of conscripts but of mercenaries, it was considered that only the dregs of the population became soldiers: 'a decent man does not become a soldier' any more than 'the best iron is used to make nails'.

It is curious that the period which became notorious for its weakness in the field was the one which introduced gunpowder as a military arm, early in the tenth century. Discovered in the Tang period and used at first for fireworks, gunpowder was adapted during the Sung to propel the first military rockets. By the eleventh century a number of explosive projectiles had been developed, together with a type of hand grenade. Cannon had not yet appeared, but artillery was increasingly used. When introduced into Europe, gunpowder helped the destruction of the feudal strongholds and eventually feudal society. The invention left Chinese society unchanged.

Although the Sung were reluctant to commit themselves in the field, they felt the need to maintain armed forces on a vast scale. In the first centuries they had an army of mercenaries of some one and a quarter million; they later supplemented their land forces with a naval force for coastal and river port defence. The land forces comprised both infantry and cavalry protected by armour made of metal and leather. They were trained in archery, the use of the crossbow, swordsmanship, wrestling and boxing, and were equipped with many kinds of catapults (some needing to be manned by scores of infantry) which hurled stones, molten metal, poisoned bullets and bombs. From the eleventh century on, war junks too were armed with catapults hurling explosive bombs.

These forces were not particularly effective. The cavalry especially was weak, lacking horses from the steppelands of the north which were no longer part of the empire. The mercenaries were ill-trained and of low morale.

In the early days of the Sung there was an increase in agricultural production. Water-control projects helped to irrigate the paddy fields, and to bring waste land into cultivation. The use of a wooden frame for transplanting paddy seedlings had eased in part one of the most arduous tasks in rice production. The plough was adapted to suit human labour where draught animals were lacking. High yielding varieties of rice and other crops were introduced. On the hillsides the cultivation of tea had been extended; a water-mill was devised for grinding tea-leaves. Agricultural production expanded, accompanied by an increase in population. The total population of the Middle Kingdom seems to have doubled in the eleventh century, reaching some hundred million towards the end of the Sung period.

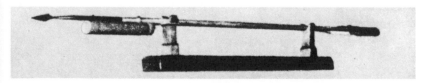

Model of a fire-arrow, invented during Northern Sung period. Gunpowder was discovered in the Tang period, but was used at first for fireworks. During the Sung it was used to propel the earliest military rockets, set off by igniting a cartridge attached to an arrow. This model had a range of 150–200 metres.

The lower reaches of the Yangtze particularly benefited from drainage schemes; it was said that every inch was planted with rice or with mulberry trees.

Agriculture developed but the condition of the peasants was miserable. The power of the big landlords was very great. They owned three-quarters of the land which they rented out to tenants. The landlord was entitled to half the produce of the tenant as rent, but he often claimed more. A good harvest scarcely left enough for the basic needs of the farmer; bad years brought debts and very often famine. The abandonment or sale of land, accompanied by the sale of children to the great houses, brigandage, or suicide—the same traditional pattern of social distress in the countryside appeared despite the technical advances during the Sung centuries. Contracts have survived showing that rates of interest for loans were 20 per cent per month for cash, and 50 per cent for cereals at harvest time. One document, no doubt typical, registers the sale of an impoverished craftsman's son for agricultural labour:

'The monumental-stonemason, Chao Tsu, because . . . he is short of commodities and cannot procure them by other means, sells today, with the option of repurchase, his own son Chiu Tsu to . . . the lord Li Chien Ting. The sale price has been fixed at 200 bushels of corn and 200 bushels of millet. Once the sale has been concluded, there will neither be anything paid for the hire of the man, nor interest paid on the commodities. If it should happen that the man sold, Chiu Tsu, should fall ill and die, his elder brother will be held responsible for repaying the part of the goods (corresponding to the period of hire which had not been completed). If Chiu Tsu should steal anything of small or great value from a third person either in the country or in town, it is Chiu Tsu himself (and not his employer) from whom all reparation will be demanded. . . . The earliest time-limit for the repurchase of Chiu Tsu has been fixed at the sixth year. It is only when this amount of time has elapsed that his relations are authorised to repurchase him. Lest a higher price should then be asked for him, this contract has been drawn up to establish proof of the agreement.'

This contract dating from the Sung was discovered at Tunhuang, on the north-western frontier, terminus of the Old Silk Road.

The wars against the Khitan and the Hsia, although not pursued to a military conclusion, were extremely costly, and the annual indemnities which ensued strained the resources of the exchequer; the burden was shifted in customary fashion onto the backs of the weakest section of the community, the peasantry. The imposition of taxation had reached a high level of ingenuity. In the days of the Five Dynasties when the warlords were fighting it out, a range of supplementary agricultural taxes had been introduced. When an ox died the owner was obliged to sell the hide at a low price to the government, for making army equipment. This was followed by outright confiscation of the hide by the government, without payment. The next stage was the demand for the payment of an 'ox-hide' tax, irrespective of possession of an ox, alive or dead. Taxes were raised on farm implements owned by the peasants; they paid tolls for crossing bridges and taxes on table salt. A wine tax was levied on the peasant even though he drank none. A 'sparrow and rat tax' had been added to the land tax, to make up for presumed loss of grain caused by sparrows and rats.

Although some of these impositions were removed in the early days of the Sung, tax and other burdens soon returned to help meet the military expenses of the state and the indulgences of the court.

In Szechuan, agricultural labour was organised like a military operation: 'Communal labour in the ricefields was regulated by a waterclock. A drum was beaten to call the workers together, to provide work rhythms, to spur them on in their tasks, and to prevent them from chattering. The sound of the drum could be heard in the fields from morning to night.'

Within three decades of the founding of the Sung, peasant risings occurred. These were suppressed, but unrest continued. After the first century of Sung rule, the emperor appointed to the post of prime minister Wang An Shih, a statesman who had studied the reforms of forerunners and who proposed a series of measures to prevent the recurrence of unrest. Many of his 'New Laws' as they were called were in fact traditional measures, or the revival of earlier reforms: the reclamation of waste land was to be encouraged through water-control projects. Pre-harvest loans from the government at interest rates of 20 per cent were designed to release the peasant from the grip of the landlord and merchant moneylenders. Peasants were enabled to secure exemption from corvée by payment of a remission fee. A new survey of the land of every household was decreed to ensure the inclusion of the estates of officials and landlords in the taxation system. Measures of price control were re-enacted, abundant goods were purchased for resale at reasonable prices when supplies were scarce, in order to discourage merchant speculation. The production of luxury goods was restricted. A militia was proposed on the basis of a quota from groups of families; peasant conscripts were to be recruited and drilled during the slack season in the countryside and were gradually to replace the mercenaries. Landlords were to supply horses for cavalry.

These measures had a temporary success; but they were opposed by the people who were most hurt by them, the landlords, officials and merchants. With the death of Wang An Shih (1086), and of the emperor his patron, the New Laws were withdrawn and the old abuses returned.

Kin Tartars

The Sung government was in no mood, or position, to deal with the continuing menaces from the northern neighbours. The Khitans had succumbed to Chinese cultural pressures if not to her might of arms. Giving up nomadism for a settled life they had adopted Chinese customs and language. In so doing, they lost their standing amongst their own people. One of the vassal tribes, the Kin (Golden) Tartars from the Sungari valley, overthrew their master; the remnants of the Khitan went west and settled in the Ili valley in central Asia. The Sung had thought this the moment to regain the ceded northern provinces from the Khitan; before the defeat of the Khitan they made an alliance with the Kin Tartars, promising to transfer to the Kin the tribute previously paid to the Khitans, if the latter were defeated in a joint attack, and the provinces restored to the Sung. Once on the attack, however, the Kin could not be halted. Having driven the Khitan from Peking they descended on Kaifeng, the Sung capital.

Kaifeng was besieged in 1126. One faction at the Sung court, with strong popular support, was in favour of outright resistance to the Kin Tartars. The emperor and a number of officials favoured appeasement, hoping to secure peace terms from the Kin with the offer of a huge quantity of silver.

In 1127 Kin troops captured Kaifeng after a half-hearted resistance on the part of the Sung emperor, who abdicated in favour of his son. Father and son, together with the imperial court, some 3,000 prisoners in all, were taken captive and transported to Manchuria.

Another imperial son fled south, assumed the imperial yellow, and after a period of wandering established his court at Hangchow, which became capital of the southern remnant of the Sung kingdom. The Kin Tartars continued their drive south and crossed the Yangtze. Despite the achievements of the Sung general Yo Fei in driving the Tartars back beyond the Yangtze and Huai rivers, the peace faction triumphed at court. Yo Fei was executed on a trumped up charge and peace was concluded with the Kin, whose rule was recognised as far south as the Huai. The Sung retained dominion over the Yangtze valley and the southern regions. This partition once more into north and south lasted one-and-a-half centuries.

9. Southern Sung

1127–1279

Commerce

Despite the political disruption that followed the fall of the Tang in the tenth century, and the loss of the northern part of the Middle Kingdom to the Kin Tartars in the twelfth, trade continued to expand in the remnant of the Kingdom, so that, by the thirteenth century something like a commercial revolution occurred, at least in south China.

The taste for Chinese products, especially for tea and silk tissues, which the barbarians in the north had acquired, was further stimulated by the accession of millions of Han people to the empires of the Kin Tartars and the Hsia. The flow of annual tribute by no means satisfied this demand, which was catered for by a growing trade between the Sung and the people of the north. Horses for cavalry were the main item of Sung import.

Maritime commerce, too, had developed to huge proportions by the time of the Southern Sung. Improvements in navigation contributed to this. The Chinese had known about magnetic polarity since the third century AD, and the compass (in China a 'south-pointing needle') was used by them in their trade with south-east Asia by the early twelfth century, several decades before its introduction to Europeans by the Arab mariners. Huge sea-going junks, carrying several hundred men, plied the southern seas each year, sailing with the monsoons, and bearing cargoes for the East Indies, India and the eastern coast of Africa. These ships relied on sails, made of matting or canvas; and on oars, each of which would be worked by four men in calm weather. The junks towed behind them boats carrying supplies of food and water. Paddle-ships driven on the treadmill principle were also in use.

The oceanic and coastal trade was concentrated in large ports like Canton, Hangchow and Chuanchou (Marco Polo's Zayton), where the Government superintendants collected customs duties and taxes (between 10 per cent and 20 per cent of the sales value of the goods) and anchorage fees. Chinese exports at this time consisted not only of silks but also of porcelain, which went in large quantities to the Middle East and eventually to Europe. From Japan and Korea, whose cultural development had derived much from the Middle Kingdom, came a demand for texts, paintings and general works of art. Sung China imported from Asia luxury articles such as gems, spices, ivory and fine woods. Cotton textiles were also imported on a large scale.

Foreign trading communities settled in the ports. These included Koreans, who in the main dominated the trade with the eastern isles, and Persians and Arabs who controlled the commerce across the wes-

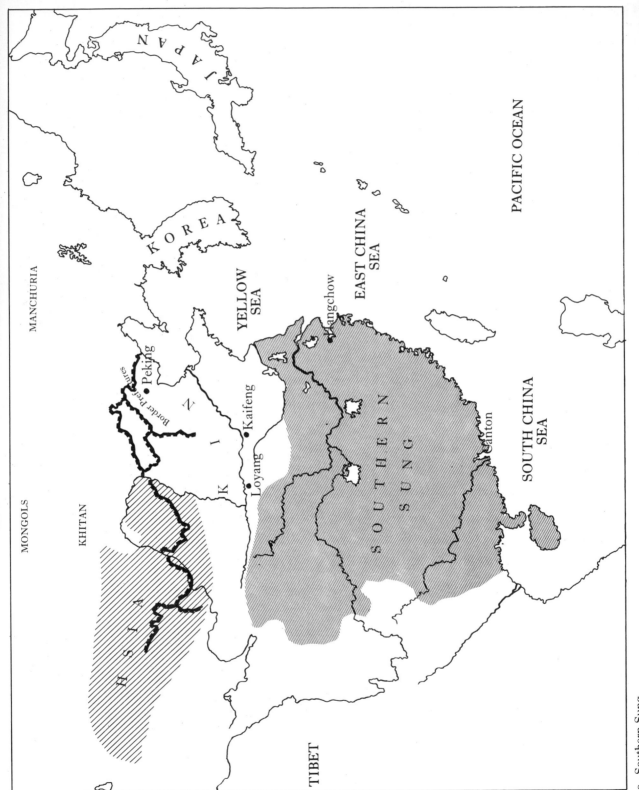

9. Southern Sung.

tern seas. The coastal areas and ports of east China began to replace the north-west corridor to central Asia as the gateway to the outside world, and as the region of contact with the outer barbarian.

This commercial growth was sustained by the development of a highly articulated monetary economy.

Increasing commerce had brought an increasing demand for currency. The unit of state accountancy was the string of one thousand cash coins tied together by a cord through the square hole in the centre. In the markets, the general unit was a string of a hundred cash. The operation of the law of supply and demand meant that the unit of 'hundred cash' in Sung times was in reality frequently a string of many fewer. In Kaifeng, for example, during the Northern Sung period, the exchange value of the 'hundred' was some seventy cash. Each year the government had millions of copper cash minted, but they still failed to meet the demand at home and abroad.

Moreover, both government officials and merchants were faced with the inconvenience and danger of the transfer of quantities of bulky copper cash over great distances. In the Tang period merchants had deposited stocks of cash with wealthy families in exchange for receipts ('flying money') which could be cashed in other places by accredited agents. During the Sung, these notes, a form of paper money, made their appearance on a large scale. Notes issued by the government permitted merchants who bought them to trade them for tea or salt at source or from state warehouses. Conversely, traders making deliveries in distant regions could be paid in notes which were convertible into goods at the capital. Early in the eleventh century, notes issued by private bankers were taken over by the state. Like the private notes, the government certificates were subject to a 3 per cent service charge. They were valid for a three year period, which was a necessary restriction because of the deterioration of the paper. By the second half of the thirteenth century, the government was putting into circulation notes which were negotiable throughout the empire. While none of the original notes from these times have survived, a plate for printing them has been discovered in Jehol. The notes it produced bore in addition to the serial number, the warning, or challenge, 'Counterfeiters will be decapitated', and 'The denouncer will be rewarded with three hundred strings of cash'.

Rapid accountancy was promoted in later Sung times by the introduction of the earliest computer, the abacus, a device still in use in many parts of Asia and Europe.

State revenues also adjusted to the increase of commercial activity and the expansion of the monetary system. During the period of the Southern Sung, after the loss of the agricultural lands of the north, the state began to receive a larger proportion of its taxes in currency than in grain and textiles. There was a greater dependence, too, on revenue derived from commercial sources. Up to the early Tang period, the government revenues had been derived almost entirely from agricultural taxation. Later, especially towards the end of the Tang, government monopolies like tea, salt and wine, together with various commercial taxes, provided an increasingly significant proportion of state revenue. During the Southern Sung, the income from commercial sources (which provided half of the cost of maintaining the army) came to outweigh the income derived from the land tax.

The Sung was a period of considerable technical progress. The advances in craft and industry were the basis of the great commercial development. Mining, metallurgy and shipbuilding expanded. Bellows powered by a waterwheel were introduced into iron-smelting, and enabled this industry to meet in part the greatly increased demand for agricultural implements and craftsmen's tools.

Sericulture also made big advances, and the silk industry, either state run, or in the hands of individual merchants, flourished. In Kaifeng, Loyang and elsewhere there were large government run spinning and weaving mills. The government also made purchases of silk from other enterprises. Cotton textiles began to be produced in China at this time.

The fine craftsmanship of the Sung period was especially distinguished in the production of porcelain. The subdued shades of green, grey and blue celadon ware, the ivory and moon-white glazes, the elegant form and simple design of the products of the Sung kilns, are world famous.

The trend towards urbanisation of Sung society was concomitant with commercial expansion. Kaifeng, the capital of the Northern Sung, contained at the beginning of the twelfth century over a quarter of a million households, or a million and a quarter individuals. Hangchow, towards the end of the next century, contained nearly 400,000 households. There were many other large urban centres. But the scale of the urban population was perhaps less important than the fact that society at this time became increasingly dominated by urban dwellers. Officials and gentry lived not on their country estates but in the towns, which supported also an immense number of artisans, merchants, shopkeepers and labourers.

The shift in emphasis from the countryside to the town occurred at the same time as the shift in orientation in the Middle Kingdom from the Yellow River valley in the north to the southern regions. The Yangtze valley and the lands to the south were better watered and richer in general than the north; the provinces of the centre and the south were the great rice, tea and silk producers. Fleeing before the nomad barbarians, increasing numbers of families from the north had come south and established themselves there. In the past, the dynasties of the Celestial Empire had been based on the north, with capitals in the valleys of the Yellow and Wei rivers. The capital of the Southern Sung, Hangchow, was south of the Yangtze.

Ching Ming (Spring) Festival at Kaifeng, capital of the Northern Sung. Detail from a handscroll painted by Chang Tse Tuan.

Hangchow

In Sung times, the population increases occurred most dramatically in the south, and here too arose the most dense urban concentrations. Sung towns were no longer centres exclusively of regional administration, divided into wards, where markets were confined by ramparts, curfews, and other restrictions. The development of Hangchow illustrated the adaption from bureaucratic to mercantile exigencies.

When the court established itself at Hangchow in the first half of the twelfth century, the town was no greater than many another provincial centre, and had certainly no claim to grandeur. It was a modest town, flanked by a lake, and the sudden increase in inhabitants meant that many officials were quartered with their wives and concubines in military camps; others found shelter in monasteries, with which Hangchow was well provided. Apart from the fact that Hangchow was reassuringly distant from regions threatened by nomad invasion, and was encircled by lakes and paddyfields, a difficult terrain for mounted archers, it had at first few advantages to offer as capital of the Celestial Empire, apart from its charm. A very old Chinese saying goes: 'Above, Heaven; below, Hangchow!' and a thirteenth-century Chinese commentator described it:

Green mountains surround on all sides the still water of the lake. Pavilions and towers in hues of gold and azure rise here and there. One would say, a landscape composed by a painter. Only towards the east, where there are no hills, does the land open out, and there sparkle, like fishes scales, the bright coloured tiles of a thousand roofs.

Houses, temples and palaces had a different structure from those in the west. They did not build foundations and bearer walls, but erected strong wooden pillars on stone supports sunk into the ground. The buildings were rectangular in shape and normally had a ground floor only or were one storey high. The roof was the most important and most expensive item, and was supported, not by walls, but by the pillars which were spaced about three metres apart, and by a number of beams and crossbeams. The finest roofs were covered with glazed yellow, pale or jade green tiles; official buildings, and those belonging to people of high rank, were permitted to have elegant curved roofs; these harmonise well with natural landscapes. Such walls as were built were light and independent of the main structure; they rose as a surround a few feet only above ground. Other partitions consisted of blinds, screens and bamboo trellises. The buildings were open to the view, shady and cool. Windows were made of square trellis work with the spaces covered by oiled paper. The ground level of the buildings was slightly higher than the courtyards in front. Sumptuary laws controlled the size of the gateways which admitted to the courtyards. Ordinary folk were not allowed to have gateways more than one span wide.

The parts of the roof timbers exposed to view were decorated with carvings, and were painted in bright colours. In the houses of the rich the furniture was frequently of black lacquer. (An imperial decree restricted red lacquer beds to the use of the emperor.) Rush matting was generally used for bedding, with covers lined with silk floss. Pillows were made of plaited rush, lacquered wood or painted pottery. Painted scrolls, hung vertically or unrolled horizontally, were a usual form of decoration, as were flowers and interesting plants. More attention was paid to the decoration than to the comfort in these houses. The wealthy burned incense to freshen the atmosphere.

The great extent and strenuous commercial activity of Hangchow made almost as much impression on Chinese contemporaries during the Sung as they did on Marco Polo somewhat later. According to Chinese descriptions, traditional Chinese single storey houses gave way in Hangchow to multistorey buildings, to cope with the increased density of population. High officials lived on the Hill of Ten Thousand Pines; merchants who had made their fortunes from the maritime trade lived on Mount Phoenix further to the south. There, summer houses and pavilions were scattered about amidst groves and gardens.

The imperial way, the finest thoroughfare in Hangchow, was sixty yards wide and stretched for more than three miles. Barriers, one painted black and another painted red, partitioned the route along its length, leaving a central passage, prohibited to ordinary people and to horses, reserved for the emperor. Other traffic was confined to the arcades beyond the barriers. Narrow canals ran along these arcades, their borders planted with lotuses and flowering trees, plum, peach, pear and apricot. The city was full of canals, and seemed to Marco Polo, when he came, like an eastern Venice. The canals of Hangchow were congested with rice barges, with boats laden with wood, coal, bricks, tiles, sacks of salt, and with the boatmen and the families that lived on board.

Formerly, according to one author, the quays along the canals had no continuous railings, only parapets constructed here and there by waterside landlords. Drunken revellers, confused by the lights, and failing to notice the twists and turns of the canals, often used to fall in, and tens, even hundreds, of them were drowned each year, until the day came when the town governor had solid balustrades placed along the banks, with gates at places of embarkation. In spite of the canal network and the popular preference for boats, there was frequent traffic congestion in the streets, especially at the town gateways which were too narrow for the seething mass of carriages, horses, donkeys and porters, and also at the approaches to the narrow humpbacked bridges (known in Chinese as 'rainbow bridges'). One inhabitant wrote that a person turned off the main streets into the seething confusion of the alleyways in the poorer districts, at the risk of his life. Pole-porters, animals laden with sacks, and pedestrians, jostled and bumped into each other in a constant pandemonium.

The two products consumed in the largest quantity by the towns-folk were rice and pork. The pig market was right in the centre of the town, near the imperial way. In two lanes there, several hundred beasts were slaughtered daily. Portions of pork and offal were sold to noodle merchants, tea houses, taverns and pickled pork shops, as well as to street vendors who hawked snacks of roast pork. One citizen, exhilarated by the sophistication of the marketing, recorded:

There are numerous varieties of rice, such as early rice, late rice, new-milled rice, winter-husked rice, first quality white rice, medium quality white rice, lotus pink rice, yellow rice, rice on the stalk, ordinary rice, glutinous rice, ordinary yellow rice, short-stalked rice, yellow rice and old rice . . . the town of Hang always likes rice barges to be coming in pellmell from all parts and finds it very convenient that they should arrive all day without pause. . . . In no matter what districts, in the streets, on the bridges, at the gates, and in every odd corner, there are everywhere to be found barrows, shops, and emporiums where business is done. The reason for this is that people are in daily need of the necessities of life, such as firewood, rice, oil, salt, soya, vinegar and tea, and to a certain extent even of luxury articles, while rice and soup are absolute essentials, for even the poorest cannot do without them. To tell the truth, the inhabitants of Hangchow are spoilt and difficult to please . . . .
. . . Let us take fish for example . . . I list all the various items sold by the fish-mongers . . . silver-fish, crabs, dried fish from the Huai, small crabs, salted duck, fried mullet, frozen fish, frozen dried fish, fried bream, loach fried in batter, fried eel, boiled fish, and white shrimps fried. In addition, these goods are sold by hawkers in the streets, to satisfy the needs of customers in the little lanes and alleyways, which is very convenient.

Salted fish took next place after rice and pork in the diet of the people. There were nearly two hundred shops selling nothing but salt fish. Then there were the specialised markets for vegetables out-side the New Gate, the fresh fish market to the south-east of the city, outside the Gate-Where-One-Awaits-The-Tide; the crab market on the river bank; and the cloth market outside the south ramparts. There were markets for olives, for oranges, for flowers, for gems, for medicinal plants and for books. In addition, there were in the streets the numerous entertainments which the towns people could enjoy, jugglers and acrobats, marionette shows and shadow plays, and the storytellers. 'Quinsai (Hangchow) . . . is the greatest city which may be found in the world,' said Marco Polo, 'where so many pleasures may be found that one fancies himself to be in Paradise.' But it is questionable whether the beauties that made such an impression on Polo were of the natural order.

This merchant of Venice estimated that in the temporary capital of Hangchow there were 'twelve guilds of the different crafts, and each guild had 12,000 houses in the occupation of its workmen . . .

the number and wealth of the merchants, and the amount of goods that passed through their hands was so enormous that no man could form a just estimate thereof.'

Of the merchants he recorded:

The leading and wealthy owners of these shops do no work with their own hands and affect on the contrary a grave and decorous behaviour. The same is true of their ladies who are very handsome, as we have just said: they are brought up to acquire habits of great timidity and delicacy, and their dress displays such magnificence of silks and jewels that it would be impossible to estimate the cost.

Both men and women, amongst the wealthy, wore ankle-length tunics, with long loose sleeves. Coats lined with silk floss or fur, protected against the cold. Common people wore a tunic blouse and trousers of a light coloured material. No one went about barefoot or bareheaded. Even the poorest wore some kind of sandal; and only Buddhist monks went about without anything at all on their heads. They were in fact cleanshaven. Women wore scarves as headwear, or were sometimes content with ornamental hairpins and combs. The wealthier women had elaborate combs and ornaments of flowers and jewels. Servant girls could be recognised by their hairstyle—a fringe and two tufts, brought to the front of the head, and tied by coloured ribbons. Children had their heads cleanshaven except for a tuft sticking up in front. Craftsmen and traders wore a kind of turban, the colour and shape of which indicated the man's trade.

When a magistrate or one who has a literary degree is paying a visit, he wears a special visiting gown, which is quite different from his daily attire. . . . If perchance one should meet a person who is not wearing his top garment, which they call a courtesy vestment, he will not greet the other with the customary gestures until he puts it on. Usually when one goes out he has a servant with him who carries this ritual cape. However when two friends meet, if one of them has on his visiting cloak and the other is without it, the one wearing the cloak will take it off . . .

Style of clothing was especially significant for men of rank. The shape and type of headgear, the colour and decoration of the robe and the style of the girdle, all had social significance, rather like military uniforms in the west. Certain forms of embroidery, and special furs like sable, fox and lynx, were used exclusively by officials, who were also distinguished by the buttons on their caps. There were prescribed colours for different grades of officials: above the third degree, purple robes; above the sixth, vermilion; above the seventh, green; above the ninth, turquoise. Black and white were worn by ordinary folk. Yellow was the colour reserved for imperial use. After a time, however, some of these colour distinctions became blurred; the court, for example, granted the right to wear purple to officials of all grades. Ricci the Jesuit missionary, described the Confucian formality regarding dress which survived into the seventeenth century:

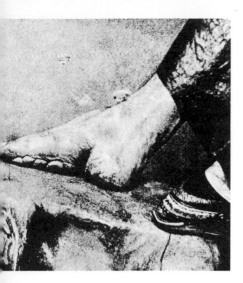

Those belonging to the literary casts may wear square hats . . . all others are round.

The headgear, like girdles, had special significance. Ricci described the caps of the mandarins:

All magistrates, high or low and of either order, wear the same kind of black hat, which has two ovate wings just above the ears and so lightly attached to the hat that they fall off very easily. The reason for this particular arrangement, so they say, is to guarantee that the one wearing the hat will walk upright and modestly—without even slightly bending the head. . . .

The Chinese can distinguish between their magistrates by the parasols they use . . . some are blue and others yellow . . . they may also be recognised by the mode of transportation in public. The lower ranks ride on horseback, the higher are carried about on the shoulders of their servants in sedan chairs.

Round parasols of turquoise silk were, in the first instance, reserved for use by princes of the imperial family. From the end of the tenth century, permission was extended to certain officials to carry these parasols. Then the right was granted to women of the palace when paying visits to town. The wide openings of the sleeves, which were often bordered like the neck with silk of a deeper colour, were used as pockets, in which small articles like fans were carried. Women's clothes were fastened on the left side, the men's on the right, by oblong buttons and toggle loops.

Among the less attractive Sung developments was the further decline in the status of women. The position of women in the Middle Kingdom had never been high; the Confucian ethic emphasised feminine subservience to men. In agriculturally based society, however, women of all social degree had tasks which were valuable, and indeed the manual labour of the peasant women was economically indispensable. In the towns, the work was less essential; a further decline in her social position took place, especially amongst the wealthy for whom women became more than ever playthings, objects of indulgence, and symbols of affluence. It was in this period that the vogue of foot-binding developed, first among upper class women, a practice which set them, and their menfolk, apart from other classes, but which spread in the course of time even among peasant folk. It has been suggested that the custom was inspired by the central Asian dancing girls, who performed like ballet-dancers. When small, Chinese girls had their feet bound until they were constricted to about half the normal size. This 'lily-foot' came to be regarded as a feature of elegance and sexual beauty, not only by men but by the women, who continued to subject their children to this torment until the twentieth century.

The urban and pleasure-seeking society, recruited to a large extent from upstarts, sometimes buying its way into the bureaucracy through its commercial successes, stimulated cultural development of a more popular nature than that of the traditional literati. In the

Lily foot. When very small, girls would have their feet doubled up and tightly bound, so that the arch broke and the toes turned under, until the foot grew into the shape of a hoof, half the normal length. When the bindings were not changed sufficiently often, festering skin added to the misery of the little girls.

big towns during the Sung, professional storytellers delighted their audiences with yarns in the vernacular, based on folk tradition, or on casual scripts—prompters notes, from which later emerged the novel as a Chinese literary form. Drama too developed in the Sung cities.

Burning incense, bamboos and rocks by Ma Yuan, one of the great masters of the Sung period.

Sung painting

Urban interests and urban entertainment replaced rustic pastimes for large sections of the community. Hunting disappeared as a patrician sport in Sung times. A characteristically urban, romanticised approach towards nature also developed, in which the individual, detached, remote and tranquil, could be attuned to the harmony of the natural order. This attitude, merging with a Taoist, mystical approach, was exemplified in many of the paintings of the Sung period, which were the artistic glory of the age. In the muted monochrome work of Ma Yuan for example, individuals are romantically dwarfed by an immense natural environment, where space and infinity are suggested with a few strokes of the brush.

This art was patronised by the court, and an Academy of Painting was established in the Ling Yin Temple at Hangchow, to which were attracted some of the greatest painters of the age, including Ma Yuan and Ksia Kuei. Calligraphy came also to rank as an art of the highest prestige, and respect for the brush of the calligrapher was no less than that for the pictorial artist.

Wood block printing of full page texts and pictures, had been practised in China since the seventh century. This was followed by printing by movable type, invented in China by Pi Sheng, during the time of the Northern Sung (1045—some four hundred years before the printing press of Johann Gutenberg in Germany). A large number of philosophical and scientific works, classics, and encyclopaedias were produced, often richly illustrated by woodblock prints which also became a highly developed art. Authorised versions of the classics could now be more widely disseminated in book form, and there was an increase in the number of private schools and academies. Education, and the mandarinate, became accessible to a larger group of families. The literary works of the Sung period come from much wider sources than the works of official recorders and scholarly poets of earlier days. They include the jottings of observant citizens and the prompt books of story tellers. The merchant citizens, as we have seen, were more interested in the details of everyday life than were the scholar officials. Medicine attracted considerable attention. Works on pharmaceutics and acupuncture were produced. Amongst the monumental achievements was a medical encyclopaedia, compiled under imperial auspices, by twelve eminent men of the day, and another compilation, by a traveller who advised on the essential items to include in one's going-away kit: he mentioned a raincoat, a chest of medicines, plenty of spare clothes and combs, a box of preserved

Sung period bronze model for training doctors in acupuncture, a traditional form of therapy. The figure had holes at crucial spots for the acupuncture needle. These were sealed with wax and the model filled with water. When the student pierced the right place, the model bled water.

foods and tea, another containing paper, brushes, ink, scissors, a rhyming dictionary and a lute. Candles, knives and chessmen were not to be forgotten, and another box should be ready to receive books which may be bought en route, together with some insecticide powder for keeping bookworms at bay.

During the later days of the Sung the court and the wealthy citizens were more active in the pursuit of pleasure than of scholarship. One statesman and scholar dared to address a memorial to the emperor on the subject of imperial extravagance:

I am informed that in consequence of the recent birth of a princess, a demand has been made on the Treasury for no less than 8,000 pieces of silk.

Now the rigour of winter is just at its height, and the wretched workmen of the dyeing department, forced to break ice before they can get water, will suffer unspeakable hardships in supplying the amount required. And judging by your Majesty's known sentiments of humanity and thrift, I cannot believe that this wasteful corvée is to be imposed, though rumour indeed has it that the dyers are already at work.

A story of the Sung period tells us that 'the capital took on a false and superficial air of wealth and prosperity'. Indeed there was evidence everywhere in Hangchow of the luxury of the Sung and its devotion to pleasure:

The most famous tea-houses of the day were the Eight Genii, the Pure Delight, the Pearl, the House of the Pan Family, the Double Honours and the Treble Honours. . . . In these places they always set out bouquets of fresh flowers according to season. . . . At the counter were sold 'Precious Thunder' tea, tea of fritters and onions, or else Pickle Broth; and in hot weather, wine of snow bubbles and apricot blossom, or other kinds of refreshing liquor.

Because of the abundance of servants, who were paid low wages, no one would dream of doing a simple task for himself; guests at banquets and even clients at cheap restaurants would not be allowed to cut up their meat themselves; everything was cut up small enough to be picked up with chopsticks. Rice wine, warmed to body temperature, was served with most dishes.

The purses and manners of the parvenus and the country bumpkins were fair game for the slick city merchants and restaurateurs: 'Towards evening lanterns and candles are lit, spreading a blaze of light everywhere.' Singing-girl waitresses were required by the owners to suggest special dishes to inexperienced customers 'so that the bill would mount up. In all restaurants, if one desired to gain esteem as a customer, the thing to do was first of all to choose one's place, consult the menu, and order the wine. Only then did one proceed in an unhurried manner to make a careful selection of several choice dishes.' 'Gentlemen from the provinces who, not being yet acquainted with the ways of the capital, began eating right away, were a laughing stock in the eyes of the proprietor.'

Not everyone in the towns, however, became a wealthy merchant. Urban poverty was a serious problem, as was the poverty in the countryside. Beggars abounded in the capital and in other towns:

In filthy knotted rags and broken hats,
They carry threadbare rugs and tattered mats;
    With batons of bamboo,
    And battered rice bowls too,
They swarm the rich man's gate and raise
    A frightful how-d'ye-do.

The birth of an additional child to a poor family was felt to be a catastrophe. It is recorded that, in the twelfth century in the country-side at the time of a birth, a bucket of water was kept ready for drowning the infant immediately, a procedure called 'bathing the infant'. In the cities the custom of abandoning the newly-born was preferred. Some poor families made over or sold their offspring to better-off families to be brought up as servants. Ibn Battuta, a Muslim traveller in the early fourteenth century, noted that 'young slave girls are very cheap in China; and indeed, all the Chinese will sell their sons as slaves equally with their daughters, nor is it considered any disgrace to do so'.

Abandonment of infants became so frequent that an edict was issued prohibiting the practice in the twelfth century; at the same time foundling hospitals were established, at the expense of the state –'in bad years, crowds of babies were brought in'. Families wanting to adopt children came and got them from the foundling hospital. Social measures were undertaken to reduce the distress of the urban poor. State granaries were revived, with stocks held against times of need, and special funds (on a limited scale) set aside for the relief of the poor. An official was appointed with the responsibility of building homes for the aged and destitute. Public and private agencies began to provide other forms of relief, such as pauper funerals. The un-employed were packed off into the army. One fund was set aside for free medicine. Only a limited amount of the relief allocations ever reached the poor, however, for there was considerable leakage into the pockets of the administrators and their friends.

Relief was also supplied by the state for victims of disasters, as, for example, the fires to which Hangchow (and other towns) were sub-ject; this despite the guard stations every five hundred yards and the watch towers permanently manned by soldiers, who ran up warning flags during the day if they sighted smoke, and lit warning lanterns at night. Hangchow, during the Sung, suffered devastation by fire on several occasions, when scores of thousands of houses were demo-lished. After one such fire in the summer of 1132, the court distri-buted 120 tons of rice amongst the poor, and the victims were authorised to camp in the Buddhist monasteries. Taxes were sus-

Sung Goblet: pale blue with purple splashes. Spotted celadon glaze.

pended from the sale of planks and waterproof rushmatting for a time after the fire, and the payment of rents was also suspended. A fire in 1208, which raged for four days and nights, was followed by similar measures. Private philanthropy in the towns sometimes took care of orphans and the aged, or provided pauper burials.

Commercial developments in China over this period, with the expansion of internal and external trade, an advanced monetary economy, technical achievements, the specialisation and sophistication of production, and the urbanisation of sections of society, were contemporary with similar economic advances in Europe on the eve of the Renaissance. In Europe these changes gave rise to the bourgeoisie and its political struggles, to capitalism and to an industrial revolution. In China state controls over commerce, and the government monopoly of the production of essentials like iron, together with the domination and ideology of the mandarinate, combined to inhibit both the investment of capital in advanced techniques and the rise to power of a bourgeoisie. Capitalism came to China several centuries later in the cargo ships of the west; it may have germinated but it did not develop in the busy Sung cities, which remained the centres of bureaucratic control.

The Sung period ended in a style similar to the decline of previous dynasties. Submerged by discontent in the countryside and corruption at court, the rulers were in no position to withstand effectively the challenge of the latest nomad empire threatening from the north, the empire of the Mongols. However, Mongol conquerors overran most of Asia and a good part of Europe before they succeeded after several decades of resistance, in reducing the Middle Kingdom to submission.

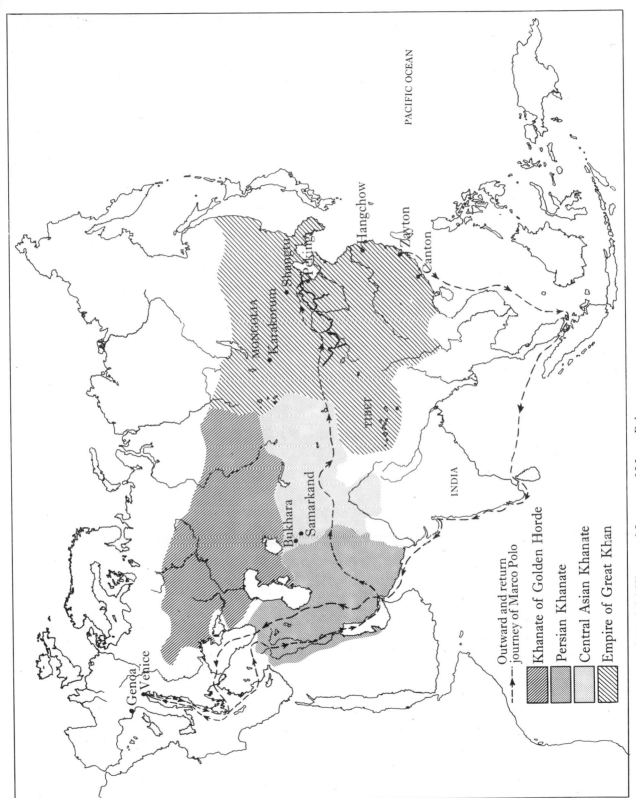

10. Mongol Empire at time of Khubilai Khan, and Journey of Marco Polo.

10. The Mongols

North of the Wall in the eleventh and twelfth centuries there was chronic warfare between the tribes of mounted nomads who had replaced the earlier Huns. Some of these tribes were know as Tartars, some as Turks, and there were many others. These names, like that of Mongol, came to be applied to them collectively. There was no unified rule and the conflicts were endless.

In *The Secret History of the Mongols*, a contemporary account written or dictated by a Mongol officer on the banks of the River Kerulen, we are told,

The starry skies are overturned
As people strain to kill each other.
There is no peace on any pallet
When all are striving after gain.
The whole wide world is being shattered
As people strain to kill each other.

The old clan solidarity had disappeared, for even kin could not be trusted, and there was no defence against rival tribes.

In the twelfth century, one Mongol chieftain Khabul Khan attempted, without success, to unify the tribes. Genghis Khan, who eventually succeeded in this task, was born *c.* 1155 into the family of Yesukai Bator, a descendant of Khabul Khan. According to the *Secret History*, Yesukai was hawking one day along by the Onon River. There he encountered a man from the Merkit tribe, who was taking his wife home in a cart. Yesukai called his two brothers and, thus reinforced, chased the Merkit away and seized the beautiful wife. 'Her screams seemed to raise waves on the Onon River and to shake the trees of the Forest. Yesukai took the woman to wife.' In due course, also on the banks of the Onon, the woman gave birth to a son, Temuchin.

The early days of Temuchin, future khan of the Mongols, were hard. When young, he lost his father, poisoned, says the *Secret History*, by Tartar rivals. His family was abandoned by their retainers and followers. Temuchin and his three brothers were reared on roots, grasses, fish broth and berries. The boy grew up, like his mates, ruthless in defending himself and in disposing of his rivals. Temuchin gained a reputation for being particularly tenacious and resourceful in battle, and generous to his supporters. He served for a period as a mercenary with the Kin, fighting against his tribal enemies and building up his own following.

The *Secret History* says:

Later in the Year of the Dog (1202), Genghis fought a battle. . . . Before hand, he instructed his men that if they got the upper hand, they were not to scramble in haste for the spoils, everyone seizing for himself; the whole booty would be divided up equally among them after the end of the battle. If anyone retreated to his own line in the battlefield, he was to summon up courage to charge into the enemy's line immediately; if he failed to do so, he would be put to the sword. Thus they eventually secured victory over the Tartars.

The Kin dynasty by this time was unable to control its distant vassals, and Temuchin succeeded in welding Turks, Tartars, Mongols and many other tribes into one nation. He was skilled in the practice of dividing his enemies and uniting his supporters, and in 1206 the process culminated at a gathering on the Kerulen River of the tribes of Mongolia when he was accepted as ruler, with the title of Genghis Khan, meaning 'Universal Ruler'. He put an end to centuries of warfare among the tribes.

In the next five or six years the Mongols overran the lands of their neighbours to the north of the Wall; then the defeat of the border kingdom of the Hsia provided Genghis Khan with camels as a reserve for his cavalry and a base for attack on the Kin of north China, who were no match for their former vassal. 'He once more led a campaign against the Kin in the Year of the Dog [1214]. . . . The remnants of the Kin defenders were reduced to cannibalism. Hitherto, the gold and silks in the central capital belonged to the Emperor of the Kin; now they belonged to Genghis.' Peking fell to Genghis in 1215.

Genghis was about sixty years old when north China was conquered.

The Mongols' way of life had diverged totally from that of their settled subjects. They respected only their own people, the horsemen of the steppe, and despised the peasant. The Chinese chronicles say that:

When Genghis invaded the western countries, he did not have in his stores a single measure of rice or a yard of silk. When [they came to the first Chinese provinces] his advisers said, 'Although you have now conquered the men of Han, they are of no use to us; it would be better to kill them all and turn the land back to pasture so that we can feed our beasts on it.' But Yehlu [his minister] said, 'Now that you have conquered everywhere under Heaven and all the riches of the four seas, you can have everything you want, but you have not yet organised it. You should set up taxation on land and merchants, and should make profits on wine, salt, iron and the produce of the mountains and marshes. In this way in a single year you will obtain 500,000 ounces of silver, 80,000 rolls of silk and 40,000 piculs of grain. How can you say that the Chinese people are of no use to you . . . ?' So Ghengis agreed that it should be done.

The pastoral economy of the nomads was in the short term self-sufficient. Their sheep supplied food, wool and pelts for clothing and felts to cover their round tents; sheep dung was burnt as fuel. At this period they were making greater use of iron for their weapons; they had no need of agriculture except to supply grain as supplementary

Genghis Khan (AD 1206–27).
Traditional presentation.

diet for their herds. In due course the nomads, or at least their chiefs, developed a taste for tea and fine textiles, and became increasingly dependent on minerals for their weapons and tools.

Many of the merchants and missionaries who came from the west during this period left accounts of the roving life of the Mongols, for most of them came via the Mediterranean across the steppelands of Asia to China, and spent some time with the nomad hordes in their own terrain.

They spend the winter in steppes and warm regions where there is good grazing and pasturage for their beasts. In summer they live in cool regions, among mountains and valleys, where they find water and woodland as well as pasturage. A further advantage is that in cooler regions there are no horse-flies or gad-flies or similar pests to annoy them and their beasts. They spend two or three months climbing steadily and grazing as they go, because if they confined their grazing to one spot there would not be grass enough for the multitude of their flocks.

They have circular houses made of wood and covered with felt, which they carry about with them on fourwheeled wagons wherever they go. For the framework of rods is so neatly and skilfully constructed that it is light to carry. And every time they unfold their house and set it up, the door is always facing south. They also have excellent two-wheeled carts covered with black felt, of such good design that if it rained all the time the rain would never wet anything in the cart. These are drawn by oxen and camels. And in these carts they carry their wives and children and all they need in the way of utensils.

So reported Marco Polo, merchant of Venice.

Ibn Battuta, a Muslim merchant from Tangier, recollected:

We saw a vast town on the move with all its inhabitants, containing mosques and bazaars, and smoke from the kitchens rising in the air. On reaching the encampment, they took the tents off the wagons and set them upon the ground, for they were very light, and they did the same with the mosques and shops.

The nomads travelled complete with all possessions: the vassal herdsman with meagre tent and camel, the chief with elaborate pavilions, studs of horses, wives, and slaves.

The Mongols lived in families or households, each household having one or more tents (yurts), according to the number of wives. The families were grouped in patriarchal clans; related clans formed the tribal unit. They moved together as a horde or camp. The institution of polygamy, and the prohibition of marriage within the clan or closely related clans, meant that the practice of seizure of wives was common. Otherwise wives were purchased; they were paid for with animals, household goods, water or pasturage rights, and sometimes with luxuries, according to the status of the family. On marriage, the girl moved from the yurt of her parents to that of her husband. It was the ancient custom that the Mongol son married all the wives of his deceased father, except his own mother; he took over also the wives of a dead brother.

Genghis Khan, with wives and sons. Reproduction for shrine of Genghis Khan at Echen Horo, in the Ordos region, north China.

Among the nomads vital tasks were carried out by both women and men. The duties of the women were to drive the carts, to erect or pack their tents on the carts and to take them down again, and to dress and to sew skins for garments. The duties of the men were to build the tents and carts, to churn kumiss (fermented mare's milk) and make the bags for it, and to tend and load the camels. Men and women alike tended sheep and goats. Marco Polo commented that 'the men do not bother themselves about anything but hunting and warfare and falconry'.

Friar John of Pian de Carpini, a massive Franciscan, set out at the age of about sixty-five on a mission from the Pope to the Mongol Khan, and returned after two years with the Khan's reply (which survives in the Vatican archives), and with one of the earliest western descriptions of the Mongols:

The Mongols or Tartars, are unlike all other people. For they are broader between the eyes, and the balls of their cheeks, than men of other nations. They have flat and small noses, little eyes and eyelids standing straight upright. They are shaven on the crowns like priests. They wear their hair somewhat longer about the ears than upon their foreheads; and behind they let it grow long like woman's hair, which they braid in two locks, binding each of them behind either ear.

The garments of their men as well as of their women, are all of one fashion. They use neither cloaks, hats nor capes. But they wear jackets framed after a strange manner, of bucram scarlet or brocade. Their gowns are hairy on the outside and open behind with tails hanging down to their hams. They do not wash their garments, neither will they allow them to be washed, especially in the time of thundering. . . .

They are very rich in cattle such as camels, oxen, sheep and goats. And I think they have more horses and mares than all the rest of the world. But they have no cows or other beasts. Their emperors, chiefs, and other of their nobles have much silk, gold, silver and precious stones.

Their manners are partly praiseworthy, partly detestable. Neither thieves nor robbers of great riches are to be found . . . they are also very hardy, and when they have fasted a day or two, they sing and are merry as if they had eaten their bellies full. In riding, they endure much cold and extreme heat. There are no disputes among them and although they are often drunk yet they do not quarrel in their drunkenness. Drunkenness is honourable among them. Their women are chaste. . . . Towards other people the Tartars are most insolent . . . and beyond all measure deceitful and treacherous towards them. . . . The slaughter of other people is accounted a matter of nothing to them.

The nomad horde was an instant army. All were trained in the saddle since early childhood, learning archery, to scout, and to fight, as soon as to walk. A stone memorial erected in 1225 by Genghis Khan in honour of his archer Yesunke, records that at a victory celebration, the archer hit his target at a distance of 703·5 metres. The households moved intact, whether on seasonal migrations or military campaigns. Women, children and herds were always with the troops, providing a self-sufficiency that increased their military strength and

Nomad of the time of Genghis Khan. From Ching encyclopaedia.

mobility. In the absence of plunder, the hordes could live on mare's milk alone. In the case of defeat in battle, however, the families and herds of the vanquished fell into the hands of the victors, as part of the normal booty.

Carpini observed that the Tartars were required to have at least one bow, three quivers full of arrows, an axe and a rope. The rich had single-edged swords with sharp curved ends, pointed helmets and coats of mail, while their horses had chest and shoulders protected by mail.

The main element of the army under Genghis Khan was composed of mounted archers. A subsidiary role was played by the settled peoples of the conquered territories, who were pressed into service. The settled populations provided the infantry and artillery units of the period, soldiers for labouring and siege works, operating catapults, battering rams, fire arrows and flame-throwing machines. The Mongols were quick to learn from the Chinese the explosive qualities of gunpowder, and they used it for sapping and mining. They used flame-throwers and grenades filled with naphtha to burn down enemy defences. Fire arrows made by fixing slow-burning gunpowder to arrowheads, set light to combustible materials.

Nomad fighting strength generally had been reinforced by the thirteenth century by the increased use of iron in their weapons, for instance, in their arrow heads. Carpini noticed that they carried a file in their quivers to keep their arrowheads desirably sharp. Advising Christians on the best way of overcoming these 'detestable people', he recommended in general doing as the Tartar did; and in particular, when making arrow heads, to dip them according to Tartar custom, redhot into salt-water, so that they would be strong enough to pierce the enemies' armour.

Under Genghis Khan, institutions developed which reinforced the military efficiency of the Mongols. His personal bodyguard rapidly developed into an élite corps of privileged, highly disciplined loyal warriors, from amongst whom Genghis chose his generals and advisers.

His armies were organised in tumans (ten thousand), thousands, hundreds, and tens; these units fitted into a stable pattern of organisation, right wing, left wing and so on, in which every clan and household knew its place, when camping as in battle. 'No man may depart to another unit than the hundred, thousand, or ten to which he has been assigned, nor may he seek refuge elsewhere.'

The full customary law and organisation of the Mongol horde has not come down to us. It was however made explicit by Genghis Khan who 'established a rule for every occasion and a regulation for every circumstance: while for every crime he fixed a penalty. And since the Tartar people had no script of their own, he gave orders that the Mongol children should learn writing from the Uighurs;

and that these yasas (laws) and ordinances should be written down on rolls.' An important group of rules dealt with the distribution of booty after battle; others dealt with pillaging. Severe punishment was meted out for theft, especially of horses.

The sport to which the Tartars were most attached was hunting, even when they had a sufficiency of food from their own flocks, or could supply themselves by raids on their neighbours. Genghis Khan encouraged hunting, not for the sake of the kill alone, but for the skill and endurance it developed, serving as training for the army. The hunts arranged for the khans were on a grandiose scale, with an elaborately regulated procedure.

The Mongol calendar consisted of a twelve year cycle, each year named after some animal, in the following order: Mouse, Ox, Tiger, Hare, Dragon (or Fish), Serpent, Horse, Sheep, Ape, Fowl, Dog, Pig. An old steppe legend says that when the animals came up in heavenly procession to have the years named after them, the camel, as the noblest, came first: but a mouse crept up on his head and succeeded in getting the first year named after himself, while the camel was entirely omitted. Another legend ascribes the animal cycle to the hunting activities of a Turkic khan: to escape him the animals fled, and crossed a river. The order of escape across the river became that of the calendar cycle. The animal calendar is used by some people in China and Mongolia to this day.

The Mongol empire

After the defeat of the Kin, Genghis Khan moved back with the main body of his army to the tribal lands of the Kerulen, leaving one general with a horde in China as an occupation force. Genghis sent embassies and trade caravans along the Old Silk Road to the west, to establish commercial relations with the kingdoms of central Asia. When his envoys were slaughtered, Genghis Khan, with his cavalry some 200,000 strong, rode west on a mission of vengeance, through the heart of the continent and south over the mountains, to annihilate the fleeing enemy on the bank of the river Indus.

When Genghis Khan set out from Mongolia in 1219 he was over sixty years old. Feeling no doubt intimations of mortality he summoned to his court the Taoist hermit Chang Chun, who had the reputation of a mystic possessing the secret of longevity. Reluctantly the hermit followed Genghis across high Asia, for, in nomad fashion, the imperial household and court moved wherever the emperor and army moved. The hermit was embarrassed at having to accompany the royal baggage train which included a vast number of women. When he caught up with the emperor, celebrating with his hordes in the mountains north of Kabul, the hermit urged that moderate living would be more beneficial to the health of the emperor than taking medicine.

Leaving part of the imperial horde to push further west, Genghis Khan, after an absence of seven years, turned his own horse homeward. In 1227 (the year of the Pig) he set out on a punitive expedition against the Hsia, who had failed to honour their commitment to supply troops. It was on this campaign that the Universal Khan died, the advice of the hermit having been honoured more in the breach than in the observance.

By this time his western hordes had pushed on across southern Russia, and had reached the Caucasus, Armenia, Persia and the Persian Gulf.

Genghis had, in his lifetime, divided his empire in customary tribal fashion among the four sons of his chief wife; some of the heritage was allocated in anticipation of its conquest. Four great Mongol kingdoms were formed, in Persia, in central Asia, in southern Russia (known as the Golden Horde) and in China. Ogodei, the third son of Genghis, was proclaimed Great Khan; he took up residence in his father's original dominion on the Orkhon. Here at Karakorum he established the first residential capital of the Mongols, building palaces for his household and court, and bringing here the captive craftsmen from his campaigns, to build and embellish the capital.

Led by Batu, a grandson of Genghis, the Mongol hordes in the west swept on from the steppes of Russia to the grasslands of Europe. By 1241 Hungary was in Mongol hands. The victors were establishing themselves on the great Hungarian Plain when Batu ordered a withdrawal. News had come of the death of Ogodei, who died regretting that 'after I had been raised to the high throne by my imperial father, and his many estates had been laid upon my shoulders, I committed the error of allowing wine to conquer me'.

The relays of Mongol horsemen who brought the news that the Great Khan had died suddenly in a drunken stupor crossed the Eurasian continent in a matter of days, through the imperial post route service established by Ogodei in 1235. The post stations, which were serviced by corvée labour and requisitioned goods, provided shelter, supplies and especially fresh horses, for imperial communications. Tough Mongol couriers, using relays of horses, could cover two hundred miles a day. The route across Asia, kept clear of bandits and passable for horse traffic, became in the thirteenth century busier and safer than ever before. Merchant caravans, plying the different stages of the route, multiplied.

The levy for the maintenance of the post stage service survived in Mongolia until 1949.

The descendants of Genghis Khan continued the expansion of the Mongol empire. Under the Great Khan Ogodei, the attack on China continued. After the capture of Peking, the Mongols had attacked and defeated the Hsia. They then sent envoys to the Southern Sung

to negotiate joint attack on the remnants of the Kin. Having learnt nothing from the past, the Sung agreed to the proposal. They jumped 'out of the wolf's lair into the tigers mouth', as the Chinese say. In 1234 the Kin were defeated by the joint attack, and Mongol troops occupied the whole of north China.

The third Great Khan died after a couple of years; under the fourth, Khan Mongke, also a grandson of Genghis, operations were resumed against the Southern Sung in China. The campaign was in the hands of Mongke's brother Khubilai, who succeeded his brother as fifth Great Khan (1260–1294). The campaign in the south was protracted. The Chinese army and people put up a strong resistance, and the Mongols, who were quarrelling amongst themselves over the succession, withdrew their armies for a time.

Under Khubilai the Mongols renewed the attack against the Southern Sung. They besieged the town of Hsiangyang, which was the main junction of land and water communications between north and south China, and the gateway to the middle reaches of the Yangtze River. The town held out for five years before it was finally invested. After the fall of Hsiangyang, the Mongol troops pressed eastward. In 1276 Hangchow surrendered and the Sung emperor was carried off captive to the north. Three years later the last Sung pretender, a young boy, was trapped with the remnants of his fleet at Canton; a loyal minister jumped into the water with the young emperor on his back. The Sung dynasty ended with them.

The Mongol conquerors had ridden south from the Wall all the way to the edge of the Burma jungle. Meanwhile, Khubilai Khan had

moved his capital from Karakorum in the heart of Mongolia to Peking. By 1271, he had declared himself emperor of China and founded the Yuan dynasty. For the first time, all of China was under the rule of the barbarian from beyond the Wall.

The three other Mongol kingdoms were loosely subordinated to Khubilai, the Great Khan, grandson of Genghis. Peking, capital of an empire which stretched practically from one end of the known world to the other, became the terminus of an intercontinental route which opened up between the Mediterranean and China. Occident and orient were linked by the barbarian empire.

The Mongols were regarded with mixed feelings in the west. The thunder of the hooves of Batu Khan's hordes in Hungary had sent a tremor of terror throughout Europe, reaching as far as Britain. So great was the fear of the Mongols that there was a glut of herrings at Yarmouth, in the year 1238. Mathew Paris, writing at St Albans at the time, recorded that the Dutch and Baltic seamen, fearing the advance of the Tartars in their rear, failed to come to Yarmouth for the herring fishery. Herrings as a result were selling at forty or fifty for one silver piece in places far inland from the English coast.

The eruption of the Mongols appeared, to guilt-ridden Europe, to be a diabolical visitation, no less. The same godly Mathew reported:

A detestable nation of Satan, to wit, the countless army of the Tartars, broke loose from its mountain home . . . and poured forth like devils from the Tartarus . . . swarming like locusts over the face of the earth they have brought a terrible devastation to the eastern parts (of Europe) laying it waste with fire and carnage. . . . They are without human laws, know no comforts, are more ferocious than lions or bears, have boats made of ox hides. . . . They wander about with their flocks, and their wives are taught to fight like men.

On the other hand, this was the crusading era in Europe, and the perils anticipated from the demons who had withdrawn once more to their remote eastern Hades appeared less dreadful than the horrors expected from the devils of Islam who had been battering on the Christian door since the eleventh century, and whom generations of godfearing Crusaders had failed to dislodge. Encouraged too by the Prester John legend of an oriental king who was a Christian, popes and princes in Europe, incapable of uniting effectively within their own fraternity against the common foe, saw the chance of shifting the initiative for the defence of Christendom to the unspeakable Mongols, the infidel archers of the steppes. A series of diplomatic and evangelical missions set out in the thirteenth century from the Papacy and the crusading kingdoms of the west, to seek the Mongols in their homeland and to propose a sacred alliance.

In 1247 Friar John of Pian Carpini returned with the letter already mentioned, written in Persian, from the third Great Khan, Guyug. The letter summoned the Pope to come, together with all the mon-

Khubilai Khan, founder of Yuan dynasty (AD 1271–1294). Traditional presentation.

archs of Europe, to render submission in person to the Great Khan; it added that God knew what would be the consequences to them if they did not:

By the power of eternal heavens, We the universal Khan of the entire great people of the earth, Our order: This is an order sent to the Great Pope so that he may know it and understand it. . . . In the face of God, since the rising of the sun until its setting, all the territories have been granted to us. Except by God's order how shall one act? Today you ought to say with all your heart: 'We will be your subjects; we will give you our strength.' You in person, at the head of kings, all together, without exception, come and offer us service and homage. Then we shall recognise your submission. And if you do not observe the order of God, and disobey our orders, we shall know you as our enemies.

Despite this impious response, further missions set out along the road to Tartary and China, their optimism increased in the second half of the thirteenth century by the Mongol conquest of Baghdad, seat of the Caliphs of Islam (1268).

The Polos

Merchant enterprise was no less intrepid than missionary endeavour. In the year of Khubilai Khan's enthronement, two merchants of Venice left Constantinople to do business in the Crimea. They were the brothers Maffio and Niccolo Polo, whose commercial prospects had brightened since the Mongol successes in Mesopotamia had breached the barrier of Muslim kingdoms across the trade routes of western Asia and weakened the monopoly of oriental trade which the merchants of Islam had established in their own favour. Hostilities broke out between the Mongol Khanate of the Golden Horde in Russia, and the Persian Khanate, and blocked their return route; so the Polo brothers made their way further into the heart of Asia to Bukhara, where they stayed three years. Then they joined a party of the Great Khan's envoys who were returning home, and journeyed on with them to China. They were well received by the Great Khan Khubilai, who questioned them closely about Europe, its kings and popes, and sent them back with a request that the Pope send a hundred missionaries to bring the Christian faith to Cathay, and some oil from the Holy Sepulchre to ease the process. The return journey of the Polos took three years. One pope had died during this time, and the merchant adventurers waited a couple of years for the election of the next. Then they set out again (1271) this time accompanied by Niccolo's seventeen-year-old son Marco, the blessing of the new Pope, some holy oil, and a brace only of friars for evangelical purposes. The latter got as far as Armenia on the western fringe of Asia, when rumours of wars caused them to turn tail and make for home. The Polos continued.

They reached Khubilai's court at Peking after a journey of three and a half years. When Marco had learned the language and the

Marco Polo. Seventeenth century presentation.

Marco Polo Bridge, some ten miles from Peking. Described by Polo as 'A handsome bridge of stone. Its length is three hundred paces, and its width eight paces, so that ten men can without inconvenience ride abreast. It has twenty four arches, supported by twenty five piers erected in the water of serpentine stone, and built with great skill. On each side and from one extremity to the other, there is a handsome parapet formed of marble slabs and pillars arranged in a masterly style . . . all the spaces between one pillar and another, throughout all the length of the bridge, are filled with slabs of marble curiously sculptured . . . surmounted with lions.'

The bridge was built in the twelfth century; it has 140 balustrades each topped with a carved stone lion and its young. Till recently no one has been able to say for sure how many lions there are—numberless restless cubs peep out momentarily from their mothers' manes and then disappear. The Chinese recently held a census and established a leonine population of 485 on the bridge. The bridge still serves heavy traffic.

customs of the Mongols, the Khan employed him on official business, sending him on missions to the south. The Polos lived seventeen years in China, and became very rich. By then the Khan was ageing and the Venetians no doubt feared for their position under his successor. Khubilai at first refused their request to return home. It happened however at this time that the Mongol ruler of Persia, Arghun, had lost his favourite wife Bolgana; according to her dying wish he sent envoys to the court at Peking to secure another bride from the same Mongol tribe. As the overland routes were unsafe through continuing Mongol strife, Khubilai prepared a fleet of junks and a seventeen-year-old princess, to send back to the west. The Polos, because of their seafaring experience, were allowed to travel back with the princess and her suite. The voyage took nearly two years. Six hundred men of the expedition were lost, but the Princess and the indefatigable Polos survived. When they arrived in Persia they found that the Khan Arghun had died, and had been succeeded by his son, who inherited the princess. News came through at that time of the death of the Great Khan Kubilai, at the ripe age of eighty.

The Polos continued their journey to Venice (1295). The Venetians were then fighting it out with their rivals the Genoese, and Marco was called upon to equip a galley against them, on which he sailed as commander. He was defeated and carried off as a prisoner to Genoa, where he remained about three years. He dictated his story to a fellow prisoner who wrote it down in bad French. Several versions in translation have survived, but not the original. This work brought to Europe a knowledge of Asia and in particular of China, a knowledge which was already available to the Islamic world; in Europe it was widely dismissed as fantasy. Accused on his death bed, it is said, of having grossly exaggerated, Marco Polo replied that he had not told half of what he had seen.

Two hundred years later, a Genoese sea captain, Columbus, inspired by Polo's book, sailed west in the expectation of finding the Indies and China. He discovered America.

The tenacity of Christian travellers was equalled by that of Muslims, one at least of whom left a long record of his travels. Ibn Battuta left his home town Tangier in 1325, travelled through central Asia to India where he entered the service of the Sultan of Delhi. Then he joined an embassy from the Sultan bearing gifts for the emperor of China. He embarked with the envoys on one of a fleet of Chinese junks returning home after a trading mission, and was among the few survivors of the storm that wrecked the fleet. He travelled extensively in China, and returned home after an absence of twenty-four years, having settled down and as a good Muslim started families in several parts of the world.

Nor was the traffic all one way. There is the record of Rabban Sauma, born near Peking, who was a Nestorian Christian. He left China in 1275 with a colleague to make a pilgrimage to Jerusalem. He arrived in the Mongol kingdom of Persia, where the Khan received him warmly. The Khan, inspired by motives similar to those of the Christian monarchs, sent Rabban Sauma on a further mission to Europe to propose an alliance between the Crusaders and the Mongols, against his enemy the Muslim rivals of Egypt. The Khan Arghun, in Mongol anticipation of victory, promised the King of France Jerusalem if he would participate. Rabban Sauma was received by the Pope and by the King of France; he also saw Edward I of England in Gascony; but the Mongol-Christian alliance did not mature.

The Mongol empire also facilitated Arab trade along the caravan route from Baghdad to Peking, and by ship from the Persian Gulf to south China ports. The traffic from east to west contributed significantly to the dispersal of Chinese technical achievements (especially printing and gunpowder) throughout the rest of the world during the thirteenth and fourteenth centuries.

Lions and cubs on Marco Polo Bridge.

143

Porcelain of Yuan period.
The kilns of north China declined
during the Yuan period, but those of
the south developed. Yuan blue and
white porcelain ware was almost
exclusively for export and a few
specimens only are to be found in
China. This example of blue and
white, in underglaze red with floral
decoration, was recently unearthed
in Hopei province.

11. Yuan
1271–1368

Mongol rule in China lasted about a century; the epoch of imperial unity which was restored endured until the twentieth century. But despite the military supremacy of the Mongols and the range of the Mongol empire, final victory lay not with the riders of the steppe but with the peasants of the sown lands.

The Mongols, with little urban culture and no bureaucratic experience of agrarian society, were obliged in China to set up an administration based not on their own kin but on foreigners. While prepared to accept Chinese in the lower ranks of the administration, they suspected their victims too much to place political power in their hands. The task of tax organisation and collection they entrusted in the main to Muslim financiers and merchants of central Asian origin, from the conquered trading centres of Bukhara and Samarkand. Other conquered barbarians of a superior cultural level were also used: Uighurs, Khitans and Tibetans. Non-Chinese like Marco Polo could secure positions of authority and trust from which the celestials were excluded. For example, the minister of Genghis Khan, Yehlu, who advised the Great Khan against the mass extermination of the Chinese in favour of their exploitation, was a Khitan, a descendant of the royal house.

The clash between the nomad culture of the steppe and the intensive agriculture of the Chinese plains did not at first restrict the advance of the economy of the Middle Kingdom. As the records of the travellers from the west testify, the flourishing trade of the Sung period survived under the Yuan and in some respects expanded.

Wheels motivated by manpower, by animal or water power, facilitated the work of irrigation and drainage in agriculture. Cotton, which had been grown since Sung times, began to be worked into a high quality textile, especially in the lower reaches of the Yangtze and Huai rivers, where a woman, Huang Tao Po, became famous for introducing methods of cotton spinning and weaving.

Other crafts besides textiles, ceramics for example, were maintained at a high level. It was the custom of the Mongols in China, as throughout their empire, to seize craftsmen from the defeated regions and bring them to the capital cities to work for the conquerors in government establishments and workshops. Here they laboured like slaves; but their products were of a high quality and much in demand by the Mongol nobles as well as by foreign merchants. Hangchow, the old capital of the southern Sung, and Peking the new capital of the Mongols, became known for their wealth and their products, from one end of Asia to the other. 'In all occupations which men practice,'

said Friar Carpini, 'there are no better craftsmen in the whole world. Their country is exceeding rich, in corn, wine, gold, silk and other commodities.'

Khubilai Khan (1271–1294), fifth Great Khan and founder of the Yuan dynasty was a notable builder despite his nomad background, and Peking, the capital of the Mongol empire, became no less brilliant than earlier Chinese capitals. Palaces and pleasure gardens, pavilions and lakes, adorned the city. Like his grandfather Genghis, Khubilai Khan tolerated all religions, a policy dictated more from prudence than humanity. Marco Polo quoted the emperor as saying:

There are four prophets who are worshipped and to whom all the world does reverence. The Christians say that their god was Jesus Christ, the Saracens Muhammed, the Jews Moses and the idolaters Sakyamuni Burkhan (Buddha), who was the first to be represented as God in the form of an idol. And I do honour and reverence all four, so that I may be sure of doing it to him who is greatest in heaven and truest; and to him do I pray for aid.

This earthy devotee, according to Polo, would readily have become Christian had the followers of Christ been able to demonstrate powers superior to those of the pagans, or if they had at least been able to deprive the pagan votaries of their demonstrable prowess.

Khubilai Khan had a range of cultural interests. After founding an observatory, the instruments and records of which have been partly preserved, he introduced a new calendar into China, for a year of 365·2 days, remarkable for its accuracy. Geography as well as astronomy flourished. The Khan sent expeditions to discover the source of the Yellow River. The Grand Canal, linking the Yangtze rice and silk regions with the capital, was improved. Under Genghis Khan, the Mongols, who till that time had no single form of written language, had adopted from their western neighbours the Uighur alphabet. Khubilai Khan wanted to create an alphabet that would enable all the subjects of his multilingual empire to communicate, an alphabet that could be applied to all languages. He appointed as his minister the great Tibetan scholar Phagspa Lama, and Phagspa received the Khan's instruction to create an alphabet capable of this task. The incredible Phagspa, Grand Lama of Sakya, ruler of Tibet under Khubilai, in a few years worked out an alphabetic table of a thousand letters. The syllabic writing he created was based on the Tibetan alphabet. It consisted of forty-one basic symbols with another fifty used for transliterating Sanscrit and Tibetan. These symbols could be combined into some 1,200 syllables. The writing, known as square writing, could render faithfully the phonetics of many languages. In 1269 Khubilai decreed that the square writing become the official written language of his empire; it was used for imperial decrees, tallies, paper money, etc., until the latter part of the fourteenth century, when the Yuan dynasty was overthrown. Some books too were printed in the square alphabet.

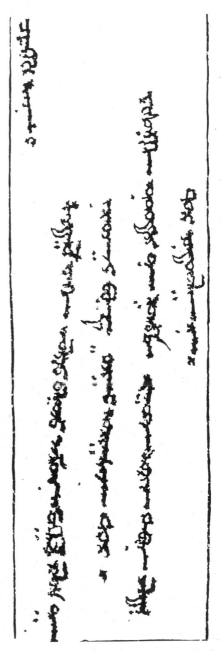

Inscription in square writing, the universal script devised by Khubilai's minister Phagspa.

Stone tablet erected by Genghis Khan in honour of his archer Yesunke, who hit his target at a distance of 703·5 metres.

The Yuan period saw the flowering of two literary forms which had taken root during the Sung period, the novel and the drama. It is thought that the lack of opportunity for Chinese scholars to advance far in official service resulted in the redirection of their talents to a field where there was a demand for literary skill, though not in the old classical form. One of the greatest Chinese dramatists, Kuan Han Ching, wrote comedies and tragedies during this period; many were based on social themes, such as the clash between human emotion and social bonds of filial piety, and the struggle of individuals against social injustice. A number of his dramas, like *Snow in Midsummer*, deal with the struggle of women against traditional oppression.

One of the most popular novels dating from the Yuan period was *Water Margins* translated also as *All Men Are Brothers*. This novel, based on tales popular in the preceding two centuries, describes the Robin Hood type of adventures of 108 braves, daring outlaws, who defeat officials and succour the oppressed.

The decline of the Yuan dynasty in China coincided with the decline of the Mongol continental empire, which began in the time of Khubilai, fifth and last of the Great Khans. When Khubilai turned from cavalry to naval expeditions, he met disaster. A great fleet sent against Japan was totally destroyed by storms and Japanese resistance.

The unity and discipline of the royal house of Genghis weakened. The authority of Khubilai as Great Khan was challenged from the outset by his brother, who set himself up in opposition and gained the support of the Khanate of the Golden Horde. The rift with this Mongol kingdom spreading across the Russian steppes, was aggravated by the Horde's conversion to the faith of Islam at the end of the thirteenth century, with the result that they joined their Muslim brothers of Egypt in attacking their kin the Mongol rulers of Persia.

Throughout his reign, moreover, Khubilai was at war with the Mongol prince of the fourth khanate in central Asia. Khubilai was in fact the last nominal sovereign of the Mongol empire. The Muslim khans refused to recognise his successor, who was Buddhist. Within the Mongol homeland too the power of the Great Khan had diminished. The removal of the court from Karakorum to Peking had contributed to this. Many Mongol hordes outside China became impatient with control from Peking, where, in the eyes of the steppe nomad, the settled life was effete, alien and degrading.

In China itself the oppressive rule of the conqueror was felt to be intolerable even in the days of the relatively enlightened Khubilai Khan. The administration of the foreign officials, especially the central Asian Muslims, who with their keen business sense frequently added usury to their official activities, was especially detested. Marco Polo observed this:

You must understand that all the Cathayans hated the government of the great Khan, because he set over them Tartar rulers mostly Saracen, and they could not endure it, since it made them feel they were no more than slaves. Moreover the Great Khan had no legal title to rule the province of Cathay, having acquired it by force. So putting no trust in the people, he committed the government of the country to Tartars, Saracens and Christians who were attached to his household and personally loyal to him and not natives of Cathay.

Ahmed, Khubilai's finance minister, provoked such hatred that he was assassinated in the Palace itself, an event recorded by Polo, who also noted that since the Mongol occupation the citizens of Hangchow had been obliged to post on the doorway of every house a list of the inhabitants, as a security measure.

In the towns, a curfew had been introduced. Other restrictions included the prohibition of all meetings between Chinese, of fairs, and of night travel. Celestials were not allowed to keep or manufacture weapons; this included even vegetable knives and meat choppers, of which only one was permitted between ten families. They were also prohibited from participation in any sport which might contribute to fighting skill. In the towns a spy or agent was allocated to every ten households, to report any hint of rebellious activity.

The repressive measures were particularly severe for the Chinese of the south. The Mongols divided the people of the Celestial empire into four categories: first, the Mongols themselves, fully privileged; second, their central Asian auxiliaries, including some of the Tartars from the border regions, who were used in positions of responsibility; third, the north Chinese; and fourth, the southern Chinese, the Han, bearing the full weight of political and economic oppression. If a Mongol beat a Han, the latter was not allowed to retaliate, and had no redress whatever.

The extension of canals and the building of fleets to carry supplies from the centre and south of China to support the swollen population of Peking, meant the raising of corvée labour. Breaches in the dykes of the Yellow River caused distress and famine in the north-east regions, and resulted in serious price rises. Religious toleration had encouraged the growth of religious establishments of great wealth, which exploited peasant labour but escaped taxation. Above all, the Mongol nobles had seized arable land from the peasantry, converting it to pasturage or leaving it waste. This reversion from arable in the north-west contributed to the formation of dust-bowl and desert areas. Despite the great displays of wealth amongst the privileged in the cities, in the fourteenth century, it seems that one sixth of the population of China was starving.

Red Turban rising

Khubilai Khan was the last of the strong Mongol rulers; he was succeeded by khans not only less competent but also debauched, especially Toghon Temur, the last of the line, who appears to have been depraved in the extreme, even allowing for the tendency of the

Yuan dynasty coin cast in 1279 and inscribed in four languages: Mongolian, Arabic, Tibetan, and Tangut.

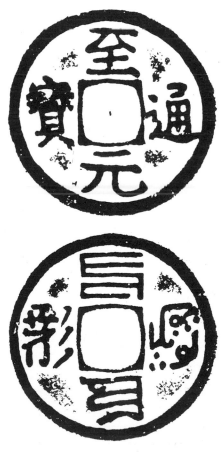

Bronze cannon of AD 1332 – the oldest known in the world.

Chinese annalists to ascribe the downfall of each dynasty to the depravity of its later members.

The Mongol hordes in China had lost their fighting interests and skills by the middle of the fourteenth century. Many had been born south of the Wall, far from the steppelands, and lacked the childhood training in mounted archery which distinguished their forebears.

Secret societies became more and more active in the Middle Kingdom. The Chinese annals say: 'In the east was attack, in the west oppression, in the south reprisals, and in the north war. On all sides people were joining forces secretly, for everyone hoped that a liberator would appear.'

In the 1350s a movement known as the Red Turbans spread throughout the north. The leaders were peasants, craftsmen and in some cases small merchants.

In 1356 Nanking, near Hangchow, fell to these rebels, who were led by Chu Yuan Chang, a poor peasant. This man in his destitute youth had become a Buddhist monk and had survived by begging. After joining the rebels, he rose quickly to power. In ten years he had won control over the important economic regions of the middle and lower reaches of the Yangtze, driving the Mongols north before him.

In 1368 he declared himself emperor as Hung Wu, first of the Ming dynasty, with his capital on the lower Yangtze at Nanking. In the same year the Yuan were driven from Peking. The Mongol emperor fled to his summer residence in Shangtu, but this too fell. The emperor had just time to escape with his empress and concubines, under cover of darkness. He took refuge in Karakorum, the original Mongol capital, which had since fallen into decay.

12. Ming

1368–1644

Hung Wu, First Ming Emperor (1368–99).
Known as the Beggar King, because of his humble origins; he had been a peasant who became a Buddhist priest and begged for his living.

In two main senses, the Ming centuries were a typical dynastic period. In the first place, this period shows most of the features associated with the dynastic cycle: the initial rehabilitation of agriculture and reduction of taxation pressure on the peasantry; the establishment of unified and effective administration by the bureaucracy and the restoration of imperial revenues; the effort to contain the attacks of nomads from the northern steppes; then the growing concentration of land and resources into the hands of landlord/officials, at the expense of the peasantry; the vain efforts of later governments, grown corrupt and effete, to control mounting peasant discontent; finally the destruction of the dynasty in nationwide peasant revolts accompanied by barbarian invasion.

In a completely different sense the Ming period was traditional, by virtue of the striving to reestablish customary modes and standards in the political and social life of the Middle Kingdom. The Ming was the one period, after the Tang, when imperial China was united under native rule.

When Chu Yuan Chang seized power and became the first Ming emperor, known as Hung Wu (1368–98), restoration of agriculture was a more than urgent issue. North China in particular had been laid waste by the Mongols, and for several decades had suffered from recurring famine, followed by floods when the Yellow River burst its banks. To encourage the reclamation of land, peasants were granted as their own property the land they restored to production; they were moreover granted tax exemption on such land for the first three years. New land registers were compiled and the tax levies were somewhat reduced. The Ming collected taxes twice annually, in silver as well as in kind (grain and silk). One decree insisted that a certain proportion of all plots of land was to be planted with cash crops, such as mulberry trees for silk, cotton and hemp. This provided raw materials for the textile crafts as well as an income for the peasants. Corvée labour was adjusted to the number of adult males in the household.

Agricultural production responded to these measures, which were coupled with the overhauling of neglected water conservancy works. Handicrafts and trades were similarly stimulated. Artisans could be conscripted for government work, but when not working for the government these craftsmen were permitted to work for themselves and to sell their products in the market. The quality as well as the quantity of the products was raised by this relaxation. The craftsmen of the Ming period produced excellent textiles and are renowned for

their porcelain; mills with many looms and large-scale kilns arose.

Hung Wu modelled his government on the Tang system, restoring the doctrine and practices of Confucianism. More power, however, was concentrated in the imperial government, and especially in the hands of the emperor himself. The powers of provincial governors were curtailed. They were limited to civil and financial matters. Other officials dealt with judicial and military questions. Control of military affairs was put in the hands of five officers of equal rank, who dealt with recruitment and administration, but who were not in command of the troops. When war broke out the Emperor appointed a commander-in-chief for the duration only.

Hung Wu abolished the post of prime minister, and himself controlled the six traditional ministries (civil offices, rites, revenue, war, punishments and works) with the aid of Grand Secretaries, who formed an executive somewhat similar to a Cabinet. The power of the bureaucracy was restored, and the examination system revived. It became highly institutionalised. Matteo Ricci, Jesuit missionary, described the procedures in detail:

There is an immense palace built especially for this examination in every metropolitan city, closed in by a great wall. In it there are a number of suites, secluded from all distraction, which are assigned to the examiners just mentioned, while they are discussing the submitted manuscripts. In the centre of this palace there are more than four thousand small cells, just large enough to contain a small table and a seat for one person. The cells are so constructed that the occupant cannot converse with the one in the next compartment, or even see him.

During the time the manuscripts are being examined both day and night, a guard of magistrates and of military sentinels is in continual circulation to prevent all contact by word or by writing between those who are engaged in the palace and those outside. The same three days are set aside for this examination throughout the kingdom. Those taking part in the examinations are permitted to write from dawn to sunset, behind locked doors, and they are served with light meals, prepared the day before at public expense. When the candidate bachelors are admitted to the palace, they are carefully searched to see that they have no book or written matter in their possession. Entering the examination, they are allowed to have several brushes for writing, the writers' palette, and also ink and paper. Their clothes and even brushes and palette are carefully examined lest they should contain anything deceitful, and if fraud of any kind is discovered, they are not only excluded from the examination but are severely punished as well.

When the bachelor candidates are admitted to the palace and the doors closed and sealed on the outside with a public seal, each of the two presiding officers appointed by the king, explains in public three passages. . . . He then presents these passages as the general subject matter, and a separate paper must be written on the selection made by each examiner. Then four passages are selected from any one of the Five Books of Doctrines and assigned for additional matter for examination . . . these seven written papers must show evidence not only of proper use of words but also of a proper appreciation of the ideas contained in the doctrines and a strict observance of the rules of Chinese rhetoric. No dissertation should exceed five hundred characters.

On the second day of examination, after two days of rest, and behind closed doors as formerly, topics are offered for examination relative to things that have happened in the past, to the annals of the ancients, and to events which may be expected to happen in the near future. These papers are written in triplex, in the form of an advisory document addressed to the king, as to what would be the best course to follow for the good of the empire in such eventualities.

On the third day three difficulties or arguments are offered for examination . . . . Each one must also recopy his manuscript into a copy book prepared for that purpose. At the end in addition to his own name he signs the names of his parents, grandparents and his great grandparents.

Then the book is so sealed that it can be opened only by the deputies.

Each one does this with as many copy books as he may have used, and he presents them personally to the deputy. These books are again recopied by the librarians appointed for that purpose. To prevent any partiality, the books are marked with a particular character in red, before they are presented to the examiners, and the autographs are omitted. These are the ones that are presented to the examiners for rating. The autographed copies are numbered to correspond with the markings on the manuscript presented. This method is followed to prevent recognition of manuscript and to conceal the author's identity and his handwriting.

The first set of examiners is chosen from the local magistrates who go through the papers and reject the poorer ones . . . the number of papers coming up to the regal examiners will not be more than double the number of candidates for the degree. If 150 degrees are to be granted, three hundred manuscripts are chosen

When the examinations are over and the ceremonies at an end, the royal examiners publish a book distributed throughout the whole empire, containing the results, the names of the new licentiates, the outstanding manuscripts on the various subjects. The book is published as a de luxe edition.

The examination system was administered by the Board of Rites. Quotas for successful candidates were established for each region. Examiners were sent out from the capital to supervise the provincial examinations. The process was further ritualised by the introduction

Examination cells for candidates in the imperial examinations. Late nineteenth-century photograph.

of a formula to be observed in the writing of answers; the essays were to be produced under eight main headings, using no more than seven hundred characters in all, a style which became known as the 'eight-legged essay'. The subject matter was confined to the Five Classics and the Four Books, in which during the Sung period, the orthodox interpretation of Confucianism had been established.

Insistence on orthodoxy was not restricted to the mandarins. For the benefit of people at large, Confucian doctrine was regularly recited in local temples, and the imperial injunctions of Hung Wu for correct living were posted in all villages. These enjoined the population to observe the Confucian proprieties, to be filial and have respect for elders and ancestors, to instruct the children, and to go peacefully about their livelihood.

Hung Wu did not himself observe one of the fundamental Confucian precepts that the ruler should set an example to his people, that he should control through the exercise of virtue. True to his earlier monkish vocation he was abstemious in the extreme and avoided extravagance; however he seems to have been of an anxious disposition, suspicious to excess; he constantly feared that he was the butt of veiled insults on the part of his ministers, and he punished them in arbitrary and brutal ways.

The Son of Heaven was deeply aware of the danger of eunuch power and eunuch factions at court; in fact a tablet was erected in the palace ordering that eunuchs should be kept out of the administration. Hung Wu himself set limits on their powers and their ranks, and decreed that they should remain illiterate. He did not abolish the institution, however, and the dynasty later suffered from rivalries between eunuch factions and officials in the same way as earlier dynasties had suffered. The problem was exacerbated by the accession subsequently of a series of minor Sons of Heaven.

Hung Wu established his capital at Nanking, near the economic heart of the Kingdom; in addition to the palaces built for the new capital, massive walls sixty feet high were constructed to defend the town. His successor, Yung Lo (1403–24) transferred the capital back to Peking in 1421, a change designed to strengthen control of the northern frontier. Peking continued to be the capital until the end of the imperial era. Under Mongol rule, defences against incursions from the barbarian north had been unnecessary. The Wall had fallen into disrepair. One of the early concerns of the Ming emperors was the restoration of this and other defences. The Great Wall was repaired, and in some places reconstructed. City walls and defence posts were among the many major construction works undertaken when the capital moved from Nanking to Peking. Armies of peasants were mobilised for this labour; the palaces and temples they built for the emperors may be seen in Peking to this day, but now as public parks and museums.

Guests arriving at the Palace. Traditional picture by Feng Chu, Ming period. View of Imperial Palace, Peking.

Temple of Heaven, Peking. One of the most beautiful of Ming architectural achievements; its threefold roof, covered with blue glaze tiles, represents, and reflects, the sky. Now part of a public park.

153

The Ming reconstructed the walls of several hundred other towns. Their military activities were not, however, wholly defensive. After the fall of the Yuan most of the Mongols withdrew to their native steppes and became absorbed in their own tribal wars. They were still active enough to mount expeditions against the Ming, and too near for the peace of mind of the Ming emperors, who themselves organised several expeditions against the Mongols. On one of these occasions the Ming armies reached Karakorum, the Mongol capital, and burnt it to the ground. These conflicts did not last long, and peaceful relations were established, troubled only by border skirmishing from time to time. Those Mongols who remained in China became integrated with the Middle Kingdom; indeed some Mongol nobles even retained their domains south of the Wall and paid allegiance to the Ming Son of Heaven.

Tribute system and maritime expeditions

The traditional empire of the Middle Kingdom was consolidated under the Ming and in some regions extended. Yunnan and the southwest were incorporated and settled; Manchuria was annexed and colonised with settlers. In the north-west the Ming were satisfied to establish their hold on Hami, the first station on the Old Silk Road, but they pushed no further into central Asia. Hung Wu at least was more concerned to secure the recognition of his dynasty by foreign powers than with conquest. Soon after his accession he sent a series of envoys with a conciliatory manifesto to the rulers of all accessible foreign states, with offers of friendship and trade and an invitation to seal the arrangement by the despatch of 'tribute' to the Ming court. The manifesto said:

Since the Sung dynasty lost the throne and Heaven cut off their sacrifice, the Yuan dynasty arose from the desert to enter and rule over China for more than a hundred years, when Heaven, wearied of their misgovernment and debauchery, thought fit to turn their fate also to ruin, and the affairs of China were in a state of disorder for eighteen years. But when the nation began to arouse itself, We a simple peasant of Huai-yu, conceived the patriotic idea to save the people, and it pleased the creator to grant that Our civil and military officers effected their passage eastward to the left side of the River. . . . We have established peace in the empire and restored the old boundaries of our Middle Land. We were also selected by Our people to occupy the imperial throne of China. . . . We have sent officers to all foreign kingdoms with the manifesto. Although We are not equal in Our wisdom to our ancient rulers whose virtue was recognised all over the universe, We cannot but let the world know Our intention to maintain peace within the four seas. It is on this ground alone that We have issued this manifesto.

The annals of the Ming dynasty, where the manifesto is recorded, add that the ambassadors were provided with presents of silk for transmission to the countries concerned, which thereafter sent embassies with tribute:

The Ming tribute system was no more than the traditional expression in ritual form of the Middle Kingdom's assumption of superiority over all other states. At most it involved the exchange of missions, good trade relations, and the transmission of gifts which could be formally accepted as tribute, accompanied by the kowtowing of envoys.

Many countries responded to the overture and sent tribute, among them, according to the Ming annals, Korea, Annam (Vietnam), Siam, Cambodia, Borneo, Java, Sumatra and subsequently Syria on the Mediterranean. The annals also record envoys from Holland and Italy.

A special problem was created by Japan, whence pirates were constantly raiding the Chinese coast. A number of missions were sent to the Japanese ruler, but with no result; the piracy continued. Hung Wu's irritation overflowed:

'You stupid eastern barbarians!' he wrote to the Japanese ruler, 'living so far across the sea . . . you are haughty and disloyal; you permit your subjects to do evil. . . .' The reply came back from far across the sea: 'Heaven and earth are vast; they are not monopolised by one ruler . . . the world is the world's world; it does not belong to a single person.'

By 1401, honourable civilities had been restored, and a Japanese mission brought impressive tribute of horses, fans, screens, armour, swords, and a thousand ounces of gold, submitted with a polite memorial from the Japanese ruler expressing 'real fear and dread and kneeling again and again'. The Son of Heaven was magnanimous:

'Japan has always been called a country of poems and books, and it has always been in Our Heart. . . . Keep your mind on obedience and loyalty and thereby adhere to the basic rules.'

The Japanese were provided with facilities for trade in Chinese ports. In the 1590s however the Japanese made attacks on China by way of Korea, which was twice invaded. The Japanese eventually withdrew, but the Ming was much weakened by the struggle against them.

In the time of the Han and Tang, the easiest trading route with the western world had been the overland desert trail through central Asia. In the Ming period the Mongols still harassed this area; indeed another nomad conqueror, Tamburlaine, claiming descent from Genghis Khan, had arisen in central Asia. The hordes of Tamburlaine camped astride the Old Silk route, threatening to engulf all the kingdoms that had composed the Mongol empire at its height. Tamburlaine's long-prepared campaign against China began at the turn of the fifteenth century, but was abandoned shortly after, when he died not many days distant from his capital Samarkand in central Asia.

The bulk of trading during the Ming, as during the Sung, was carried by sea. Shipbuilding had made great advances in China by the end of the Sung:

Cheng Ho on board ship. Woodcut of Ming period.

Reconstruction of sea-going junk of early Ming period.

The ships which sail the southern sea and south of it are like houses [wrote Chou Ku Fei]. When their sails are spread they are like great clouds in the sky. Their rudders are several tens of feet long. A single ship carries several hundred men. It has stored on board a year's supply of grain. They feed pigs and ferment liquor. They take no account of dead or living, there is no going back to the mainland when once they have entered the dark blue sea. When on board the gong sounds the day, the animals drink gluttonly, guests and hosts by turn forgetting their perils. To the people on board all is hidden, mountains, landmarks, the countries of the foreigners, all are lost in space . . . the big ship with its heavy cargo has naught to fear of the great waves, but in shallow water it comes to grief.

It was in such ships that the mariners of the Ming sailed the western oceans, in an outburst of maritime activity in the early years of the fifteenth century. According to the Ming annals, in 1405 the emperor ordered Cheng Ho to set out on an expedition to the west at the head of 28,000 men. He was given large quantities of gold and silk and built a great fleet. Cheng Ho was a court eunuch, and proved himself an able commander. He led seven major expeditions, some of them consisting of fleets of over sixty treasure-laden ships. They sailed west to Indonesia, Malaya, India, and as far as Africa and the Persian Gulf.

The main motive for the expeditions is not known. The annals say they went in search of the emperor's young nephew, Hung Wu's heir-elect, who had taken flight after losing the dragon throne to his uncle, but it is hardly likely that the search would have drawn the ships to Africa. In any case Cheng Ho appears to have been equipped with manifestos to the rulers of the western kingdoms proposing in the usual style trade and tributary relations. It is likely that Yung Lo, the uncle who had usurped the throne, felt the need for confirmation that he had received the Mandate of Heaven in the form of tributary recognition by the barbarians. The inscription on a stele erected by Cheng Ho in a temple near Shanghai says:

The countries beyond the horizon and at the ends of the earth have all become subjects, and to the most western of the most western or the most northern of the most northern countries however far they may be, the distances and routes may be calculated. Thus the barbarians from beyond the seas though their countries are truly distant . . . have come to audience bearing precious objects and presents.

No doubt the tribute itself was not unwelcome, consisting of luxury goods as well as rare and marvellous creatures from the lands of the barbarian west. One ambassador, from Egypt, brought lions, tigers, oryxes, zebras and ostriches for the Celestial zoo. The new ruler of Bengal passed on the present of a giraffe which he presumably had received from Africa.

Trade and tributary relations were established with over thirty countries, and do not seem to have been impaired by the energy with which Cheng Ho carried out his diplomatic mission, bringing back, in the case of Ceylon and Palembang at least, the local kings under duress to do homage in person before the Dragon throne.

The tribute system helped to reinforce the illusion that the ruler of the Middle Kingdom had dominion over 'all under heaven'. Except in the case of immediate neighbours, the relationship was no more than a ritual bond, with no basis in real suzerainty or subordination. Tributary status was the only relationship known to, or understood by, the Chinese state. The question of mutual ties on a basis of equality with foreign countries, did not arise for the Middle Kingdom.

Ming dish painted in blue and maroon underglaze: dragon playing with pearl among clouds. Writhing dragons were a favourite theme with Ming potters.

These expeditions, on the eve of the great western voyages of discovery and maritime commercial ventures, stopped in the 1430s for reasons which are not clear. The initiative in the southern oceans was left to the Arabs, the Portuguese, the Dutch and, later, the British. It may be that the maritime activity was dropped because of the rivalry which began to dominate the Ming court, between the factions of officials and of eunuchs. Cheng Ho's own narrative of his voyages was destroyed by jealous officials; the accounts that survive are those left by his staff. The voyages gave impetus, however, to Chinese emmigration to neighbouring lands and to islands in the Southern Seas; thus a sea-faring branch of the people was maintained.

Although Chinese maritime efforts had waned by the sixteenth century, western missionary and mercantile interest in China had grown intense. In 1582 a Jesuit mission led by Matteo Ricci reached the offshore island of Macao and after about twenty years succeeded in reaching Peking. The missionaries were well received at court, despite the initial opposition of the mandarins who were no doubt influenced by the fact that the westerners were first introduced to the emperor by a eunuch. They poured scorn on the Christian pictures and sacred relics brought by the mission. The annals tell that the Ministers of the Board of Rites made a long report to the Emperor pointing out that the foreigner seemed to be a liar. Ricci had stated that he was a man from the Great Western Ocean, but they knew of no ocean of that name.

Moreover this man has appeared at court twenty years after his arrival in China. And what did he offer to the Emperor as tribute? Nothing but strange things which have no resemblance to those rare and precious presents usually offered by the envoys from distant countries. He has brought for instance portraits of the Lord of Heaven and of his mother, and also some bones of immortals (saints). As if an immortal who soars up to heaven should be provided with bones! Hanyu (a Tang scholar) has said that such unclean things can only bring mischief, and therefore ought not to enter into the Palace.

After this the report blamed Ma Tang the eunuch, who should have applied to the Board of Rites before introducing Ricci into the palace, for the Board usually examined the gifts presented as tribute.

This man Ricci is staying privately in a Buddhist temple of Peking, and we know nothing about him and his intentions. It is a rule that in the case of foreign countries sending tribute to the court, the envoys are rewarded and entertained as guests. Now we propose to bestow upon Ricci a cap and girdle, and to send him back. He ought not to be allowed to live secretly in either of the two capitals, nor to enter into intimacy with our people.

However, the Son of Heaven could not make up his mind to send the foreigner away, and the Board of Rites again laid a report complaining that they had been waiting vainly five months for His Majesty's decision in the matter of Ricci. They now tried to prove that their only concern was the wellbeing of the barbarian, fearing the effect of prolonged stay on Ricci's health: 'Just as a bird or a deer when put into a cage is mourning for its forests and luxuriant grass, likewise men also do not feel easy in a city.' The Board of Rites suggested he be dismissed to the mountains and deep valleys of the province of Kiangsi, where people were said to attain to a very great age. The emperor paid no attention to these manoeuvres; he was pleased with the man who had come from so far, and he ordered that he remain in the capital, giving him a house, paying his maintenance, and bestowing other gifts on him. Ricci in fact stayed in Peking until his death in 1610, and came to be held in high esteem by many people, including officials. The Jesuits cooperated in the reform of the Chinese calendar, and introduced western science and technology to China, though they were restrained by the Vatican from teaching the Copernican system of astronomy. Ricci, a mathematician and astronomer of distinction, translated into Chinese many specialised works which aroused considerable interest. On the other hand he and his colleagues developed a sympathy with the Chinese outlook even in matters religious, a sympathy not cultivated by later missions which accompanied the trading magnates. 'Of all the pagan sects known to Europe,' avowed Ricci, 'I know of no people who fell into fewer errors in the early stages of their antiquity, than did the Chinese.'

Cultural developments

During these centuries Europe was enjoying one of the most dynamic periods of its history: it was the time of the Renaissance, of exploration and discovery in many fields, of the growth of nation states, a period which was the precursor of great political and industrial revolutions.

China on the other hand, as a reaction to Mongol rule, was looking back over her shoulder to her own past, and concentrating on the restoration of established Chinese modes and traditions. There was a deliberate attempt to oust the alien and to restore the native. This was evident in the revival of Tang and Sung methods of government, and in the wider field of culture. The first Ming emperor, Hung Wu, tried to ban foreign styles of clothing in favour of Tang styles. He was a great traditionalist. One of his early acts was to ensure even that the history of the previous Mongol dynasty should be preserved, according to custom. He said, 'Recently on the fall of the Yuan capital [Peking] we obtained the Veritable Records of these thirteen rulers. Although their state has been destroyed, its events should be recorded. History marks success and failure and offers lessons of encouragement and warning, so it should not be abandoned.'

The Ming restored the study of the classics. There was much compilation but little innovation. One of the most remarkable achievements was the production, under the third emperor Yung Lo, of an immense encyclopaedia. Two thousand scholars and more were

Chen Hung Shou, painter of Ming period.

Shih Chin, one of the heroes of the popular novel *Water Margins*.
Illustration by Chen Hung Shou, Ming period painter.

employed for four years on this work. Rare books were collected from every corner of the Celestial Empire and copied before being returned. All the principal writings inherited from the past were included in the 11,095 volumes, many of them unique works. Unfortunately it was too long to print, but two copies were made by hand. The greater part of the collection was destroyed at the end of the last century during the western attack on the imperial Summer Palace. Fewer than 400 volumes have survived.

Li Shih Chen was a medical scientist of distinction as well as a compiler of the Ming period. He produced an encyclopaedia of pharmacology, giving over 8,000 prescriptions based on animal, vegetable and mineral drugs. He described amongst many important medical advances the method of inoculation against smallpox, used in China, according to tradition, since the eleventh century.

In literature, the most important works were novels, a literary form which had developed during the Sung. Some of the greatest Chinese novels date from these days. The *Romance of the Three Kingdoms* was a glamorised account of the struggles in third century China, and *Water Margins* of twelfth century China. *Monkey*, a satire on popular fables about the spirit world, was based on the journey of Hsuang Tsang to the west to secure the Buddhist texts. The main character, who makes the fabulous journey, is Monkey, a rebel against authority, a cheeky creature with supernatural powers who creates havoc in heaven.

Drama continued to flourish in the Ming period. From those times has developed much of the drama and opera of today. In Chinese drama, parts are sung and a small orchestra including gongs is indispensable. For a long time, all parts were played by males, and even in this century some of the most outstanding actors made their reputation through their female roles. The stage is bare of curtains and sets; scenery is replaced by elaborate conventions; a flourish from the orchestra indicates a change of scene or a new act; city ramparts or a mountain can be indicated by a table or a chair. A horsewhip signifies that the actor is mounted; when he lifts a leg he dismounts. A stage fight is a skilled acrobatic performance. Sumptuous costumes, a development of Ming styles, indicate on the stage to this day the social position of the characters. Stage scholars carry fans; people dressed in black are accepted as invisible. Make-up is heavy and masklike, and is used to indicate personality traits. The villain can be identified by the large white patches on his face, symbolising craftiness. Green is another derogatory identification. Red represents loyalty, and black integrity of character. The face of a lovable type is suffused with pink.

Audiences three centuries ago, as today, identified themselves readily with the performance, and the skill of the actor and the sophistication of his technique was as keenly appreciated as the theme of the drama. The story is told that, in the seventeenth century, a play was

An avenue of stone beasts and generals guarding the highway to the Ming tombs, where thirteen Ming emperors are buried, in the hills to the north-west of Peking.

One of the guardians along the route to the Ming Tombs.

Ming tombs in a quiet valley near Peking. The site was chosen by Emperor Yung Lo, who moved the capital from Nanking to Peking. Wan Li, the thirteenth Ming emperor (1573–1620), began building his tomb as a young man of twenty two: when, six years later, it was finished, the chronicles say that he gave an entertainment there. The place is called Ting Ling, royal Tomb of Security.

The tomb of this emperor was excavated in 1956. It consists of a man-made hill planted with sombre pines, beneath which is the huge burial chamber. There was no trace of plundering. The chamber had been closed by a self-jamming device; when the stone doors were closed another slab fell automatically into a recess behind the door, preventing it from opening again. All the doorways were sealed in this fashion. The vault contained three precious thrones in white marble, and three lacquer coffins side by side on a stone couch. The colours were fresh, despite three hundred years in the tomb. Here the emperor and his two empresses were laid. All three skeletons wore gold and black gowns. The bones of Emperor Wan Li remained, with a few remnants of hair and beard. He wore a dragon robe with long wide sleeves, and a spare robe was buried with him. There were many rolls of silk in the tomb, with other precious articles. Two boxes contained a wooden imperial seal and wooden tablets. In a third were an iron helmet, decorated with gold and jewels, a coat of scale armour, a sword, a composite bow, and iron tipped arrows. From other rotted wooden boxes had rolled ornaments and wooden figurines, jewels, pendants, belts, clothes, shoes. One box contained about 200 miniature pewter vessels, and other sets of gold objects—two pairs of chopsticks, one pair each of spoons, ewers, washbasins. There were also models of sedan chairs, coaches, spears, bows and arrows, and other articles used in imperial processions.

There were gold crowns and many jade objects. Jade was supposed to have the power to protect the body from decay. Beside the thrones there were huge porcelain vats for burning oil, 'everlasting lamps', with some of the oil remaining in them.

Above: crown of the empress, decorated with kingfisher blue feathers, from the Ming Tombs.

performed showing the execution of the patriotic Sung general, Yo Fei, caused by the treachery of a rival. The latter part was played by an actor to such effect that one of the spectators, aroused beyond forbearance, leapt on to the stage and stabbed the actor to death.

The first century of Ming rule was one of stability, despite some dynastic upheaval. The heir elect of the founder emperor died before coming to the throne, which passed to his sixteen-year-old son. An imperial uncle (fourth son of Hung Wu), who commanded the northern frontier and resided at Peking, rose against the young heir, seized the capital Nanking, and mounted the Dragon throne. This was Yung Lo, who moved the capital to Peking. The dispossessed nephew escaped and spent the rest of his life as a mendicant, wandering throughout China. (According to the annals the search for this prince was the motive for the expeditions of Cheng Ho.) He eventually returned to Peking, during the reign of the great grandson of Yung Lo; he was recognised, but managed to live out his days peacefully if obscurely in the capital.

After the reigns of Hung Wu and Yung Lo there were a succession of infant or weak emperors under the influence of eunuchs. By the middle of the fifteenth century, the restrictions on eunuch power were relaxed; they had become literate and were granted state positions. Their numbers increased and so did the wealth and estates which they secured for themselves. Royal princes joined in the race with the greedy eunuchs for land, and built up huge domains.

By the seventeenth century, the position of the government had seriously deteriorated. The avarice and corruption of the eunuchs reached extremes: the treasure of one eunuch was found to include 3,000 gold rings and broaches, 4,000 jewelled belts, and immense hoards of gold and silver.

Peasant rising and Li Tse Cheng

The indulgence of the court went hand in hand with impoverishment of the peasantry. Peasants were driven from their farms to make way for the domains of the courtiers. Landlords throughout the Middle Kingdom had been increasing their estates and, by the middle of the Ming period, the bulk of the land was in the hands of the emperor and royal princes, government officials and big landlords. All this was exempt from taxation. Ricci, who found much to admire in the Middle Kingdom, wrote

Below: golden jug and jar, encrusted with jewels.

Those who are reputed to be of royal blood are supported at public expense. At present they are supposed to number somewhat over sixty thousand, and as they are continually increasing, one can readily imagine what a public burden they constitute. Removed as they are, from all public office and administration, they have developed into a leisure class given to loose living and to insolence.

The rural economy deteriorated. Ninety per cent of peasantry were landless. At the same time taxation increased. The military efforts of the Ming against the Japanese in Korea had been expensive. Over a third of the state revenues went for army supplies. The Middle Kingdom became the beat of a multitude of tax collectors. Their victims were to be found in the villages and in the towns. 'So great is the lust for domination on the part of the magistrates,' wrote Ricci, 'that scarcely anyone can be said to possess his belongings in security, and everyone lives in continual fear of being deprived of what he has, by a false accusation.' The Jesuit missionary also commented that children were sold into slavery

when the family becomes too numerous to be supported . . . for about the same price that one would pay for a pig or a cheap little donkey. . . . the result is that the whole country is virtually filled with slaves: not such as are captured in war or brought from abroad, but slaves born in the country and even in the same city or village in which they live. Many of them are also taken out of the country as slaves by the Portuguese and the Spaniards.

He also noted 'the far more serious evil–in some provinces of disposing of female infants by drowning them–their parents dispair of being able to support them', and further,

the practice of committing suicide in desperation of earning a living, or in utter despair because of misfortune, or out of spite for an enemy. . . . This is frequently done by hanging or choking oneself to death in a public place or perhaps before the home of an enemy. Jumping into rivers and swallowing poison are other common methods . . .

He commented on:

the custom of castrating a great number of male children, so that they may act as servants or slaves of the king . . . almost the whole administration of the entire kingdom is in the hands of this class of semimen, who number nearly ten thousand in the service of the royal palace alone. They are a meagre looking class, uneducated and brought up in perpetual slavery, a dull and stolid lot, as incapable of understanding an important order as they are inefficient in carrying it out.

Mercantile taxes had multiplied with the expansion of handicraft and commerce. By the end of the sixteenth century, the Ming emperors were sending eunuchs as tax collectors into the cities. They frequently arrested and killed at will and their arrogance and oppression provoked revolt in urban centres. In 1599, the people of Wuchang rose against the tax collector, Chen Feng. Chen Feng ordered out the troops, but the rising spread. Chen Feng fled, but some of his staff were captured and tossed into the Yangtze. In the following years textile workers rose against the tax collectors; other urban revolts followed. This was a new development in the history of China, the first time that the waves of revolt involved urban workers.

In the countryside there was also widespread resistance to the tax-collectors. Famine hit the north-western provinces for several seasons, and large numbers of people starved to death. The pay of the troops stationed in the area was two or three years in arrears; the troops rioted and looted the local treasury. In the 1630s, risings occurred throughout the north-west. Landlords and officials were killed and their estates were distributed to poor peasants. The un-coordinated risings in different provinces became unified at the end of the 1630s under the leadership of the peasant rebel Li Tse Cheng. By 1640 the peasant armies under Li numbered hundreds of thousands. The following year Loyang was captured, together with prince Chu Chang Hsun, the owner of two million mou of land.

Chu Chang Hsun's stores of grain, gold and silver were distributed to the poor. A feature of these peasant armies was their discipline. The men were forbidden to acquire personal loot, or to occupy peasant homes by force. The death penalty was imposed for offences like riding through fields of crops. Early in 1644, Li's immensely strong army set out from Sian and marched on Peking. The demoralised court, torn with factions, offered little resistance. Many of the Ming troops surrendered to the peasant forces. In April Peking fell to them. On the previous night the emperor commanded the empress to commit suicide and sent his three sons into hiding. The Son of Heaven tried to kill the eldest princess but only managed to cut off her arm. At dawn the bell was struck for the court to assemble; no one came. The Son of Heaven climbed Prospect Hill behind the imperial palace, and hanged himself with his own girdle from a locust tree in the grounds, as did one faithful eunuch. The emperor had written a miserable note: 'Poor in virtue and of contemptible personality, I have incurred the wrath of God on high. My ministers have deceived me. I am ashamed to meet my ancestors: and therefore I myself take off my crown, and with my hair covering my face, await dismemberment at the hands of the rebels. . . . Do not hurt a single one of my people!'

The Manchus

In the early years of the seventeenth century, tribes called Nuchens had grown strong in the north-east region, Manchuria. They were Tartars of the same stock as the founders of the Kin dynasty, but practised a mixed economy of hunting, animal husbandry and agriculture. Led by Nurhachi these tribes were united by 1616 and during the next two decades overcame Ming power in Manchuria and set up their own state, under the dynasty known as Ching. Manchurian troops made repeated attacks south of the Wall, and at one stage the peasant leader Li Tse Cheng offered to cooperate with the Ming army in beating them off. The offer was rejected; on the contrary, one Ming general preferred to call in the help of the Manchu against the peasant rebels. The triumph of Li Tse Cheng after the collapse of the Ming at Peking, was shortlived. The Manchu troops drove south and occupied Peking, a month only after the suicide of the Ming emperor. Li Tse Cheng retreated to Sian. In 1645 the Manchu troops attacked and captured Sian; Li was assassinated. Other peasant leaders emerged and continued the struggle against the Manchu for another decade or so. In 1659 the last of the Ming pretenders was destroyed. The Manchu, like the Mongols four centuries earlier, had come to stay. Barbarian conquerors and popular revolt had put a traditional end to the dynasty. The Ming downfall was one more in the long series of dynastic collapses.

13. Ching
1644–1911

The Manchus occupied northern China unopposed, at the treacherous invitation of a Ming general; serious resistance to them continued in southern China for another four decades, and in these regions anti-Manchu sentiment remained strong. Among the more distasteful reminders to the Chinese in general that they had come under alien barbarian rule, were the measures compelling men to adopt the Manchu style of headdress. Instead of long hair gathered in a topknot, the traditional Chinese mode, men were compelled to shave the front of their heads and wear a pigtail at the back, in Manchu style. This was long regarded as a symbol of servitude, which could be avoided only by becoming a Buddhist monk, with a completely shaven head, or a Taoist priest, wearing a topknot.

To prevent internal resistance being reinforced by external stimulus, the Manchus (as the Nuchen were now called) turned their attention to the frontier regions. Through political intrigue and conquest Turkestan, Mongolia and Tibet were incorporated into the empire; Burma, Korea and Annam became tributary states. After about a century of Ching rule, the Celestial Empire extended once more from the Pacific to the Pamirs, and from Siberia in the north to the offshore islands in the south. In the outlying provinces, especially Sinkiang (Turkestan) and Manchuria, land was brought under cultivation and settled.

The Manchus, during the earlier formation of their own state, had organised their whole people into groups of companies or 'banners', of which there were originally four, yellow, white, blue and red. The banners were both military and administrative groupings, through which all the Manchu tribesmen, slaves and serfs, were registered, taxed and conscripted. Appointed officers took the place of hereditary chiefs, but Nurhachi's descendants remained the clan imperial. When military forces were required, each banner provided an appropriate quota.

The Manchu banners were distributed throughout China. They had no occupation other than the service and protection of the Manchu state, and were prohibited from undertaking commerce or industry. They were maintained by tribute rice and other levies brought mainly from the south. They were forbidden to inter-marry with Chinese. The Manchus kept political control firmly in their own hands, but having no administrative tradition of their own (they had not acquired even a script for their language until the seventeenth century) they were obliged to accept the Chinese system of civil administration, serviced by Chinese who were willing to support the

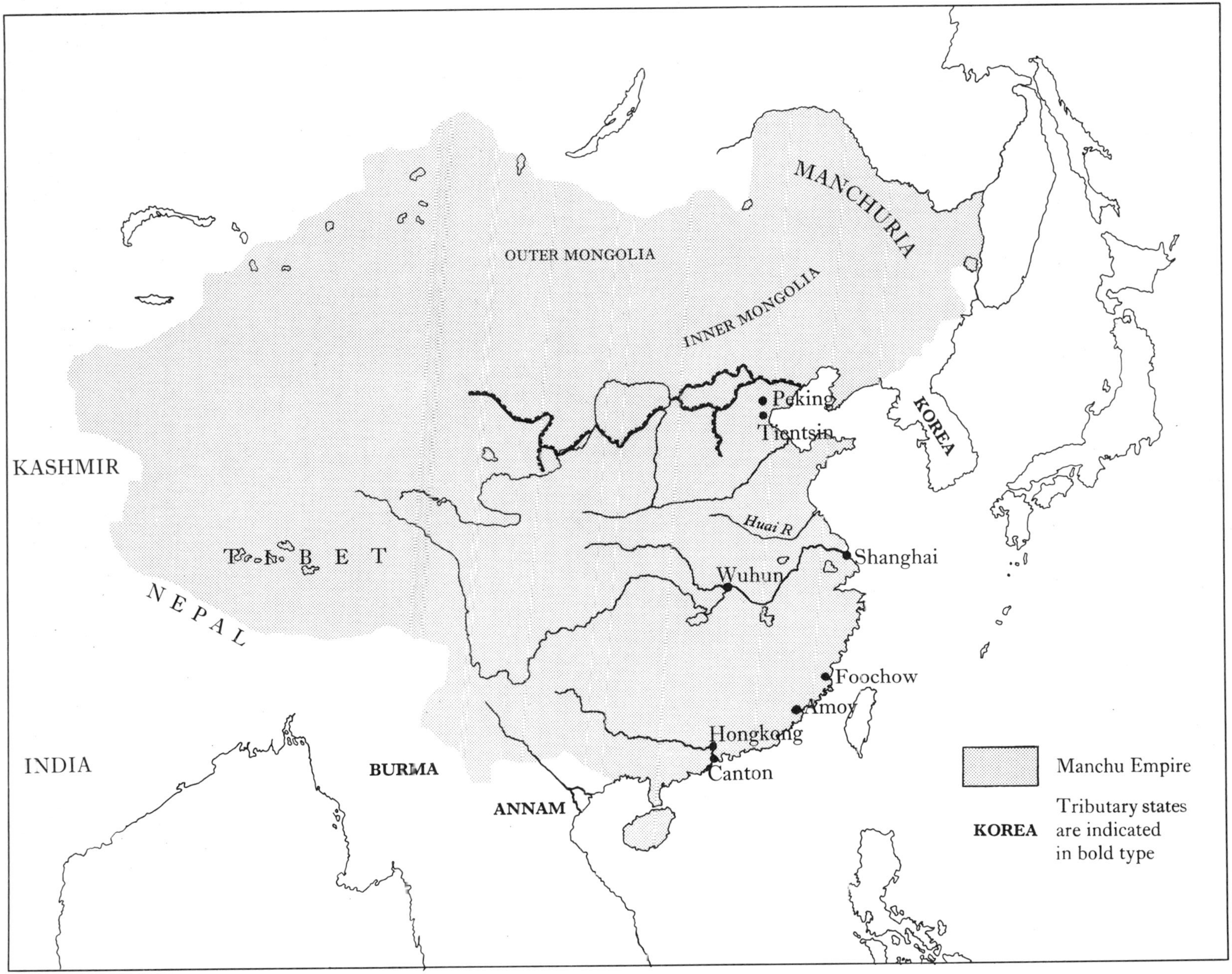
MANCHURIA
OUTER MONGOLIA
INNER MONGOLIA
KASHMIR
Peking
Tientsin
KOREA
Huai R
Shanghai
Wuhun
T I B E T
NEPAL
Foochow
Amoy
Hongkong
Canton
INDIA
BURMA
ANNAM
Manchu Empire
KOREA
Tributary states are indicated in bold type

11. Manchu Empire.

regime. The Ming examination system for the selection of officials was adopted practically intact, together with a highly centralized version of the administrative structure and the laws of the Ming; these were sustained by an inflexible Confucian orthodoxy, which remained the basis of social control throughout the empire. Confucian maxims were expounded once a fortnight in every village by officials and gentry, exhorting the people to carry out their filial obligations, to work and be frugal, to respect authority and be law abiding, and to pay their taxes. In the latter part of the seventeenth century, and during the eighteenth, the Celestial Empire came under the rule of capable Manchu emperors who secured internal peace, advanced irrigation works and agriculture, and became patrons of Chinese culture. The most outstanding of these was Chien Lung (1735–95) himself a scholar and poet.

Unified government during this period was of benefit to economic and cultural development within the empire. The central regions traded iron implements, cotton textiles, tea and salt with the frontier provinces, in exchange for musk, saffron and rhubarb from Tibet; skins and livestock from Mongolia; jade from Sinkiang; drugs and timber from the south-west. Agriculture, handicraft industry and commerce made modest but steady progress.

The Manchus, unlike the Mongols, attempted to preserve Chinese society intact. Adopting the most rigid Confucian traditions, they became resistant to change. A period of stagnation set in, during which innovation and change were blindly resisted. While in Europe industrial capitalism was fast developing, the Manchus in China were consolidating their rule on the basis of the past: China remained socially as well as politically moribund, an empire dependent on scarcely self-sufficient village economy, where the peasants produced the grain they consumed and most of the articles in everyday use. Landlords and officials collected huge amounts in rents and taxes, but this disappeared immediately in luxury consumption and there was no significant investment in capital products or commerce.

The Manchu and the West

Part of the conventional mandarin mythology readily absorbed by the Manchu was the belief in China as the Middle Kingdom, the cultural as well as the geographic core of the earth, surrounded by uncouth, insignificant, but potentially inconvenient barbarians. One Manchu official of Canton, wrote at the beginning of the eighteenth century:

To the extreme west there are the red-haired and western foreigners, a fierce violent lot, quite unlike the other barbarians of the western islands. Among them are the English, the Islamists, the French, the Dutch, the Spaniards, and the Portuguese. These are all very fierce nations; their ships are strong and do not fear typhoons; their guns, powder and munitions of war generally are superior to those of China. Their natures are dark, dangerous and inscrutable;

wherever they go they spy around with a view to seizing other people's lands. Of all the island barbarians under heaven the red-haired barbarians, the western barbarians and the Japanese are the three most deadly. Singapore originally belonged to the Malays, who were in the habit of trading with these red-haired barbarians. Subsequently they were ousted by them, and the place became a barbarian harbour and emporium. During the Ming dynasty, Japan rebelled, and many provinces were overrun by them, so that even now the people of those parts cannot remember the name of the robber dwarfs without a shudder.

Such views about the 'barbarians' had some empirical justification. It was in recent centuries only that the flow of Chinese trade changed its direction from east to west. During the period of world exploration by western mariners in the early sixteenth century, the Portuguese had seized the initiative and the trade in eastern waters. Despite their plundering and massacring manners which brought them expulsion from Chinese mainland ports, they later secured a base on the offshore island of Macao, where they built a fort and supplied gunners for the Ming.

Matteo Ricci had commented, that 'the Chinese look upon all foreigners as illiterate and barbarians, and refer to them in just these terms. . . . No one in the whole kingdom is ever permitted to do business with foreigners, excepting at certain times and in certain places, as on the peninsula of Macao, where a trading mart was established with the Portuguese.'

The English had been beaten in the race for Chinese trade not only by the Portuguese but also by the Dutch. The Chinese called the Dutch 'redheads' and this derogatory title which likened them to demons who were traditionally painted with red or blue hair (in contrast to the blackhaired Chinese), came to be applied to northern Europeans in general. The British East India Company in its efforts to open up trade with China in the first half of the seventeenth century, sent three ships to Canton. Impatient of restrictions and delays, a party landed and started hostilities, tearing down the Chinese flag, and as John Weddel, the commander said, doing 'all the spoile we could unto the Chinese'. The British enterprise was a failure and the Portuguese at Macao retained their monopoly.

The Manchus, anxious for the security of their dynasty, especially in the south, feared opposition launched not only from the mainland but from an overseas base, and adopted an even more restrictive policy. In the early Ching period Chinese were removed from the offshore islands; restrictions were placed on the movement of coastal vessels, and inhabitants of the south-eastern coastal strip were moved inland. Foreign trade was restricted to Canton, where the official market was organised, and where all foreign merchants were required to transact their business through official intermediaries. Foreign merchandise was subjected to import taxes and to limitations of kind and quantity.

'The men of old see not the moon of today; yet the moon of today is the moon that shone on them.'

Chinese proverb.

Autumn moon over dew platform. Traditional painting by Yuan Yao. Ching period.

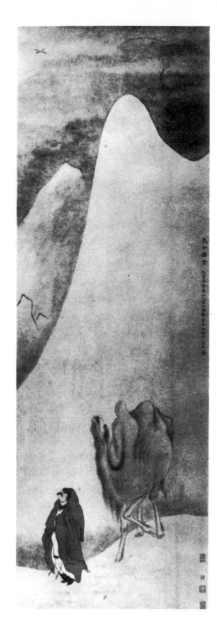

Such conditions were intolerable for western merchants, especially the British, for whom freedom of trade was sanctity itself. In 1793 Britain's first formal embassy to China, led by Lord Macartney, an Ulster grandee, arrived at the Manchu court of Emperor Chien Lung. The Son of Heaven was then eighty-three, but carrying his years well, according to Macartney. The British government wanted to open negotiations to remove trade restrictions, and to establish an ambassador permanently in Peking. Neither of these ends was achieved. Lord Macartney was taken to be an envoy bearing tribute from a vassal state, and he caused a considerable flurry at the celestial court by refusing to kowtow in the manner traditional in such circumstances, three genuflections and nine prostrations before the emperor. The Manchu officials reluctantly accepted the compromise suggested by Macartney, that he should behave before the Son of Heaven as he would before his own ruler George III, and kiss the hand of the sovereign.

The celestial response sent to George III said that the Middle Kingdom had no need of barbarian geegaws: 'The Celestial Empire possesses all things in prolific abundance and lacks no product within its borders. There is therefore no need to import the manufactures of outside barbarians in exchange for our own products'.

First Opium War

Perhaps this reply was no more shortsighted than the attempt to persuade the Chinese to be interested in such British products as bronze figures, elastic garters, waistcoats and stockings of fleecy hosiery, which were mentioned on Macartney's list of possible exports, or in the huge stock of opium which the British East India Company had brought illegally to China the year before Macartney's arrival. The British East India Company began making headway in Chinese markets, especially after the defeat of maritime rivals in the Napoleonic wars. They originally sent ships for cargoes of silk, tea and porcelain, for which they paid in part with European luxury goods such as clocks and with some textiles, but in the main with silver. Payment in silver produced an increasing trade deficit for the Company, because the Chinese, relying on their village and handicraft economy, had little interest in textiles or the luxury gadgets the Company was eager to market; later on pressure from textile manufacturers in England secured a regulation which imposed a quota of textiles as cargo on all ships sailing from England.

The development of the opium trade changed the situation. The opium habit (new to China) increased and a ready market developed, to such an extent that the balance of payments was reversed, and instead of silver flowing in, it began to flow out. The British East India Company was the principal carrier of the drug from India to the coast of China; the first shipments came in the 1780s, and by the

In the ice-capped peaks of the Tienshan mountains, a traveller in a red cloak leads a camel which, like him, is gazing at a solitary wild goose flying across the wintry sky.

Painting by Hua Yen, Ching period.

beginning of the nineteenth century grew to some 40,000 chests annually, valued at twenty million silver dollars. The Ching government became alarmed at the drain on silver. The import and smoking of opium were made illegal. Commissioner Lin Tse Hsu was appointed to deal with the problem. Lin was an engaging mandarin, a scholar and man of principle. One of his first acts was to compose a moral address to the Queen of England indicating the error of the English ways. His letter to Queen Victoria pointed out:

The ways of God are without partiality; it is not permissible to injure another in order to profit oneself. The feelings of mankind are not diverse; for is there anyone who does not hate slaughter and love life? In your honourable nation, which lies 20,000 li away, separated by several oceans, these ways of God and feelings of mankind are the same; there is no one who does not understand the distinctions between death, life, profit and injury.

He represented trade with Britain as a benevolent concession by a self-sufficient power to a people liable to extinction through constipation:

Is there any single article from China which has done any harm to foreign countries? Take tea and rhubarb, for example; foreign countries cannot get along for a single day without them. If China cuts off these benefits with no sympathy for those who are to suffer, then what can the barbarian rely upon to keep themselves alive? . . . On the other hand, articles coming from outside to China can only be used as toys. We can take them or get along without them. . . . There is however a class of treacherous barbarians who manufacture opium, smuggle it for sale, and deceive our foolish people, on order to injure their bodies and derive profit therefrom. Formerly smokers were few in number, but of late the contagion has spread, and its flowing poison has daily increased. . . . Not to smoke yourselves, but yet to dare to prepare and sell to and beguile the foolish masses of the Middle Kingdom—this is to protect one's own life while leading others to death, to gather profit for oneself while bringing

Canton in the seventeenth century. Nineteenth-century oil painting.

171

Destruction of ten million dollars worth of foreign-owned opium on the beaches of Canton, by order of Commissioner Lin Tse Hsu. His address to the Spirit of the Sea, apologising for the pollution, began: 'Spirit whose virtues makes you chief of Divinities, whose deeds match the opening and closing of the doors of Nature, you who wash away all stains and cleanse all impurities . . .' and it ends with a prayer that the Spirit will 'tame the bestial nature of the foreigners, and make them know their God'. Lin was a fine scholar, respected for his caligraphy and his verse, and for his just and merciful exercise of office. Modern representation.

injury upon others. Such behaviour is repugnant to the feelings of human beings, and is not tolerated by the ways of God . . . I now propose that we shall unite to put a final stop to this curse of opium; in the Middle Kingdom by prohibiting its use, and in your dominions by prohibiting its preparation . . . and being thus in harmony with the feelings of mankind, you will receive the approbation of our Holy Sages . . . our divine House controls the myriad nations by a spiritual majesty which is unfathomable; do not say that you were not warned in time! And on receipt of this letter, make haste to reply stating the measures which have been adopted at all sea ports for cutting off the supply.

These were the days, however, of gunboat diplomacy by the west, and even if the letter had reached Queen Victoria, which is unlikely, it is equally unlikely that it would have found a responsive 'harmony with the feelings of mankind' in the heart of politicans of the Palmerston vintage. The trade continued. Later, in 1839, Commissioner Lin blockaded the section of Canton where British and American merchants were permitted to operate, and forced them to surrender the stocks of opium they had on hand, some 20,000 chests. These he publicly destroyed on the beaches of Canton, apologising in an Address to the Spirit of the Sea for the ensuing pollution of her waters.

The British Government declared war. Palmerston despatched troop-carriers and men of war. The first of two Opium Wars (1839–42) ended in a decisive defeat for the crude fire arms, bows and arrows of the Manchu bannermen, who after two centuries of indolence were in no shape as fighters. Hostilities ended with the Treaty of Nanking, the first of a long series of humiliating exactions by foreign powers, who sought to partition China amongst themselves during the course of the next hundred years. The Treaty of Nanking (1842) opened five ports to foreign trade – Canton, Amoy, Foochow, Ningpo and Shanghai. Hongkong island was ceded to Britain. By further concessions the following year, British nationals were granted 'extraterritoriality', which meant they were not to be subject to Chinese

laws. Chinese customs duties were limited to 5 per cent, a provision which protected manufactured imports from abroad, and impeded the growth of Chinese industry. A huge indemnity was imposed in payment for the destroyed opium.

Two years later the Government of the U.S.A. and the French Government extracted similar concessions from the Manchus for their own traders.

The long isolation of the people of the 'south-pointing needle' was ended.

Taiping Rebellion

After this war the import of opium into China grew considerably; but the import of British, American, and French manufactured goods, especially textiles, increased even more. From being an exporter of textiles China became an importer. Weavers and other handicraftsmen in China were ruined. The old inland transport system which used to carry the Canton trade was superseded by the opening of new ports to foreigners and thousands of boatmen and porters in the south of China no longer had a livelihood. The drain of silver from China increased, to pay for the imports, and to pay the indemnity to Britain. The price of silver rose, and as usual the tax burden on the peasants was increased to meet escalating demands. One mandarin reported to the emperor in connection with the rising price of silver: 'The court collects the regular amount but the small people actually have to pay double. Those who have no power to pay are innummerable. . . . Soldiers and government servants are sent out pursuing and compelling them day and night, whipping them all over the houses so their blood and flesh are scattered in disorder.'

During the early Manchu period there was a heavy increase of population. Then, with the neglect of irrigation, famines were recurrent. The corruption of officials reached new depths. A further element had been added to the traditional crisis of China's peasant economy: the exactions of the westerners. A saying current in the Canton area went: 'The people fear the officials; the officials the foreign devils, and the foreign devils fear the people'. But by this period faith even in the classical scholarship of the mandarins had disappeared. It was commonly held that success in the public examinations resulted from one or more of the following influences, important in the order given: first, luck; secondly, predestination; thirdly, the influence exerted by the propitious siting of the ancestral graves; fourthly, good deeds, especially those done in secret; and lastly, study. The novel *The Scholars*, by Wu Ching Tsu, written in the Ching period, satirised the corruption and ignorance of the mandarins. Another masterpiece of the period, Tsao Hsueh Chin's *Dream of the Red Chamber*, portrayed the hollow life of the gentry.

The additional levies imposed on the peasants after the first Opium War came at a time when productivity was in decline. The trade introduced by the 'ocean devils' was dislocating the old economy. A number of peasant revolts gathered force in China during the 1840s, and came to a head in the Taiping Rebellion, the biggest revolt in Chinese history; possibly the world's greatest civil war. Risings occurred in many parts of China, but the unifying force was the Taiping Tien Kuo, the Heavenly Kingdom of the Great Peace, a movement which started in the south-east around Canton. The founder was a poor scholar of peasant origin, a village schoolteacher named Hung Hsiu Chuan, who shared the general hatred of the Ching dynasty. Earlier in life he had come into contact with Christian teaching, and as a result of 'visions' experienced during a serious illness, he believed he had received divine revelation and was called upon to spread the faith. He preached that men could move paradise from heaven to earth by building a state of equal, free men, which he named Taiping Tien Kuo, the Heavenly Kingdom of the Great Peace. In 1843 he set up the 'Godworshipping Society' in his native town near Canton. The godworshippers admitted no god other than the Christian god, were intolerant of Buddhist and Taoist worship, destroying many of these temples. They distributed free copies of the Bible in Chinese to their supporters and converts. The Ten Commandments were the foundation of their creed and the first thing that their children were taught.

The Taipings marked a new stage in Chinese peasant rebellions: they aimed not merely at the overthrow of the dynasty, but at the transformation of society. The rebels were no longer looking back to a mythical 'Golden Age'. They advocated a revolutionary programme of land redistribution, to give each peasant sufficient land to maintain an ordinary standard of living. 'Where there is land, we will till it together; where there is rice, we will eat it together; where there is clothing, we will wear it together; where there is money, we will spend it together. No place without equality; no one cold or hungry.' This simple egalitarianism appealed to the poverty-stricken peasants, and when in 1851 the Taiping Rebellion was formally declared after a series of famines in the south, thousands rallied to the Taiping cause. Amongst the scattered peasant forces that became united under the Taiping, there were many from the national minorities oppressed by the Manchus.

Other reforms enacted or envisaged by the Taipings were equally radical: they included the development not only of water communications but of railways; not only measures for flood and famine relief, but the establishing of institutions for the blind and the deaf; they included the prohibition of infanticide, the abolition of group punishment and of all cruel physical punishment, of slavery and of concubinage. Trade in opium was banned, gambling and corruption made punishable. One observer, speaking of Taiping justice, commented:

The disgusting scenes, the inseparable concomitants of the Manchu magisterial dwelling, such as torture of litigants, criminals and prisoners, are entirely abolished . . . the infamous system of bribery is entirely unknown in a Taiping court of Justice. . . .

Taipingdom is one of the last places in the world to please a lawyer; plaintiff, defendant, and the prisoner having to plead their own cases. The Taiping have one very singular custom in connection with the 'Judgment Halls'. Two large drums are always kept hanging, just outside the porch of the outer gate, and are at the use of any person who may consider himself aggrieved, or who may wish to represent a complaint, when he is at liberty to strike upon the drums and demand justice from the chief.

The same observer noted that many of the reforms of the Taipings were of special benefit to women, who were granted complete equality. Regulations in the areas under Taiping control prohibited the sale of slaves (a traffic mainly in females), houses of prostitution, adultery, and footbinding:

All children born since the earliest commencement of the Taiping rebellion have the natural foot. This great benefit to the women, their consequent improved appearance, and the release of the men from the tail-wearing shaven-headed badge of former slavery . . . cause the greatest difference and improvement in the personal appearance of the Taipings as compared with their Tartar-governed countrymen. A plebian Taiping is allowed but one wife, and to her he must be regularly married by one of the ministers . . . in contradistinction to the Manchus, the marriage knot when once tied can never be unloosed; therefore the custom of putting a wife away at pleasure, or selling her, as in vogue among the Chinese—or the proceedings of the British Court of Divorce, has not found favour in their sight.

The civil service examinations were opened by the Taipings to men and women alike. The emancipation of women reached also the military sphere; guerrilla detachments of women were formed. Another observer estimated that one-fourth of the units he had seen were women, 'many held military rank and were in charge of companies'.

The Taipings encouraged art and set up Boards to supervise the production of embroidery, weaving and sculpture; a number of these works have survived. They established a disciplined army, banning looting and corruption on the one hand, but dealing ruthlessly with Ching officials, big landlords and moneylenders on the other. They seized their wealth and distributed it among the poor. Unpaid and voluntary, the Taiping forces increased their numbers from the original twenty thousand or so to over a million. The armies of the imperial court, degenerate and corrupt, were no match for the forces of the Taiping. At the beginning of 1853 the Taiping occupied Wuhan, an important city on the middle Yangtze, and by spring they had entered Nanking, where they established their capital. They set up a revolutionary peasant state which ruled nearly half China for eleven years,

under Hung Hsiu Chuan, who became Tien Wang (Heavenly King),
temporal and spiritual head of state.

The radical reforms which they enacted were impracticable in
existing conditions, but many were enlightened, and some attempt
was made to enforce them. Fundamental to Taiping reform was the
Agrarian Law of 1853, based on the principle of peasant ownership.
According to this law, every man and woman over sixteen years of
age was entitled to a share of land, and everyone under sixteen to a
half share. Land was to be divided into nine grades according to its
fertility. The unit of administration remained the family, each of
which was expected to raise five hens and two sows. Every twenty-five
families formed a communal group with a common storehouse, a
church, and a head of temporal and spiritual affairs. After the harvest
this chief was to reserve sufficient grain for his group, sending the surplus to national storehouses for deficiency areas. The monthly tax
system introduced was considerably lighter than that of the Ching.
Only part of this land reform could be implemented in the prevailing
conditions of constant warfare. Title deeds were in some cases issued,
and some land redistribution took place, but many of the other provisions were unattainable. Booty and supplies captured during the
campaigns were, however, taken to the Sacred Treasury, including
the thousand or so junks of tribute grain which fell into Taiping hands
on the Grand Canal en route for Peking; these were taken to the
Taiping storehouse in Nanking.

The Taiping were friendly to foreigners, referring to them as
'foreign brothers' in place of the traditional epithets such as 'foreign
devils' or 'red-haired barbarians'. They proposed to open the whole
Chinese empire to the trade of foreigners, who might travel and

reside where they pleased. The Yellow Silk Letter of the Taiping God-worshippers to the British representative, Sir George Bonham, in 1853, struck a very different note from the message of the Manchu emperor to Britain; it said:

The Heavenly Father, the Supreme Lord, the Great God, in the beginning created Heaven and Earth, land and sea, men and things, in six days; from that time to this the whole world has been one family. . . . You distant English have not deemed myriads of miles too far to come to acknowledge our sovereignty; not only are the soldiers of our celestial dynasty delighted and gratified thereby, but even in the high heaven our Celestial Father and Elder Brother will also admire their manifestation of your fidelity and truth. We therefore issue this special decree, permitting you the English chief, to lead your brethren in or out, backwards or forwards, in full accordance with your own will or wish, whether to aid us in exterminating our impish foes, or to carry on your commercial operations.

After organising their government in Nanking, the Taipings tried to push northwards to oust the Manchu from Peking. By this time the big landlords and mandarins, seeing the futility of the Manchu forces, had mobilised forces of their own to defend themselves. Chief amongst these were the important officials Li Hung Chang and Tseng Kuo Fan, who concentrated many troops in north China. The Taiping failed to take Peking, but managed to beat off a Ching offensive against Nanking, in 1860.

The Taipings maintained their position, despite dissensions in the leadership since 1856, and other weaknesses, because of the massive support from the peasants and artisans and because of the general hatred of Ching rule. Two French observers in Canton remarked early in the rebellion that 'the population of this large city proclaims its sympathy for the new dynasty; and prays with all its might for the overthrow of the Manchus'. They also remarked that the Manchu army on campaign treated 'friends and enemies with most perfect impartiality, plundering all alike'. An English Taiping supporter, Lindley, pointed out that Taiping crimes, especially those of ill-using villagers, and opium smoking, were severely punished. He too had a low opinion of the Ching forces, many of whom were bandits and pirates turned mercenaries, the rest unwilling conscripts. He described a Manchu attack as if it were a scene from a Peking opera:

At last the Manchu warriors girded up their loins, that is to say, tucked up the bottoms of their petticoat inexpressibles, fiercely wound their pigtails round their cleanly shaven caputs, made a terrible display of huge flags, roaring gongs, horridly painted bamboo shields, and a most extravagant waste of gunpowder, and moving forward with terrific cloud-rending yells, established themselves safely out of cannon range of the walls.

Paper tigers and dragons, which they brandished to frighten the foe, were part of Manchu military paraphernalia till the end of the century.

After the rout of the Ching offensive in 1860 the Taipings strengthened their control over the rest of the wide regions of southern and

Token of the Taiping Rising, 1851–64.

central China, the rich revenue-yielding silk and tea districts. The trade of the interior was in their hands, and it seemed as if Heaven had indeed withdrawn its mandate from the dynasty in Peking. But what Heaven withdrew, the British, French and Americans stepped in to restore.

Second Opium War

Since the 1850s the western powers had been seeking further advantages in China and had been demanding a revision of the treaties signed after the first Opium War. In 1856 the Canton water-police seized a vessel, the *Arrow*, flying the British flag, on suspicion of smuggling. Great Britain, joined later by France, renewed war on China. This was the Second Opium War (1856–58). Anglo-French forces landed at Tientsin, not far from Peking, and the Manchu capitulated. In the Treaty of Tientsin (1858) they conceded to the following demands: the legalisation of the opium trade in China; freedom for missionary activity; the opening of new ports and the Yangtze river for foreign trade with settlements under foreign administration; foreign control of the customs, and tariff limitation; the right of foreigners to residence in Peking; and a further great war indemnity. In 1860 a new ministerial office was created by the Ching government, the Tsungli Yamen, to deal with foreign affairs. These had previously all been treated as vassal relations.

Foreign powers were in addition permitted to transport Chinese labour to work in their own lands and in their colonies. From this arose the coolie-trade, whereby Chinese peasants were taken as labourers to the mines and plantations of Malaya and elsewhere; in the U.S.A. they were used to help build the trans-continental railway. The chief exports from China became silk, tea and coolies. Tsarist Russia and the U.S.A. profited by securing similar concessions shortly afterwards. When the Manchu court delayed the ratification of the treaties, the war was resumed. Anglo-French forces attacked and destroyed the Taku forts which guarded the approaches to Tientsin, stormed into Peking, and, as reprisal for attacks on their envoys, burned and looted the imperial Summer Palace, a unique treasury of art. This vandalism was followed by the signing of the treaties and by further concessions to the western powers by the Manchus. For the first time in Chinese history, foreign ambassadors were permitted to reside in Peking.

At this point the Manchu court began to appreciate the effectiveness of western techniques, and, fearing the Taiping insurgents who were still established in the south with their capital at Nanking, more than they feared the 'foreign devils', modified their attitude and considered adopting western methods to suppress the rebels. At the same time the treaty powers abandoned their posture of neutrality with regard to the Taipings, who were much in earnest with regard to such matters as the ban on the opium trade. The powers undertook to supply the Manchu with modern arms and equipment, and the services of commanders to train and lead their forces. A corps of mercenaries was established by an American adventurer named Ward, calling itself the 'Ever-Victorious Army'. After Ward had been killed in battle at the head of this force, the English officer Gordon (subsequently General) took command of the 'mutinous rabble', as he called it.

Captain Fishbourne, commander of the British vessel *Hermes*, then in Chinese waters, reported that the western powers also employed Chinese pirate junks against the Taiping:

Having engaged pirates the authority was committed to them, to sanction the atrocities that these would certainly commit; and as if that were not sufficient, they encouraged them to do more than they would otherwise be inclined to, for they promised them six dollars for each head they would bring in.

The trade in heads proceeded briskly. The first thing the pirates did was to

disperse in every direction in search of heads regardless of anything save that the people who possessed them should be helpless; it mattered not to them that they were infirm and unoffending: they had heads: these they wanted. . . . At first they began taking their heads off at the adjoining pier; this was soon fully occupied, and the executioners becoming fatigued, the work proceeded slowly, therefore an additional set commenced taking their heads off on the sides of the boats. This also proved too slow for them, and they commenced to throw them overboard, tied hand and foot.

At Amoy 'for days bodies were floating about the harbour . . . many on whom sentence of death had not been passed, had their noses slit or cut off; others the ears cut off, or nailed to a post in the sun'.

In Britain and the British Parliament there was considerable criticism of the intervention in support of the Manchus, by leading politicians like Cobden, Bright, and others, as well as by the sympathisers who fought with the rebels. One of these Taiping supporters was Augustus F. Lindley, a sailor who had taken a berth as chief mate on a small steamer employed on the inland waters of the Shanghai district, trading with the Taiping for silk. He visited their leaders and entered their service. At that time (1859), they controlled a third of China. For the next four years he fought with their army under the distinguished general, Li Hsiu Cheng (the Loyal Prince), and helped with gunnery training; he bought a vessel as a blockade runner, and made frequent journeys between Shanghai, which was in western hands, and Nanking, the Taiping capital, bringing up food, such arms as he could secure and volunteers, running the gauntlet of pirates as well as of Manchu outposts. Captured on one occasion by the Ching mandarin in charge of a customs post, he secured his release by pretending to be an important western official, producing a copy of the *Hong Kong Daily Press* as his commission from 'His Majesty the King

Li Hsiu Cheng—Prince Cheng (Chung Wang or Loyal Prince), the outstanding military leader of the Taipings. He came from a poor peasant family. Lindley said of him: 'Many of the Taiping chiefs were popular with civilians; some were disliked, all were considered better than the Manchus, but none was so beloved as the Chung Wang.' There are many folk songs about him. One goes:

Sparrow, sparrow, how free you are
Flying east, flying west—carefree,
When you fly to the capital,
   Please do me a favour:
Go see how Chung Wang is,
   Is he thin or not?

Under Lindley's command, a captured steamer Firefly, renamed Taiping, launches an attack against the imperial flotilla.

Marie. Lindley's life was much like that of the young Garibaldi. Having twice rescued Marie of Macao, a Portuguese girl, from a forced marriage, Lindley made her his own bride. Marie was killed a year later in battle at his side, while Lindley was covering a Taiping retreat.

of America', a couple of Bass Pale Ale labels as his official cards, and an old Manchester rug as his banner, and representing the members of the ship's crew as his retinue.

Lindley's Portuguese wife Marie, whom he had rescued from an unwilling marriage in Macao, and his friend 'L', who married a Taiping princess, gave their lives in the war. Lindley himself was wounded in one of the campaigns. In 1864 the British authorities in Shanghai ordered his arrest, and, broken in health, he was compelled to return to England, to exchange as he said the pen for the sword in defence of the Taiping revolution whose ideals he shared. He wrote a book of half a million words in less than two years, describing the rebellion and his own activities; he died shortly afterwards.

The Taiping failed in their offensive against Shanghai, and soon their own capital Nanking, pressed by Manchu and western forces, was reduced to extremes. Of the siege of Nanking, Lindley wrote that during all their trials, the hope and courage of the Taipings never faltered for a moment: 'In the midst of his perishing people, the Tien Wang calmly and sublimely taught them to call upon God as the sure means of deliverance from their pressing danger . . . from the soldiers on the walls to the little children in their mothers' arms, the voice of praise and supplication ascended to the heavens.'

Following the advice of Gordon, the walls of Nanking were dynamited, and, as the Manchu account sent to Peking reported:

Smoke and flame from the burning buildings filled the city . . . several hundred female attendants in the palace hanged themselves in the front garden, while the number of rebels that were drowned in the city moat exceeded 2,000. We searched the city and in three days killed over 100,000 men . . . not one of the rebels surrendered themselves when the city was taken but in many cases destroyed themselves and passed away without repentance.

An Englishman, Lord Elgin, who visited the region was reminded of Pompeii. 'We walked along deserted streets between roofs of houses. . . . There was something oppressive in the universal stillness.' Another English traveller saw the ground 'literally white like snow with skulls and bones. The massacre of the unfortunate Taipings (inoffensive villagers most likely) must have been awful.'

With the fall of Nanking, in 1864, after the lengthy siege, the Taiping rebellion was defeated. The Chung Wang, the Loyal Prince, was captured and beheaded. The Tien Wang committed suicide. The Manchu dynasty and the landlords were given a reprieve of half a century; but no more. The regime had been shaken to it foundations. Estimates put the loss of life at between twenty and thirty million people, the most destructive civil war in the world's history. In the early 1950s, when the new Government took a census, provinces near the mouth of the Yangtze river that had been most affected by the rebellion were still twenty million short of their population in 1850.

The mandarin Tseng Kuo Fan, who had commanded one of the Manchu forces that had helped suppress the Taipings, was rewarded by edict of the Manchu ruler: 'We now confer upon him the title of Senior Guardian of the Throne, a marquisate of the first rank, hereditary in perpetuity, and the decoration of the double-eyed peacock's feather.' Gordon too received the imperial decoration of the peacock's feather.

The Taiping rebellion had been overcome, but not the problems which gave rise to it. The misery of the peasants under the restored Manchu regime was increased rather than diminished. The foreign indemnities added to the burden of taxation. Western products flooding in through the open ports destroyed the livelihood of many craftsmen. Receipts for the sale of children from penurious families have survived in numbers from this period. National minorities that had risen in revolt alongside the Taipings, were still oppressed and anxious to escape from Manchu dominion.

Feeling against the Manchu was as strong as ever amongst the population at large, perhaps even stronger than in the first half of the century, for it was now reinforced by the hatred of the foreigner that the Manchu had admitted within the gates of the Middle Kingdom. The corrupt court and officials were still wedded to the past, fanatically refusing to introduce reform or change of any kind, with the exception of the military know-how and help of the western powers. After the defeat of the Taipings, the Manchu dynasty found itself in possession of relatively modernised military forces. In addition, the

Scene in a Manchu court where mandarins dispensed justice. 'Trials in Chinese courts are conducted by torture,' wrote the Archdeacon of Hongkong in 1878, 'the judge when conducting a trial sits behind a large table. The prisoner is made to kneel in front of the table as a mark of respect to the court, by whom he is regarded as guilty until he is proved to be innocent. . . . Should his answers be evasive, torture is at once resorted to as the only remaining expedient.' The archdeacon then went on to describe a few of the simplest modes of torture, which destroyed the prisoners physically if not morally.

The Old Buddha – The Dowager Empress Tzu Hsi. 'Her good health and vitality were extraordinary. . . . Opium like other luxuries she took in strict moderation, but greatly enjoyed her pipe after the business of the day was done.' She was also noted for her cold-blooded ferocity and homicidal rage.

great landowners and officials, who had organised forces against the Taiping, maintained these troops under their own control and established regional warlord regimes. The forces were used to put down a number of risings of national minorities in the northern and southern border regions during the following decades.

The dynasty itself had fallen into the hands of the Empress Dowager Tzu Hsi, a latterday Empress Wu; her ability in the handling of traditional forms of control over the Middle Kingdom was matched by her tyrannous resistance to change. This Manchu woman had become the Emperor's concubine at the age of eighteen. Her son inherited the throne as an infant in 1861, and as co-regent, she became effective ruler of China at the age of twenty-five; continuing in power, with brief intervals, until her death in 1908 at the age of seventy-three. Known to the Chinese as 'the old Buddha', she ruled through her court of eunuchs and mandarins with absolute authority and coldblooded ferocity.

Shaken by foreign penetration and the reverberations of revolt, two groups developed at court. One group, favoured by the Old Buddha, clung tenaciously to old ways, trying to stem the tide of change. The other group, with the mandarin Li Hung Chang at its head, favoured learning from the industrialised west. During the sixties and seventies of the last century a number of munitions factories were established in China, financed by the government and managed by government officials. They also started shipping and mining industries. Li Hung Chang, for example, founded the China Steamship Navigation Company. Small-scale metal works, paper and match

A pavilion in the Summer Palace Gardens. The Dowager Empress reconstructed the Summer Palace which had been sacked after the Second Opium War. For this she took the 2½ million kilogrammes of silver which had been assigned for the building up of a navy. In 1910 the Summer Palace was seriously damaged a second time by the combined forces of the eight powers who entered Peking to put down the Boxer Rising. The Summer Palace is in the Western Hills a few miles from Peking; today many pavilions remain among the gardens, and the area is a public park.

factories and textile concerns started up in Shanghai, Wuhan and other centres. China was beginning to develop, if only in a small way, her own capitalist enterprises; a small group of national entrepreneurs emerged alongside the growing working class, who were mutually agreed in opposing the penetration of foreign industrial and commercial interests. Many of these early enterprises went bankrupt or passed under foreign control.

Partition

The next shock to the shaky Ching regime came in the 1890s, as a direct result of external pressures. During the 1880s the neighbouring states of Burma and Vietnam, formerly dependencies of the Middle Kingdom, were taken over as colonies by Britain and France respectively. At this point Japan joined in the race of the powers for concessions, and with ambitions directed towards Korea, secured an agreement with the Manchu that neither China nor Japan would send troops to that country without notifying the other. In the 1890s a revolt broke out in Korea against the ruler, who appealed to the Ching for help. Manchu troops were sent across the border to support her vassal against the Korean rebels, and China found herself at war with Japan (1894). The Japanese attacked the Chinese fleet, drove the Chinese forces out of Korea, and then they entered China itself, occupying the new Chinese naval bases of Port Arthur and Weihaiwei. A few months later, early in 1895, the Manchus were suing for peace, beaten this time not by an established industrial power of the west but by the 'robber-dwarfs,' a relatively tiny neighbour with newly developed industry.

The Manchus signed the Treaty of Shimonoseki, surrendering Taiwan and the Pescadores islands to Japan, renouncing all say in

Korean affairs, opening more ports to foreign trade, agreeing to pay an indemnity to Japan of 200 million ounces of silver, and granting Japan the right to set up factories on Chinese soil. It should be noted that the other foreign powers who had forced unequal treaties on China had also secured 'most favoured nation' clauses. This meant that any concession granted subsequently to any other power, was automatically extended to the original powers. At first Japan also secured Port Arthur and Dairen as bases, but Tsarist Russia, France and Germany who had their own ambitions in China, intervened and forced Japan to relinquish these claims in favour of an increased indemnity.

By the end of the nineteenth century, it seemed as if China were a completely helpless prey of the powers of both east and west. The business interests of the powers began to engage in an even more energetic carve-up. In 1898 the British stepped in to build the north China railways, for which China was mortgaged up to the year 1944. A concession for a railway in Manchuria, was gained by Tsarist Russia as a result of a million rouble bribe to the mandarin Li Hung Chang, who was then conducting foreign affairs for the Old Buddha, to whom he passed on substantial gifts.

The race to secure railway concessions was equalled by the race for naval bases and commercial ports along the Chinese seaboard. The killing of two missionaries in China provided the pretext for Germany to seize the port of Tsingtao in 1897 and a 99-year leasehold on the Shantung peninsula. Three weeks later, the Tsarist government gained a 25-year lease on the naval base of Port Arthur and the commercial port of Dairen. Within a few days, Britain secured the naval stronghold of Weihaiwei; then France seized a bay in south China.

The partitioning of China reached a further stage when the powers came to an agreement amongst themselves over their respective 'spheres of influence', where they would have a free hand to develop their interests without competition from rivals. The Yangtze valley was the British sphere; Manchuria and Mongolia came into the sphere of Tsarist Russia, Shantung province went to Germany, Fukien to Japan, and further areas in the south-west to Britain and France. The U.S.A. was a latecomer for the partition stakes, and declared a policy of 'Open Door' to break down spheres of influence (alternatively described as the 'me too' policy, through which she hoped to secure access for her interests anywhere in China). The Chinese were not invited to participate in any discussion of whether their doors should be open or closed.

The 'Hundred Days of Reform', 1898

The situation for the Celestial Empire had become so grave that a section even of the closed minds at the Manchu court realised that the crisis called for drastic remedies. A group of officials and scholars proposed reforming the archaic monarchy and giving scope for industrial development within the framework of limited constitutionalism, along the lines of Japanese development. A programme of reform measures was proposed to the young emperor Kwang Hsu, who had just attained his majority and was seeking to wrest power from his regent aunt, the Old Buddha. During a hundred days in the summer of 1898 the emperor issued a number of reforming decrees. These envisaged the abolition of the classical Confucian texts for the civil service examinations, and the establishment of modern public education, including a university; measures for the promotion of Chinese manufactures and trade, including railway and mining development; and measures to oblige the Manchu bannermen to contribute to their own support by undertaking agricultural and other work. One warlord official in the 'reforming' group, Yuan Shih Kai, betrayed the project to the Old Buddha, with the result that the emperor was seized and kept under detention until his death ten years later. The members of the reforming group who did not escape were arrested and executed by being cut in half at the waist. The old order remained.

Yi Ho Tuan: the Boxer rebellion

The next movement for reform came from the people and was led by an anti-Manchu secret society of traditional peasant type, the Yi Ho Tuan—Society of Righteous And Harmonious Fists—known as the 'Boxers' because their training included physical exercises reminiscent of boxing. This society became the centre of the rapidly mounting resentment against the foreigners. In 1898 feeling was running high against the Germans, who were exploiting and abusing the Shantung province in a brutal manner. In 1899, under pressure from France, the Manchus accorded Roman Catholics of all nationalities special privileges and powers. As a result Christian missionaries were regarded as the agents of foreign partition, and became the target of particular popular resentment. The unrest spread to Peking and the Ching government was frightened. Hoping to deflect the anger from the dynasty, the Empress Dowager proposed a joint attack by Boxer and Ching forces against the foreign legations and missions in Peking. This took effect in 1900. A number of missionaries were killed, and foreign diplomats and their families were besieged in the legation quarter of Peking for forty-five days.

The Manchus called off their troops, leaving the attack to the Boxers. Meanwhile the powers mobilised a combined force which eventually reached Peking and relieved the legations. The Manchus fled. These events were apparently recorded in a diary kept by Ching Shan, a court official and Manchu of the Plain Yellow Banner Corps. The diary has since been proved a forgery but the picture it conveys of the times is accurate. For 15 August he noted the decision of the court to flee:

At the hour yin [from 3 to 5 – Chinese hours are of two sixty-minute periods each] she [the Old Buddha] hurriedly put on a peasant woman's clothes, which she had ordered yesterday to be brought to the palace, and dressed her hair in the Chinese style. It looked very strange indeed. The Pearl Concubine [of the Emperor], who has never been dutiful towards the Old Buddha, now had the audacity to fall on her knees before the Old Buddha and implore her that the Emperor should not be obliged to go on the western 'tour of inspection' [i.e. flight] but should remain in Peking and carry on the negotiations for peace.

The Old Buddha lifted up her voice like the sound of thunder and forthwith ordered the eunuch on duty to throw this obstinate and rebellious woman down a well. At this the Emperor appeared deeply distressed, for the Pearl Concubine was His Majesty's chief favourite, and kneeling down, besought the Old Buddha to be merciful and pardon her from death . . . the two eunuchs threw the Pearl Concubine down the big well outside the Palace of Tranquillity and Longevity. It seems rather more than harsh that the well where she met death was in this place. . . .

To the Emperor, who was grieved and frightened beyond description, the Old Buddha said 'Get down into your carriage and be careful that the curtain is let down, so that people may not see you. . . .'

My womenfolk all intend to commit suicide by taking poison. This is the very worst they could think of, but as women are stupid by nature and do not listen to reason, I have not been able to dissuade them. As for myself I do not think of such a thing.

All communication of news with the outside world is now interrupted, and everywhere the foreign robbers are looting. But the rumour goes that everybody's life is spared who puts up a white flag. Very likely the foreign barbarians will have no means of finding my hidden treasure and so I shall not move elsewhere but just quietly await things here. . . . My servants have all gone to their houses, there is no one to prepare my evening meal.

Old Ching Shan survived his womenfolk by a few hours. His eldest son is supposed to have pushed him down a well in his own courtyard.

The forces of the foreign powers defeated the Boxers, occupied Peking, and once more ransacked the restored Summer Palace. The Manchu court again came to terms with the powers and signed a Protocol (1901) negotiated by Li Hung Chang, agreeing to pay a further huge indemnity, to suppress the Boxers and execute or 'condemn to suicide' (a more honourable way of dying) a number of Manchu officials who had taken part in the attack, to suspend the civil service examination for five years in all towns where foreigners had been murdered or harshly treated, and to ban on pain of death membership of anti-foreign societies. Ten powers received the right to station troops in Peking to protect their legations and the railway from Peking to the coast. The Manchus also agreed to accept amendments to existing treaties which the foreign powers required to facilitate their trade.

The Middle Kingdom, the Celestial Empire, was reduced to the condition of a colony, not of one power but of all who had the industrial strength to exploit it.

During the first decade of the twentieth century the Manchu government dragged out its doomed existence under the protection of foreign powers. Economically the position of the country declined; the annual excess of imports over exports increased to phenomenal proportions; in addition, heavy industry and railways were being further developed by foreign investors. The larger ports, both coastal and riverine, were foreign economic bases. Even in the sphere of light industry Chinese enterprise was constantly in difficulty because of foreign competition. The Celestial Empire sank deeper into debt, with most of its resources mortgaged abroad.

The Manchus were thoroughly discredited throughout the Middle Kingdom, and faced a number of threats, some traditional, some new. Militarily, their own forces had proved ineffectual, and were becoming increasingly unreliable as funds for their pay were lacking. Mandarins and regional viceroys like Li Hung Chang had built up their own forces, and presented the same threats to the Dragon Throne as had the ambitious local rulers of earlier periods. These warlords supported themselves and their armies with a relatively new tax, the *likin*, a customs duty imposed on inland trade, in addition to the usual exactions; some of them made great fortunes from the *likin* although it restricted internal commerce.

Chinese businessmen and traders, hampered by such taxes, and especially by foreign competition, formed another section in opposition to the Manchus. The peasantry, as usual bearing the brunt of the regime's oppression, formed secret anti-Manchu societies throughout the kingdom. Chinese intellectuals, particularly those who had gone abroad for their education at the turn of the century, to learn western technology, also formed anti-Manchu groups for the expression of their indignation at the effete and obscurantist government which had no policy or means of resisting the incursions of foreign powers.

During the war between Japan and Tsarist Russia (1904–5) China was neutral, yet the main battlefields were on Chinese soil, and as a result of Russia's defeat Japan established herself in Korea, on the former Russian railways in south Manchuria, and in the Russian leasehold ports of Dairen and Port Arthur. A number of scholars and gentry who opposed the Manchus saw in the success of Japan, a recently modernised society, an example of what could be achieved with a constitutional monarchy; here was an example of an oriental people who had beaten a western power. This demonstrated even to the Manchu court some advantages of learning from the west.

A series of decrees in 1905 aimed at the military and educational reorganisation of the Celestial Empire. The purpose that inspired the changes was to be able to oppose the western powers with something more effective than bows and arrows, more decisive than the paper tigers and paper dragons which Manchu warriors brandished to

frighten their foes. The examination system for the selection of government officials, which had served imperial China for thirteen centuries, was overthrown. A plan was drawn up for the introduction of general schooling in the Middle Kingdom, in which a dash of modern learning was to be added to the inculcation of the ancient virtues. According to one syllabus, prepared for the fifteen-plus grades in secondary schools, the basic study of Chinese classics, literature, philosophy, and of the government and edicts of the Ching dynasty for the last hundred years, was to be supplemented by a comparative study of foreign geography, especially that of Russia, France, Germany, England, Japan and America, with a cursory survey of the wealth and power of these nations. For this latter part of the course a period of ten days was allocated. Military academies were set up, and recruiting began for divisions trained under foreign instructors. Able students were sent abroad to study; they went mainly to Japan, but some went to Europe or to the U.S.A. A commission was even set up to study foreign constitutional systems, with the object of preparing for constitutional reform in China.

Such tonics, however, could not restore to health the degenerate celestial carcase. There seemed little chance of any changes being carried out. Taxes increased and there was no sign of any weakening in the demands of officials and landlords, no sign of effective social or constitutional reform.

Sun Yat Sen and the Revolutionary League

In 1905 a number of revolutionary groups in China came together to form the Revolutionary League. Its programme consisted of the 'Three People's Principles': of Nationalism—freeing all China from foreign control: of Democracy—overthrowing the Manchu dynasty and the introduction of a democratically controlled political system; and of the People's Livelihood: 'Land to the tillers' a socialist principle which meant the redistribution of the land so that each peasant household would be able to support itself.

The leader of the Revolutionary League was Sun Yat Sen. Sun was born of peasant stock not far from Canton, in a region formerly a Taiping stronghold. His elder brother had settled in Hawaii, and young Sun joined him there to be educated. At the mission school of Hawaii, Sun Yat Sen became a Christian; he later studied medicine in Hongkong. Like many of his fellows, Sun was strongly opposed to the Manchu regime. In the 1890s he had formed a secret society which had attempted a rising in Canton; this had failed, and from 1895 onwards Dr Sun had a price on his head and had to live in exile. He travelled abroad, to Japan, the U.S.A., and Britain, organising support for the movement amongst the overseas Chinese.

He reached England the following year. Sun was making his way to Church in central London one Sunday morning when two Chinese

Attack on a Manchu stronghold. Notice the paper dragons and tigers included among the defenders.

Dr Sun Yat Sen (1866–1925). Provisional President of the First Chinese Republic.

hustled him into the doorway of an adjacent house. 'All at once it flashed upon me that this house must be the Chinese Legation (49 Portland Place) thereby accounting for the number of Chinamen in mandarin attire, and for the large size of the house . . .'

Sun was locked in an upper floor room with a barred window facing the back of the house. Two or three men kept guard on him, one of them a European. Sun was told that he had been seized 'by order of the emperor' who wanted him captured at any price alive or dead. He was to be taken gagged and bound 'as a lunatic' on board an east-bound steamer, transferred to a Chinese gunboat and taken to Canton for trial and execution. In his memoirs Dr Sun mentions the death he anticipated: 'first having my ankles crushed in a vice and broken by a hammer; my eyelids cut off, and finally being chopped to small fragments, so that none could claim my mortal remains. For the old Chinese code does not err on the side of clemency to political offenders.'

Sun tried in vain to attract the attention of neighbours or passersby by throwing coins out of the window, but the Manchu servants of the Legation gathered them up. On the sixth day of imprisonment Sun managed to persuade an English servant named Cole to take a message about his plight to his former professor Dr Cantlie, one of the pioneers of the Hongkong Medical College, who was then living nearby.

At 11 pm on Saturday night, a week practically since the kidnapping, Dr Cantlie who was in bed heard the doorbell ring; he went down in his nightshirt. A note had been pushed under the door: 'I was kidnapped into the Chinese Legation on Sunday and shall be

The card that brought help and saved Dr Sun's life when he was kidnapped in the Chinese Legation, London.

189

smuggled out from England to China for death Pray rescue me quick.'
The message added: 'Please take care of the messenger for me at
present; he is very poor and will lose his work by doing for me.'
Dr Cantlie went into action. He posted a watch on the Chinese Legation to make sure Dr Sun was not smuggled out of the building to
another hiding place, or the ship. The local police station (Maryle-
bone) felt the problem was outside its competence. Scotland Yard,
in the small hours of Sunday morning, was sceptical. Thinking to
enlist the help of the press, Dr Cantlie hurried to *The Times*—but no
one was due in until ten that evening. The Foreign Office was not
prepared to act, especially at the weekend, on such flimsy evidence.
Corroboration came however from a shipping line which disclosed
that a passage had actually been booked. Twelve days after his capture, Dr Sun Yat Sen was released from the Chinese Legation in
London after the intervention of the British Foreign Office.

Sixteen years later, in 1911, again on his travels in London, Dr Sun
was at the home of the Cantlies when he received the telegram which
led to his return to China as Provisional President of the First Chinese
Republic. Revolution had broken out in China, and the Manchu
dynasty had been overthrown.

14. The First Republic

1911–1949

Revolution of 1911

The year 1911 was one of natural calamities, famine and mounting discontent in China. In the spring the Manchu government took over the building rights of some of the private railway lines, preparatory to mortgaging them to foreigners. This touched off protests and armed clashes. In October, under the influence of the Chinese Revolutionary League, the imperial garrison stationed at Wuchang, a key industrial city on the middle Yangtze, rose in revolt and called for the overthrow of the dynasty. They gained possession of the arsenal. Townspeople, students and peasants joined the revolutionaries. The Manchu officials fled. The court ordered the navy to sail up the Yangtze to suppress the rising; the navy sailed, anchored, but did not fire on the rebels. One province after another rose in revolt and over-threw Manchu authority. The revolution is known as the 'Double Ten' because it broke out on the tenth day of the tenth month.

Three years before on the death of the Manchu emperor and the Old Buddha (1908) the three-year old Henry Pu Yi assumed the imperial yellow. Faced with revolution in 1911, the court, in the name

Henry Pu Yi, Emperor Hsuan Tung, last of the Ching dynasty, at the age of two. In his autobiography Henry Pu Yi described his upbringing in the imperial court:
'Whenever I went for a stroll in the garden a procession had to be organised. In front went a eunuch from the Administration Bureau whose function was that of a motor horn: he walked twenty or thirty yards ahead of the rest of the party intoning the sound "chir . . . chir . . ." as a warning to anyone who might be in the vicinity to go away at once. Next came two chief eunuchs advancing crabwise on either side of the path; ten paces behind them came the centre of the procession—the Empress Dowager or myself. If I was being carried in a chair there would be two junior eunuchs walking beside me to attend to my wants at any moment; if I was walking they would be supporting me. Next came a eunuch with a large silk canopy followed by a large group of eunuchs of whom some were empty-handed and others were holding all sorts of things: a seat in case I wanted to rest, changes of clothing, umbrellas and parasols. After these eunuchs of the imperial presence came eunuchs of the imperial tea bureau with boxes of various kinds of cakes and delicacies and of course jugs of hot water and a tea service; they were followed by eunuchs of the imperial dispensary bearing cases of medicine and first aid equipment suspended from carrying poles . . . At the end of the procession came the eunuchs who carried commodes and chamberpots. If I was walking a sedan-chair, open or covered according to season, would bring up the rear. This motley procession of several dozen people would proceed in perfect silence and order . . . when I heard people telling the story of the last emperor of the Ming dynasty who had only one eunuch left with him at the end I felt very uncomfortable.'
Henry Pu Yi, as boy emperor for ten days in 1917.

of the boy emperor, appointed the erstwhile emperor-betrayer, Yuan Shih Kai, premier and commander-in-chief of the imperial forces.

The Revolutionary League meanwhile had declared the establishment of the Republic of China, and had set up a provisional government at Nanking; Dr Sun Yat Sen, returned from Europe, was elected Provisional President. In Peking, Yuan Shi Kai, a warlord of the old pattern, was quick to seize his opportunities. He accepted a massive loan from a group of foreign bankers to rehabilitate the country, on terms similar to those which had roused popular opposition to the Manchus. He also sent his forces south to attack Wuchang.

Fearing civil war and another partition of the country, Dr Sun yielded to pressure from some members of the Revolutionary League, and agreed to negotiate. He offered to resign as President of the Republic in favour of Yuan Shih Kai, if the latter agreed to break with the Manchus, and to uphold the Republic, with its capital in Nanking, and its provisional constitution. Yuan, grown no more loyal with the years, arranged the abdication of the boy emperor. The abdication decree provided a substantial income for the deposed Son of Heaven, who was allowed to retain the imperial private property including the palaces. The Manchu aristocrats also retained their properties and a number of privileges. Yuan Shih Kai was empowered by this decree to organise a provisional Republican government.

Yuan Shih Kai

The Manchu abdication occurred in February 1912; two days later Dr Sun resigned, hoping thereby to maintain peace and unity within the Republic. Yuan Shih Kai became President; he kept the capital in Peking.

The following month the new, modified, constitution of the Republic was proclaimed. It contained a property qualification for the vote, which meant that the majority of the people was excluded from the franchise. It ignored the question of the equalisation of land ownership; it withdrew a provision for equality between men and women. In fact little had changed, except the name of the ruler. As in the past, dynastic change left the basic problems unsolved; the agrarian problem—greedy landlord, ruthless official and penurious peasant—remained. The Republic moreover continued to mortgage China's resources to foreign interests. And it provided the warlord Yuan with the opportunity to establish his own dynasty.

He became a military dictator, using his generals and troops to enforce collection of rents and taxes. Political opponents were removed by assassination, and other opposition was quickly suppressed by the sword. Yuan Shih Kai's personal ambitions were not long in coming to the surface. By early 1914 the constitution had been altered again to make him President for life, and to make the post hereditary so that it would pass to his son.

China has had a number of emperors remarkable in their rise to power or in their exercise of it. Few have exceeded Henry Pu Yi in their demission of power; he abdicated twice. This yo-yo emperor ascended the throne at the age of three, abdicated in 1912 after the revolution. In 1917 he was reinstated by a warlord, for a few days. When the Japanese overran Manchuria he was enthroned (1932) as puppet emperor of the new Japanese controlled state of Manchukuo. Japan capitulated in 1945 and Henry Pu Yi was taken by the Russians; he spent five years in Siberia. In 1950 he was returned to China. In 1959 he was released from prison under a special pardon, and became a gardener in Peking.

In 1914, on the outbreak of the First World War, China at first remained neutral. Japan joined the Allies ranged against Germany and Austria–Hungary. Once more Japan fought on Chinese soil, seizing the opportunity to take over Germany's concessions in China. The European war gave Japan the chance to secure bases with a view to the total subjugation of China, which provided a wide market for Japanese products, and a valuable source of raw materials. 'Such an opportunity will not occur again for hundreds of years', said a Japanese militarist. There was no resistance from Yuan Shih Kai.

Twenty-One Demands

At the beginning of 1915 the Japanese presented Yuan Shih Kai with Twenty-One Demands, which amounted to a request for a free hand in China, an attempt at a full takeover. These points included, in addition to the transfer to Japan of Germany's former 'rights' in China, control of the Manchurian railways and ports by Japanese; they demanded that no harbour, bay or offshore island along the entire China coast be leased to any power other than Japan; that Chinese iron and steel works, arsenals, and mines be placed under joint Sino-Japanese control; and that the police in important centres be put under Sino-Japanese control. Japanese 'advisers' were to be employed to take part in the political, financial and military control of China. In May, Yuan Shih Kai accepted the main demands, in return for Japanese support for his imperial ambitions, and he made arrangements to ascend the dragon throne.

Risings in protest against the capitulation to the Japanese demands, and against Yuan's imperial plans, swept through the country. The would-be Son of Heaven, clearly lacking the divine mandate, cancelled his accession, and died a few months later, consumed with chagrin. The government of the Republic passed into the hands of northern warlords – Yuan's generals, adventurers backed by the treaty powers. The Peking Republican government became a mere figurehead; central authority disappeared. Groups of generals, each courting the support of one or more foreign powers, struggled for supremacy. At one point the Manchu boy emperor was reinstated on the throne. His restoration lasted ten days. A new 'warlord era' opened up, to consume yet another generation of the Chinese people.

A participant in the 1911 revolution, Wu Lao (Wu the Elder, later President of the China People's University) described the mood of despair after the Yuan betrayals:

The Revolution of 1911 had indeed brought a ray of light to the agelong darkness of China. It brought joy and encouragement to the people, but in a short time, Yuan Shih Kai usurped state power, and threw the whole nation into a dark abyss again. The people's disappointment and despair was so great that they could hardly bear it, and a number committed suicide. . . . When my elder brother, who had become blind and was suffering both sickness and

Henry Pu Yi learning from a gardener in Peking where he worked after his pardon:
Describing his prison experience in China, Henry Pu Yi says:
'For the past forty years I had never folded my own quilt, made my own bed, or poured out my own washing water. I had never even washed my own feet or tied my shoes. I had never touched a rice ladle, a knife, a pair of scissors, or a needle and thread; so that now I had to look after myself I was in a very difficult position. When other people were already washing in the morning I would only just have got into my clothes . . . when I put my toothbrush in my mouth I would find there was no tooth powder on it, and when I had finished cleaning my teeth the others would be almost through with their breakfast. So it went on all day . . . On our first day in Fushan a rota of duties had been made for each cell by which everyone took it in turn to sweep the floor, wipe the table and empty the chamberpot . . . Was I to empty the chamberpot for others? I felt worse about this than I had about the secret agreement between 'Manchukuo' and Japan; I thought that I would be humiliating my ancestors and disgracing the younger members of my clan.'
In his last years Henry Pu Yi took up historical writing, and published his autobiography. He died in Peking in 1967.

193

poverty in Chengtu, heard about my threatened arrest, he lost hope and felt there was no future for our home and country. He also committed suicide by hanging himself. . . . Personally I have always been against the idea of committing suicide. I believe that it is unwise for a man to kill himself because if he has courage enough to sacrifice his life it is far better for him to go and fight his enemy and risk death that way. In addition I have always been extremely optimistic with regard to the future of our motherland.

The preoccupation of the western powers with the war in Europe led to a relaxation of their industrial activity in China, with the result that industry, partly Chinese and partly Japanese controlled, expanded rapidly. In the cities light industry was developed mainly by Chinese entrepreneurs, and a large force of industrial workers grew up. The conditions of the industrial workers was no improvement on those suffered by the peasantry. Long hours and low wages, were the lot of men, women and children alike in the factories; whipping was a common method of disciplining the workers; before long the cities became centres of industrial strikes.

During this period a vigorous cultural movement arose amongst writers and intellectuals, who wrote attacks, not in the classical style, but in simple popular language, on the old social system that the Republic had failed to overthrow. Their writings had a considerable influence amongst student and youth groups that were formed to discuss them.

In August 1917 the Peking warlords joined the Allies and declared war on Germany; Chinese labour battalions were sent to Europe and the Middle East. When victory over Germany came in 1918, and the Allied representatives gathered at Versailles near Paris to formulate a Peace Treaty, the Chinese claimed that foreign concessions in China, including the Twenty-One Demands, should be annulled, in conformity with the principle of national self determination which was being canvassed by the U.S. President Wilson and other Allied leaders. This request was ignored. The Allies accepted Japan's claims and transferred all the interests formerly held in China by Germany to Japan.

May Fourth Movement

In China, anger and indignation were boundless. Protests rocked the country. The movement started with the students of Peking. They gathered in the Legation quarter on 4th May in an attempt to influence the representatives of the Allies who were still assembled at Versailles. The Legation police turned them away. They stormed the residence of the Minister of Finance. Troops were called out to crush the demonstration, and many students were arrested. A protest strike was organised the following day by the Peking students; in other cities students, workers and school children organised strikes, demanding the repudiation of the Peace Treaty, freedom of speech and assembly,

Peking students on their way to join The May Fourth demonstration, 1919.

and the release of those arrested. Professor John Dewey, the American educationalist, who was in Peking at this time, wrote: 'We have just seen a few hundred girls march away from the American Board Mission School to go to see the President and to ask him to release the boy students who are in prison for making speeches in the street. . . . We are witnessing the birth of a nation, and birth always comes hard.'

The pressure was such that the government eventually gave way. The jailed students were released, with apologies; officials who in 1918 had reached agreement with Japan, were dismissed (they fled to Japan). The Chinese representatives at Versailles refused to endorse the Peace Treaty; but the provisions remained unchanged, and were carried into effect.

The anger and humilitation was felt even more deeply in China than the original submission by Yuan Shih Kai to the Japanese demands. Chinese confidence in the equity of the Allies was undermined. The eyes of revolutionary China turned away from the Far West. 'No sun rises in the west for China.'

The May Fourth Movement marked the opening of a revolutionary period of heightened intensity in China. It was directed against imperialist intervention and against the warlords who submitted to foreign demands. It reinforced the cultural movement for educational language reform, and the movement for the emancipation of women. More writers began to write on social themes and to use the vernacular, like the author Lu Hsun. The movement was influenced by the Russian Revolution of 1917, which had profound repercussions in

China. In Russia the autocratic rule of the Tsar and the old social order had been overthrown by the Bolsheviks, led by Lenin; they were communists, inspired by the writings of Karl Marx, who aimed at establishing a communist society in Russia. The 'whites' who opposed the 'red' Bolsheviks in Russia, were supported by armies and other forms of aid by the foreign powers who were clinging to their privileges in China. The Chinese people's sympathy with the potential Bolshevik ally against their common enemies was reinforced when the new Soviet government of Russia renounced the concessions and privileges that the old Tsarist government had secured in China. Moreover, when Japan attempted to annex eastern Siberia, a part of Soviet territory, the Bolsheviks threw the Japanese forces out. This was the first time that Japanese aggressive ambitions had met a check in Asia.

The failure of the Chinese Revolution of 1911 to change the social order and to improve conditions increased Chinese interest in the experience and ideas of the Russian Revolution. The new cultural movement in China became interested in Marxist philosophy, and many publications and groups were devoted to its study. By 1920 the first communist groups had been formed in Shanghai and some other cities, as well as by Chinese studying abroad, and in July 1921 these groups came together to form the Chinese Communist Party based on the theories of Marx and Lenin.

Kuomintang and warlords

After the overthrow of the Manchu dynasty and the establishment of the Chinese Republic in 1911, the old Revolutionary League had been reorganised and became the Kuomintang, the National People's Party, still under the leadership of Dr Sun Yat Sen, and dedicated to the Three People's Principles. The party had gained a number of supporters less revolutionary than the former League. These were people who wanted to go no further than the overthrow of the Manchu, and were content to assume the powers and privileges of the former rulers. After the death of Yuan Shih Kai, Dr Sun Yat Sen had established himself in Canton in the south with the support of a southern warlord, and had assumed the post of Emergency President of the Republic.

The May Fourth Movement was followed by a rapid growth of trade unions amongst town workers, railwaymen and seamen; there were numerous strikes especially against foreign employers to gain improved conditions. The warlord government in the north tried to suppress the strikes by sending in troops. Amongst the peasantry, too, the demands for reform became louder. In 1920 another famine in the northern provinces caused the death of millions; in addition, the warlord armies ravaged the countryside, pillaging the villages and slaughtering defeated enemies.

Main thoroughfare, Shanghai. Until 1949 the city was divided into three parts: the international settlement, the French concession, and the Chinese area of Greater Shanghai. At the beginning of this century a notice on the gate of the Bund Park, by the main thoroughfare, read, 'No admittance to Chinese or dogs'.

By 1923 Dr Sun Yat Sen had become convinced that it was necessary to make a complete break with the old order – the old military commanders and warlords. He turned to the newly formed Chinese Communist Party and to the Soviet Union for an alliance. This was achieved. The Kuomintang, with the Three People's Principles still the basis of its policy, was reorganised, and communists were admitted to membership. The Kuomintang pledged its support for the workers' movement. A new revolutionary government was set up in Canton, and a military academy was established to train the forces that could defeat the warlords: the Whampoa Military Academy. Chiang Kai Shek, who had been Dr Sun's military adviser since 1917, became Dean of the Academy, and the political director was the communist leader Chou En Lai. Advisors and equipment came from the Soviet Union.

Sun Yat Sen planned to send an expedition north to defeat the warlords and unify China, in 1925, but he was a sick man, and died in the spring of that year. Before he died, he wrote a Testament to the Kuomintang, saying:

The revolution is not yet finished. Let our comrades follow . . . the Three People's Principles . . . and make every effort to carry them out. Above all, my recent declarations in favour of holding a National Congress of the People of China and abolishing unequal treaties should be carried into effect as soon as possible.

Another letter addressed to the leaders of the Soviet Union said:

You stand at the head of a union of free republics . . . By the will of fate, I must leave my work unfinished . . . I have charged the Kuomintang to continue the work of the revolutionary nationalist movement, so that China, reduced by the imperialists to the position of a semi-colonial country, may become free . . . I have instructed the party to be in constant contact with you.

I firmly believe in the continuance of the support you have hitherto accorded my country.

After the death of Sun Yat Sen, who was mourned throughout China like a lost father, Chiang Kai Shek became leader of the Kuomintang. Born into a well-to-do landowning family, he had followed a military, anti-Manchu career, before he became Sun's adviser in military affairs. When the Expedition set out from Canton in mid-1926 against the warlords in the north, it was under the command of Chiang.

In the path of the Northern Expeditionary Army, working people prepared active support. They helped with transport and provisions. Peasant associations, especially in the Hunan region, attacked local landlords and warlord supporters, who were forced to reduce rents and interest demands. In the cities, strikes affected all branches of industry and commerce; foreign interests were particularly attacked; bloody clashes occurred with the alien concessionaires. Aided by these events, the Northern Expedition reached the Yangtze by the beginning of 1927, bringing south China under the control of the Kuomintang Government, which transferred from Canton to Wuhan (Wuchang).

In preparation for the seizure of Shanghai, China's richest city, at the mouth of the Yangtze, the communists, led by Chou En Lai, called a general strike there. Industry closed down; the workers seized the police station, the arsenal, overthrew warlord control and proclaimed a citizens' government. By the time Chiang Kai Shek arrived with the Expeditionary Army, the victory had been won.

These events caused some right-wing sections in the Kuomintang to have second thoughts about social revolution and about cooperation with the communists. In the countryside the gentry realised that 'land to the tillers' could become a reality; in the cities the businessmen feared similar confiscations at the hands of the workers. Some of them, both foreign and Chinese, made secret advances to Chiang Kai Shek. Chiang himself had important business connections, and shared these fears. Two weeks after the expulsion of the warlords from Shanghai, he used his troops and gangs from the Shanghai underworld to attack the trade union leaders, communists and anyone associating with them. Thousands were shot down. Similar massacres took place in other cities under his control, and in the countryside.

A few days later, Chiang set up his own Nationalist Government in Nanking, 1927. He repudiated the alliance with the communists and with the Soviet Union. Membership of the Communist Party of China became a crime punishable by death. Sun Yat Sen's widow and other Kuomintang leaders loyal to the original policies had to flee into exile. The Wuhan government collapsed. All power passed to Chiang Kai Shek and his Nationalist government in Nanking.

Chiang Kai Shek

Chiang Kai Shek had assumed the mantle of Sun Yat Sen but he played the role of Yuan Shih Kai. The Northern Expedition was resumed, and met with little resistance; in 1928, Chiang took Peking; and the warlord government was dissolved. Nanking remained the capital. China was formally unified—under the dictatorship of Generalissimo Chiang Kai Shek. His government was recognised by the western powers and supported by loans from foreign banks.

The internecine warlord problem had at that time been settled; but the 'national' problem—the control by foreign powers of territories, ports and a large part of China's economy, was in no way resolved. Feeling ran very high on this issue; many of the clashes in Shanghai and other ports in the 1920s occurred on this account.

Japanese aggression

The Japanese, entrenched in Shangtung, the former German concession, were still looking for an opportune moment to sail west and extend their foothold on the mainland of Asia, with a double aim in view—of renewing the attack on the eastern provinces of the Soviet Union, and of extending their subjugation of the Middle Kingdom. They had consolidated their influence in Manchuria, for during the warlord period the generals in that region had frequently been in liaison with them.

In autumn 1931 the Japanese army attacked the Chinese forces at Mukden, in Manchuria. Within a few months they drove the Chinese south of the Wall, and seized the whole of Manchuria, one of China's most industrially developed provinces. The matter was referred to the League of Nations. The League had been set up after the First World War to prevent aggression and to preserve world peace. Japan's action was condemned but no steps were taken by the League or any of its members to secure Japanese withdrawal from Manchurian territory; Japan withdrew from the League but stayed in Manchuria. She declared it to be an independent state, under the name of Manchukuo, and installed the deposed Son of Heaven, Henry Pu Yi, as emperor. He was of course a puppet prince, acting only under the orders of the Japanese.

Chiang Kai Shek offered no resistance to the Japanese.

In 1932 the Japanese attacked Shanghai. Army units in that area and inhabitants put up a strong resistance. Chiang nevertheless signed an agreement with the Japanese which permitted them to station troops in the region, while China withdrew her own garrisons.

Despite popular anger at Japanese aggression the Nationalists of Nanking mounted no opposition; they yielded at each stage. Chiang Kai Shek was in fact preoccupied. Those communists who managed to escape with their lives in 1927 had taken to the hills where they were winning support from the peasants. Chiang conceived his mission to be the total elimination of the communists before he tackled the Japanese invasion, a policy he defined as 'internal pacification before resistance to external attack'.

A million people are believed to have been slaughtered in the five years following 1927. Chiang's rule resembled more and more a fascist dictatorship. He himself employed officers from Nazi Germany and fascist Italy as advisers and gave them state appointments.

The Red Army and the Kiangsi Soviet

Not all communists were eliminated in these attacks. Transferring attention from the cities, where the Kuomintang and foreign powers were strong, they concentrated on organising the peasants in the countryside. Shortly after the Shanghai massacre a section of the army revolted at Nanchang, in Kiangsi province, against the Kuomintang. This was followed by a series of peasant risings led by communist leaders like Mao Tse Tung and Chu Teh. They established a revolutionary base in the mountains between Kiangsi and Hunan, and here the first units of the Chinese Workers' and Peasants' Red Army were formed. The failure of the Kuomintang to introduce land reform, and the ferocity with which they executed not only communists but thousands of ordinary peasants, drove many of the people in the countryside to join the communists. By 1930 there were fifteen Red Army bases in the region. Their soldiers became skilled guerrilla fighters. In the areas under their control an agrarian revolution was carried out. The estates of rich landowners were confiscated and given to poor peasants and farm labourers; debts to usurers were cancelled and taxes were reduced; the old officials and landlords were driven away or killed; many fled to the cities. The peasants elected their own councils—'soviets' to take charge of their affairs. Edgar Snow, an American journalist, described a typical situation:

There was a peasant lad who had joined the Reds in Szechuan, and I asked him why he had done so. He told me that his parents were poor farmers, with only four mou of land (less than an acre), which wasn't enough to feed him and his two sisters. When the Reds came to his village he said, all the peasants welcomed them, brought them hot tea and made sweets for them. The Red dramatists gave plays. It was a happy time. Only the landlords ran. When the land was redistributed his parents received their share. So they were not sorry but very glad, when he joined the 'poor people's army'.

Failure by the Kuomintang to carry out the promised agrarian reform provoked widespread discontent and open rebellion in many parts of the country, especially during the late twenties and early thirties, which were famine years. Edgar Snow was in China in 1929 at the time of one of the famines in Suiyuan near Mongolia:

In those hours of nightmare I spent in Suiyuan [he wrote], I saw thousands of men, women and children starving to death before my eyes . . . I don't mean to dramatise horror . . . Millions of people died that way in famine . . . But these were not the most shocking things after all. The shocking thing was that in many of those towns there were still rich men, rice hoarders, wheat hoarders, moneylenders and landlords, with armed guards to defend them, while they profiteered enormously. The shocking thing was that in the cities–where officials danced or played with singsong girls–there was grain and food, and had been for months; that in Peking and Tientsin and elsewhere were thousands of tons of wheat and millet, collected (mostly by contributions from abroad) by the Famine Commission, but which could not be shipped to the starving. Why not? Because in the north-west there were some militarists who wanted to hold all their rolling stock and would release none of it toward the east, while in the east there were Kuomintang generals who would send no rolling stock westward–even to starving people–because they feared it would be seized by their rivals.

While the famine raged the Commission decided to build a big canal (with American funds) to help flood some of the lands baked by drought. The officials gave them every cooperation–and promptly began to buy for a few cents an acre all the land to be irrigated. A flock of vultures descended on this benighted country, and purchased from the starving farmers thousands of acres for the taxes in arrears, or for a few coppers, and held it to await tenants and rainy days.

Yet the great majority of those people who died did so without an act of protest! 'Why don't they revolt?' I asked myself. 'Why don't they march in a great army and attack the scoundrels who can tax them but cannot feed them, or who can seize their lands but cannot repair an irrigation canal? Or why don't they sweep into the great cities, and plunder the wealth of the rascals who buy their daughters and wives, the men who continue to gorge themselves on elaborate thirty-six-course banquets while honest men starve? Why not?' . . .

I was profoundly puzzled by their passivity. For a while I thought nothing would make a Chinese fight.

I was mistaken. The Chinese peasant is not passive; he is not a coward. He will fight when he is given a method, an organisation, leadership, a workable programme, hope–and arms.

Chinese peasants have themselves since then described how they came to fight. Pai Yu Teh, a peasant of Liuling village in northern Shensi, gave an account stage by stage.

In 1927 a peasants' organisation was set up here and that was when I first heard of communism. 'Destroy the landowners and do away with taxes,' was the cry. We wanted everyone to be equal and all bureaucrats and landowners to be destroyed. So, one night, Han Pei Hsin and I set off across the mountain to see if we could find the Red Army. It was chilly and we had only one quilted coat between us, and that was seven years old. . . . It was now my job to organise people of the neighbouring villages. I had to find leaders who could help the Red Army and see that it was given food and information and kept up to date with the landowners' plans. In the district there were two detachments of the landowners' armed forces, and also a dozen or so police, so I had to work in secret. They used to cut off the head of any of us they happened to get hold of. . . . In the end the landowners no longer dared stay in the villages at night, but made fortified places for themselves up on the hillside and withdrew to those. After I had organised twenty villages, one of the landowner's armed forces fled. . . . We went to Chaochia, where there was a money-lender and landowner called Chen Chin Ho. We allowed him to escape with his life, but we confiscated all his possessions and all his land. . . . We agreed that we would send a 'feather-letter' round the villages. This is a letter with a feather. As soon as it reaches one village, it is sent on to the next, and so everyone knows what is going to be done. By next morning six hundred farmers had arrived, and we arranged a mass meeting and elected a revolutionary committee.

That then was our new government. There were various departments in the committee: a defence and a land department and a grain department and a department for women's affairs and a department for young communists. . . . I was chosen brigade leader for the Red Guard . . .

We had now seized control in both valleys. . . . But we had no arms. Not all landowners had been able to escape with their arms, but it wasn't much they left behind. So the village blacksmiths took the surplus agricultural implements and made spears out of them; but as there were not even enough of these to go round and we weren't all armed, we made dummy ones. Each of us had three wooden hand grenades. Our uniform was a red armlet. At a distance it looked as if we were heavily armed. We got hold of some silver paper in a shop and used it to cover our wooden bayonets. They glinted in the sun. We frightened the landowners.

Such developments and such forces also frightened Chiang Kai Shek. Between 1930 and 1932 the Kuomintang sent four expeditions to surround and exterminate the multiplying Red bases in Kiangsi and Hunan. Although the Kuomintang had overwhelming superiority of numbers and equipment, the successes that they constantly announced were wishful thinking. On the contrary, their German-trained armies lost the cream of their troops, and much of their equipment passed into the hands of the Chinese Red Army.

The military tactics which the Red Army employed with such success then as later, were based on mobile guerrilla tactics, avoiding static, positional warfare, pitched battles. These tactics were expressed in four slogans:

When the enemy advances, we retreat!
When the enemy halts and encamps, we trouble them!
When the enemy tries to avoid a battle, we attack!
When the enemy retreats, we pursue!

Such methods, which left the Kuomintang expeditions little opportunity of getting to grips with the Red forces in a decisive encounter, could not have succeeded without the active support of the peasants in the areas where they were based. At last a new order in the countryside became a reality instead of a promise. As Mao Tse Tung reported:

Sun Yat Sen devoted forty years to the national revolution; what he wanted but failed to achieve has been accomplished by the peasants in a few months. . . . The major targets of their attack were the village bosses, bad gentry, and illegal landlords, as well as the old patriarchal ideology, corruption of city officials, and undesirable village customs. . . . After the overthrow of the gentry's power, the peasant Associations became the only organs of power.

By the end of 1931 the communists were able to proclaim a 'Chinese Soviet Republic' in Kiangsi, with Mao Tse Tung as Chairman of the provisional government. Two years later Chiang mounted a fifth expedition of 'annihilation' against the communists; they were to be crushed by a total encirclement and economic blockade. But the 'Nationalist' troops of the Kuomintang antagonised popular support as much as the Reds won it. Peter Fleming, a British journalist who visited the Kiangsi front of the Kuomintang, wrote:

For the last three years there have been permanently garrisoned in Kiangsi between 100,000 and 200,000 Government troops. . . . Press gangs, conscript labour, extra taxes, and many forms of indignity and extortion have made [the inhabitants'] lives a burden to them, and in return they have received only the most inadequate protection. If anything is calculated to make the Chinese peasant turn spontaneously to communism (or anything else that presents itself) it is having troops permanently billeted on him. . . .

The thing that struck me most on the front was that every officer to whom I spoke was thinking in terms of defence, not of attack . . . an order had been issued to all villages of more than two hundred families to build three forts if they had not got them already. . . .

The Chinese soldier . . . is a mercenary. . . . In billets he seldom pays for what he eats, and the division to which he belongs was almost certainly created by diverting some part of the national or provincial revenue from more legitimate and needful expenditure. Should his general meet with a reverse, whether military or financial, he will be turned loose on a district, which is probably far from his home, with a rifle, a few rounds of ammunition, and a grievance against society. . . .

Most of the time there was nothing for the troops to do. . . . Those romantically situated forts were prosaically evacuated at the first serious threat of danger, and expeditions which marched out against the Reds returned minus their rifles and their officers.

The fifth annihilation campaign was a serious affair. Chiang threw in over half a million troops supported by four hundred aircraft. The Red forces could muster about a hundred thousand rifles; they totally lacked artillery and aircraft.

After nearly a year it seemed as if the Reds were indeed caged in and on the point of extinction. The first stage of Chiang's policy might be yielding results. Meanwhile the Japanese problem had intensified; in 1931 they had occupied Manchuria; in 1932 they had gained a base for their troops in Shanghai. Larger and larger Japanese forces were stationed in north China, and the Chinese demand for resistance to Japan grew stronger; it affected even sections of the Nationalist army, which by 1933 began to offer local resistance to the Japanese.

The Long March
On 16 October 1934 the Red Army in south Kiangsi launched a two-pronged attack on the Nationalist forces blockading them in the south and the west. They broke through, and the 300,000 men of the Red Army, accompanied by thousands of peasants, men, women and children, equipment and dismantled workshops, began the Long

March, which was to become one of the outstanding feats of Chinese history.

In the course of a year they traversed, on foot, some 8,000 miles of almost inaccessible mountains, and crossed some of the mightiest rivers of China. They were under daily air and ground attack from the pursuing Nationalist forces. They outmanoeuvred and outpaced their pursuers. Despite their desperate physical circumstances they were in better heart than their opponents. The Kuomintang soldier was not welcomed by local populations, and he often wondered why he was fighting his fellow Chinese and not attacking the Japanese. But the Red Army, after driving westward, swung north through Szechuan to Shensi region, where soviets had been set up similar to those in Kiangsi-Hunan. This army was going north, however, not for rest, but to fight the Japanese.

The natural obstacles along the mountain flanks to the north were formidable, and at each stage Chiang hoped to intercept the route and trap the Red forces. The first major obstacle was the upper reaches of the Yangtze river, which flowed deep and swift through gorges. Chiang ordered his troops to destroy all boats for crossing the river, but the Kuomintang advance guard withdrew them to the north bank. Using a village official as a decoy, the Red Army on the south bank seized from the north a boat sent over to ferry some 'government' troops. With this they despatched a detachment of Red soldiers who disarmed the Kuomintang guards on the other side, and brought back five more boats. Six boats ferried the entire Red Army over the Yangtze, working non-stop for nine days. When the main body of pursuing Kuomintang troops reached the river, their enemy was out of reach on the other side, and all boats by then had indeed been destroyed.

An even better known incident was the crossing of the Tatu River the next strategic point to the north. This time a speedy crossing was essential for the Red Army because Chiang was determined not to lose his quarry for a second time. Some boats were captured by the Reds, but the water flowed so swiftly that each crossing with a load of men took four hours. Further up river, where the cliff faces of the gorge were almost perpendicular, was a famous iron suspension bridge – the Liuting Bridge, built centuries ago in traditional fashion. Sixteen heavy iron chains were slung from the cliff tops across the river. Planks lashed to the lower chains formed a roadway. The White troops on the north cliff set up a machine-gun post at their end of the bridge, and removed the planks. When the Red Army led by Lin Piao came up, thirty men volunteered to capture the crossing. With hand

The Long March.
Storming the Liuting Bridge over the Tatu River, May 1935.
Contemporary painting by Li Tsung Tsin.
A century earlier a famous general of the Taiping and his army had been wiped out by the Manchu troops at this spot. Here, too, the legendary heroes of the 'Three Kingdoms' had met defeat.

205

grenades strapped to their backs they swung hand over hand along the iron chains, under enemy gunfire. Three were hit, and dropped into the swirling current below. Towards the northern end, some of the planks had been left in place, and these to some extent protected the volunteers who reached the other side. Their grenades put the machine-gunners to flight, but not before they had set fire to the bridge planks with paraffin. More Red troops now swung across the bridge, and the fire was put out. Planks which had been removed by the Chiang forces were replaced, and the Red Army raced across, protected not only by the advance group but also by those who had made the crossing lower down stream by boat. Chiang's planes, sent over to destroy the bridge, were not good marksmen; their bombs fell in the river.

Particular acts of heroism were matched by the feats of endurance of the whole Red Army, which was ill-clad and undernourished. A survivor of the Long March, Chao Hung Chin, recollects how one day he found the skin of a broken drum when his detachment was resting by the temple of a mountain god. He first used it as a rain hat; later as a sunshade. Then as his straw sandals blistered his feet he made the skin into sandals:

As the days went by, there was less and less to eat. After our grain was finished, we ate the horses, and then we lived on wild vegetables. When even the wild vegetables were finished, we ate our leather belts. After that we had to march on empty stomachs.

One day we camped at the foot of a steep cliff, so high that the summit was out of sight. We were in such bad shape that we could not climb this cliff without first having something to eat. . . . I collected some dry twigs to make a fire and resolutely started roasting my shoes . . . after we had baked the shoes for a time, we washed and scraped them clean, then boiled them in a basin. Boiling turned the leather yellow and soft, and its appetising smell made us hungrier than ever . . . when the 'shoes' were cooked our squad leader cut them into small bits and distributed them among the men to eat before climbing the cliff the next day.

Much of the region of the Great Snow Mountains along their route, which bordered on Tibet, was inhabited by hostile tribesmen, the Mantzu, who hated all Chinese, Red or White. The Mantzu queen threatened to boil alive anyone who helped the travellers. After that came the Grasslands, muddy swamps, deep seas of wet grass where many dropped from sight into the treacherous ooze, beyond reach of their comrades. Finally, in October 1935, after a year's march, they reached the border of Shensi, just south of the Great Wall, where another Chinese soviet base had existed since 1933. Of the 300,000 who set out, some 20,000 reached Shensi.

But they had won millions of supporters along their route. Unlike the Kuomintang troops, they were welcomed as the 'poor people's army'. In the regions under their control, a new way of life had developed alongside the redistribution of land. Opium-smoking and gambling were forbidden. The sale of children, and all forms of slavery, were also forbidden, together with arranged marriage, prostitution, and begging. When the Red Army was on the march it was required to maintain exemplary behaviour. This distinguished it sharply from the Nationalists. Red Army soldiers were forbidden to confiscate articles from peasants, and any wealth taken from the landlords had to be promptly delivered to headquarters. The Red Army had an eight-point code in relation to the peasantry: replace any article used; roll up and return the straw matting you slept on; be courteous and help out wherever you can: return all borrowed articles; replace all damaged goods; be honest in all transactions with the peasants; pay for all articles received; maintain hygiene and establish latrines at a distance from people's houses. Two other points were added: do not flirt with women; do not kill prisoners of war.

The Red Army travelled light. Much of the equipment taken with them when they left Kiangsi-Hunan was soon abandoned, buried or given to the villagers, because it held up progress. In general they provisioned themselves by confiscations from the rich—landlords, officials, big gentry. If there were surpluses these were distributed among the local poor. In Yunnan when the Reds seized thousands of hams from a rich packer, the peasants came from miles around to receive their free portions.

The Red Army had no armament production of its own, and could not survive indefinitely with silver paper bayonets. They equipped themselves almost entirely with supplies captured from the Kuomintang armies, so much so that they came to call the Nationalists 'their ammunition-carriers'.

Yenan

In Shensi, the Red Army set up its headquarters in Yenan. Here a river runs through a deep gorge. In the cliff face a cave city was established in which some 20,000 people lived. Living quarters, a military academy, hospitals, a college of art, and many other facilities were organised in these grottoes. Some of these rock caverns held several hundred people. They were excellent shelters against the bombing raids of Chiang. Edgar Snow said of the Red Academy that it was 'probably the world's only seat of higher learning whose classrooms were caves, with chairs and desks of stone and brick, whose blackboards were walls of limestone and clay, and whose buildings were completely bomb-proof'.

Every active commander in the Red Army was supposed to spend at least four months at the Red Academy during each two years of active service. There were waiting lists of applicants. These came not only from the Red forces but from all over China. If accepted, the

students were smuggled across the Kuomintang lines to attend. The curriculum included military, political, and social questions. There was also a theatre which trained about sixty theatrical troups; these performed in the villages and at the front.

In 1932 from its southern Kiangsi base the Chinese Soviet government had made a formal declaration of war against Japan. At that time they were in no position to carry the declaration into effect. By 1935, with the new northern base of Yenan, where the guerrilla units from different regions were unified under their control, conditions had changed. By then Japan had made further inroads into China, with the connivance of the Kuomintang government in Nanking, which had declared the autonomy of five northern Chinese provinces; these had become zones of Japanese influence. The Kuomintang turned a deaf ear to demands throughout Nationalist China for resistance to Japan.

In August 1935, before the conclusion of the Long March, the Chinese Communist Party sent out a call to all groups and parties in China to unite to set up a government of national defence, to fight against the Japanese. Their slogan 'Chinese do not fight Chinese' echoed throughout the Middle Kingdom. In December, for example, a demonstration of students in Peking demanded a reversal of Kuomintang policy and resistance to the invader. Organisations for 'National Salvation' were set up, and strikes occurred in many centres.

In February 1936 units of the Chinese Red Army moved east from Shensi to join battle with the Japanese. Their policy was to subordinate all other issues to the main one of opposing Japanese aggression; they offered to cooperate with all—even landlords—who would join in this struggle.

The answer of Chiang and the Kuomintang was to mount another extermination campaign against the communists in Shensi. By their obstinate failure to meet national demand, the Kuomintang 'Nationalist' leaders were losing all popular support.

Yenan, Shensi province. In the hillside caves of this valley the Chinese Red Army had its headquarters for eleven years.

Sian Incident

One of the more strikingly inept features of their policy was the selection of Marshal Chang, the 'Young Marshal', son of a former warlord of Manchuria who had been assassinated by the Japanese, and the north-eastern army, as the extermination squad of the Yenan Soviet. Neither the troops, who were mainly Manchurian, nor their Marshal, had their heart in this job; they would have preferred to be fighting to regain Manchuria. The peasant Pai Yu Teh, of Yenan region, who had earlier fought with silver paper bayonets to establish soviet power in Yenan, described what happened after the arrival of the Red Army from the south:

In October 1935 the First Route Army came here at the end of the 'Long March'. It was led by the Central Committee of the Party and Chairman Mao. . . . The Central Committee came to us with this message: 'Go north to fight the Japanese! Form a United Front! Resist Japan! Chinese do not fight Chinese!' . . . We were now to fight shoulder to shoulder even with landlords . . . we local party workers were given the job of taking the north-eastern army in hand and forming a united front against the Japanese. . . . Their fighting morale was poor, of course; they had no food, they were hungry and cold, and lost all the engagements they were in with us, for they were fighting far from their homes in a war they did not understand . . . the morale of the north-eastern army grew worse and worse. In the end they had neither food nor ammunition, having fired it all off unnecessarily. Then the enemy tried to supply his troops by air, but the planes flew too high. The pilots were Americans hired by Chiang Kai Shek and they didn't want to die, they were just flying for money. So they dropped pancakes over Kanchuan where the enemy was starving, but the wind caught them and they drifted over to us and we ate them. They were still warm . . .

The first conferences between us and the north-eastern army took place . . . about twenty li from Yenan. . . . We sat in a stone cave and had a friendly discussion. That was the first step in our collaboration that finally led to Chiang Kai Shek being taken prisoner in Sian and compelled to go to war with Japan. . . .

This agreement was of course strictly secret. Chiang Kai Shek suspected that something was brewing in the north-west, but he could not prove anything.

The Generalissimo himself decided to visit Sian, capital of Shensi province in December 1936, to deal with disaffection, and to urge on the anti-communist attack. Chiang was taken prisoner in Sian by his own generals, and held under arrest while the communist leader Chou En Lai and others came from Yenan to negotiate a top-level united front.

United front against Japan

The result of this episode, the Sian Incident, was that Chiang agreed to an armistice with the communists and a joint attack against the Japanese. An amnesty was granted to the rebels who had kidnapped him and threatened to take his life unless he agreed to the reversal of policies. The communists agreed to place their forces under the supreme command of the Generalissimo, and to acknowledge the authority of the Nanking government; the Chinese Red Army became the Eighth Route Army and the Shensi Soviet Republic was declared an autonomous border region.

The Japanese militarists did not remain on the defensive. In July 1937 their army came south and attacked Lukouchiao (Marco Polo Bridge) and occupied Peking a few days later. In support of their campaign for the total seizure of China, devastating bombing raids were made on Chinese cities, and an army nearly a million strong was put in the field. In the first stages, the united resistance of the Chinese met with some success, but their armies were pressed to the south and by the end of the year Shanghai had fallen to the Japanese; this was followed shortly afterwards by the fall of the capital Nanking. In 1938 the Japanese seized most of the coastal area, including Canton, and pressed up the Yangtze to Wuhan. With the eastern half of China, including the main urban centres, in the hands of the Japanese, the Nationalist capital moved to Chungking in the heart of southern China, on the upper reaches of the Yangtze. Here the government was almost totally cut off from the outside world; the main avenue of contact remaining open to them was through Burma, to the southwest.

In September 1939 the Second World War broke out in Europe, and the Chinese struggle shifted to the fringe of international interest. When, however, the Japanese attack on the U.S. naval base at Pearl Harbour brought the U.S.A. into the war, the Chinese struggle against Japan became part of a wider international conflict, and the U.S.A. arranged to send military aid to Chungking along the Burma Road. The seizure of Burma by Japan closed this road, and the last link between Chungking and the outside world was from north India, by air, over the Himalayas.

From 1939 the Chungking nationalists undertook no major campaigns against the Japanese; squabbles amongst their own generals, and fears of rousing amongst the peasants expectations of social revolution which they had no intention of satisfying, were factors in this reticence. Chiang Kai Shek followed the policy of playing for time, in the hope that Japan would be finished off by America and the allies, without further effort from Chungking. Communist guerrilla bands continued to harry the Japanese in the north, while in the south the Kuomintang pursued a static, defensive policy. The truce between the communists and the Kuomintang became a dead letter. The Nationalist forces in 1941 resumed attacks on communist units, and once more imposed a blockade on Yenan.

The morale of the Nationalist forces was depressed to zero. General Stilwell, the U.S. liaison general in Chungking, in charge of the reopening of the Burma Road, made no secret of his low opinion of the Kuomintang situation. Chiang Kai Shek, he wrote,

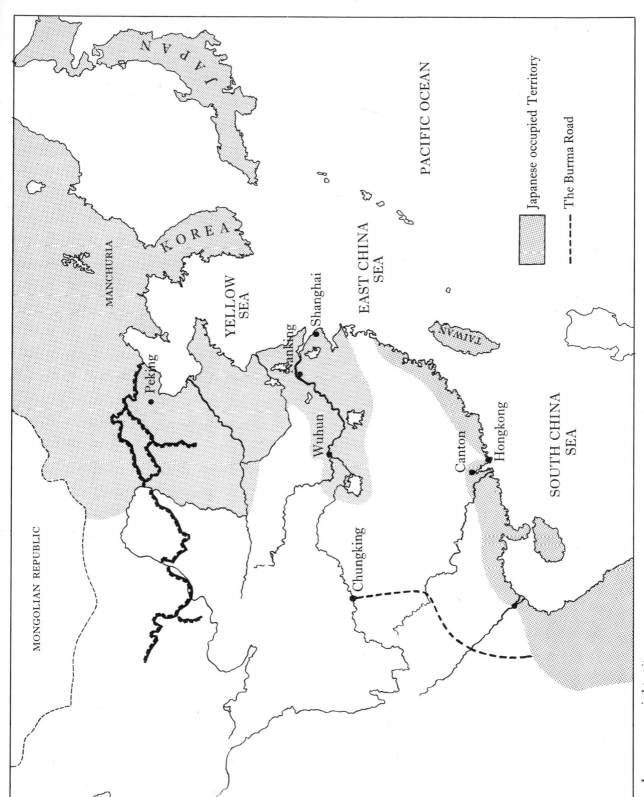

13. Japanese occupied territory, c. 1942.

knows about the rotten conditions, too, but he can't do anything. . . . Sixtieth Army can't be moved – they would refuse to obey the order. Opium traffic in Yunnan still enormous. Guarded by soldiers. Big stocks of hoarded gas, cloth, and other commodities. . . . The Chinese Red Cross is a racket. Stealing and sale of medicine is rampant. The army gets nothing. Malnutrition and sickness is ruining the Army; the high-ups steal the soldiers' food. A pretty picture.

In 1943 the central provinces of China suffered another famine. In the spring of the following year, 1944, a Japanese force driving west through central China defeated a Nationalist army nearly five or six times its size. The peasants of the region rose against the Kuomintang remnants, fighting them with pitchforks, birdguns and knives. The Japanese offensive continued through the heart of China, practically cutting Nationalist China in two. One after another the Nationalist armies rotted away.

Japanese surrender

But by 1944 the Japanese were loosing ground in other theatres of war: the Pacific and Burma.

In May 1945 the war in Europe ended with the unconditional surrender of Hitler's Germany. The total Allied war effort could be transferred to the east. The Soviet Union too joined the war against Japan. On 6 and 9 August the world's first atom bombs were dropped by the U.S. air force, on the Japanese cities of Hiroshima and Nagasaki. Within the week Japan had surrendered.

Since 1941 the communists had re-established their base in Yenan and were generally strong in the north, where they had liberated large areas: they were in a much better position to take over from the Japanese garrisons than the Kuomintang, far away in the rear. The U.S., however, gave a massive airlift to the Kuomintang troops which enabled them to take over many cities in the north in regions long under communist control. The countryside stayed with the communists.

In August 1945 agreement was reached between a delegation of the Communist Party and the Kuomintang Nationalists, in Chungking, in the hope of eliminating civil war.

Civil war renewed

But division was too deep for conciliation; the truce was short-lived. The communists could not agree to total abandonment of their forces and their aims, especially with regard to the land policy. The Kuomintang was determined to oppose social revolution and the spread of communism. The Kuomintang position, although backed by the U.S.A., was not in fact strong. Their negligible contribution to the defeat of Japan had lowered their prestige, relative to that of the communists; in the countryside their only support came from rich landlords, and these were ready to flee at the approach of the Reds. The Kuomintang were reinstated and maintained in the cities by a foreign power, in isolated units, dependent on outside support. Here too they had fallen into disrepute through their corruption. Businesses and banks had been avidly seized, after the Japanese surrender, by leading Kuomintang officials, particularly by members of the Four Big Families, the Chiangs, Kungs, Chens and Soongs, who made fortunes out of the war. Chief amongst these families was the family of Chiang Kai Shek himself – the Soong clan – relatives of his wife Meiling Soong. An American missionary and diplomant in China at the time stated that:

This party almost from the time it came into power had tolerated among its officials of all grades graft and greed, idleness and inefficiency, nepotism and factional rivalries – all the evils in short of the corrupt bureaucracy it had overthrown. These evils had become more pronounced after V.J. Day in the attempts to crush communism by a combination of military strength and secret police . . .

Inflation rising to fabulous heights made conditions in cities and in the countryside more and more intolerable; barter took the place of trade in Shanghai. In 1946 the Kuomintang armies launched another offensive against the communist bases in the north. They captured Yenan in 1947 but by the end of the year the Red Army, now known as the People's Liberation Army, took the offensive; the demoralised Kuomintang troops, hated for their brutality to peasants and workers, became increasingly isolated and were forced on the defensive in northern and central China.

Kuomintang defeated

The last revolutionary civil war was short and decisive. Yenan was regained early in 1948. By the end of the year the Kuomintang had been driven out of north-east China. Peking admitted the communists without a battle, in January 1949. At the same time Chiang Kai Shek took off in a U.S. plane for the south, announcing his retirement.

The Liberation Army, like earlier communist forces, received its military equipment either by capture from the enemy, or by bribery or voluntary surrender. There were massive desertions from the Nationalist forces.

In the spring the Red Army reached the Yangtze; after that, resistance practically disappeared – they 'captured' on average three cities a day. Nanking was taken in April and Kuomintang control came to an end. By autumn all mainland territories except Tibet had been liberated.

Chiang Kai Shek fled with a few Kuomintang remnants to the island of Taiwan (Formosa).

On 1 October 1949 Mao Tse Tung proclaimed in Peking the establishment of the People's Republic of China.

15. People's Republic of China

1949 onwards

At the proclamation of the People's Republic of China on 1 October 1949 Mao Tse Tung declared that 'The Chinese people, one-quarter of the human race, have now stood up'. After half a century of practically uninterrupted civil war, warlord strife and invasion, would China settle once again for a change of dynasty without social transformation? Only the Taipings, a century before, had attempted elementary social reform, but they had gone down before the Manchus and their western supporters.

Agrarian reform: land to the tillers

Six months after the proclamation of the People's Republic an Agrarian Reform Law was promulgated. The redistribution of the land amongst the poor peasants which had begun in the areas previously liberated was continued. This fundamental reform, 'land to the tillers', took three years to complete; it was not achieved by decree, but by methods similar to those used in the early Chinese soviets. Its object was to abolish landlordism. Meetings were held in the villages and each household, including the landlord's, was assessed: poor, middle, rich. In the redistribution, women received an allocation equal with the men. At the same time trials, or 'accusation meetings', were held to judge the crimes committed by the landlords. This was not always a spontaneous process; many peasants were still frightened. Too often in past decades landlords had been expropriated and fled, only to return in the wake of the Kuomintang or the Japanese to wreak vengeance on the peasant survivors. The fate of the landlords depended on the crimes they had committed. Many were executed; many were given prison sentences combined with farm work as a method of re-education and reform. Landlords who were not convicted of serious crimes received an allocation of land like other villagers, provided they themselves were willing to work it.

The dream of generations of Chinese peasants was realised. Each household had a plot of land, and there was no landlord to take half the produce.

This was but the first stage in the rural reorganisation, the object of which had not been to introduce a small peasant economy. The peasant households still farmed their individual plots with primitive methods and appliances; although better off they remained at the mercy of natural calamities and personal misfortune. If one of the household fell sick, the harvest might suffer; they were helpless against droughts or floods.

Cooperative farms

In 1953 the First Five Year Plan was introduced; in the sphere of
agriculture its objective was to raise production by 25 per cent and to
develop cooperation as a new stage of agrarian reform. The peasants
found that by grouping themselves together in teams and working on
each others' plots in turn they could raise larger crops in normal times
and avoid disaster in times when special difficulties arose. Team work
led to the pooling of the land and the establishment of cooperative
farms. A farmer from Liuling village, Shensi, described the transition
from work teams to cooperatives in his area: 'When there were eight
households working jointly in a labour group for mutual help, it
meant that one of the households had its land sowed roughly eight
days earlier than the last household's. . . . This led to a lot of argu-
ment . . . finally we said, 'Let us try cultivating it altogether and then
just sharing the produce . . .'. After the harvest the produce or income of the cooperative farm was shared amongst the members
according to the amount of work done – the 'labour days' contributed
– during the year.

The cooperative farms had considerable advantages over household plots. There were all the benefits of larger over small-scale
farming; both labour and land could be more rationally allocated;
a larger labour force shared the work at times of seasonal pressure;
during slack times other useful work could be organised, like the re-
claiming of waste land for cultivation, or the terracing of hillsides;
wasteful boundaries were eliminated, and so forth.

The progress from land redistribution to cooperative farms meant

Farming is now undertaken on a
communal basis. There is still great
need of agricultural machinery.

not only an improvement in farming, but a reorientation of attitudes amongst the section of the community generally regarded as the most individualistic and least adaptable. This move towards socialism generated new capabilities and a new outlook in the rural population. Peasants with no experience of management were elected to positions of authority with responsibilities never before within their scope. Some of them found these extra, unpaid tasks, which had to be fitted in before or after the day's work in the fields, onerous. They had also to become literate, in order to keep records and accounts, and to make their reports. The leader of the 'East Shines Red Higher Agricultural Cooperative', in Liuling, said, 'I have had the job for eight years now. It is a heavy responsibility . . . the leaders of the labour groups are responsible for the day-to-day work but my task is to coordinate all the work and see that all goes smoothly and that we stick to our plans . . . planning, supervising, training, solving problems, finding out members' views and listening to them.' Local self-government and initiative arising out of this reorganisation were no doubt as important as the increase in agricultural production which was necessary to support the population.

The communes

A further stage in agrarian development started in 1958 with the introduction of the Second Five Year Plan. Cooperative farms were amalgamated into larger units, called communes. This amalgamation was designed to achieve the benefits of large-scale farming. Whereas the cooperatives were restricted to a village, or to one side of a valley, the communes united a whole district. Substantial modernisation of farming techniques could be undertaken, and capital projects begun. As they pointed out in Liuling, 'Before the people's commune was set up, we had begun building a dam that was to serve three different co-operative farms. But it had been difficult getting them to collaborate. The people's commune made it possible to systematise joint effort.'

A certain proportion of the land amalgamated into communes, normally less than 5 per cent of the total, was reserved for the private use of individual households, as vegetable gardens, for keeping poultry, and so on.

By pooling resources, supplemented by government loans, the communes were able to acquire some agricultural machinery; they set up workshops for the maintenance of their machines. The communes were large enough to undertake irrigation and water conservancy works, and to develop research centres for crop improvement, and breeding stations. By 1959 the 500 million peasants of China were organised into some 26,000 communes.

The starting of small-scale industrial workshops in the communes was an important development. This was part of the policy called 'walking on two legs'. The communes were encouraged to be independent so far as the simpler industrial products were concerned. Workshops capable of keeping agricultural machinery and implements in repair began to make common tools. Brick kilns were erected to produce building materials, and pottery kilns to provide utensils. These developments were invaluable in an immense country like China with little industrial development, limited capital and serious distribution problems. In these workshops large numbers of people acquired the skills necessary for further industrial growth.

The communes thus become self-reliant units dealing with agricultural and industrial production, marketing and local distribution, as well as a whole range of social and cultural affairs. They are also the basic political units. The inclusion in the commune of people of all trades and professions is helping to eliminate the distinction between countryside and city, between manual and white-collar workers. Industrial plants are no longer being sited primarily in cities, but in rural areas, where the surrounding communes can supply not only food for the workers but the workers themselves. China's wealth of manpower is thus being used to produce capital construction and accumulation, to overcome her deficiency in capital. Industrial development takes two main forms: a limited number of large-scale state financed projects on the one hand, such as major water-control projects, heavy industrial complexes, and on the other, numerous local smaller industries, constructed by communes through labour-intensive effort.

Work on the communes, as on the cooperative farms, is organised on the basis of teams of thirty or forty families. Eight or ten teams make up a brigade. In the early days some very large communes were formed; these proved to be difficult to organise, and smaller units became normal. The income of the commune is distributed to households according to the number of labour-days worked by the family, after the state land tax has been deducted (16–25 per cent of a normal yield according to region) and an agreed proportion set aside for social welfare (usually 1 or 2 per cent). The communes have been able to give a range of social services. Besides providing help for the unattached and the aged, they have set up schools and clinics.

The period of commune development coincided with a recurrence of natural calamities over huge areas of the country. In the northern regions one of the most serious droughts in recent history occurred for several seasons running (1959–62), while in the south floods ruined the spring sowings and whole provinces lay under water. Some impetuous reorganisation and unscientific measures also led to poor harvests.

Severe rationing of food and textiles had to be introduced, but there was nothing like the wholesale famine and mortality characteristic of such disasters in the past. This was undoubtedly the result of the emergency measures that were undertaken by the government

nationally and on a local level by the communes; people were encouraged to sow quick-maturing crops to replace the sowings lost in the flooded regions; alternative supplies were mobilised for the cities. Rigorous rationing, price control and the absence of large-scale corruption and hoarding, were all new features in Chinese experience. The mass of the people were able to survive major calamities for the first time in Chinese history.

Restoration of industry

Nine-tenths of China's population still gain their livelihood from the land. Thus the agrarian revolution changed the lives of the majority of the people. But the policy of the People's Republic was not only to improve agriculture. It included the industrialisation of the country in order to raise living standards, to bring China up to the level of the great industrial powers and, sooner or later, to surpass them. To do this a socialist industrial economy was considered necessary.

The first stage was the rehabilitation of the industry that had existed up to the liberation. Railways and other communications had to be repaired, whole cities and industrial plants had to be reconstructed, and the currency stabilised. Despite shortages the new currency introduced in 1950 remained stable, and reconstruction was completed by about the same time as the first stage of land reform was achieved in 1952.

Anti-corruption measures

In addition during this period a deep-rooted problem was tackled, the elimination of the traditional corruption and dishonesty of public life. The new order was not only to be structurally different but differently motivated. A campaign called the 'Three Anti's'—anti-corruption, anti-waste, anti-bureaucratic methods—was reinforced by a 'Five Anti's' campaign: anti-bribery, anti-tax evasion, anti-fraud and theft of state property, and anti-stealing of economic information for private speculation.

First Five Year Plan

In 1953 the First Five Year Plan was inaugurated. Its intention was the establishment of the necessary foundations of modern industry in China. During this period (1953–57) more than half of the existing industrial enterprises were brought under state management. The government appointed the managers; on some cases they were the former owners, 'national capitalists', who had not collaborated with foreign enemies of China, and who were willing to work with the new regime. Some found the new situation had considerable advantages over the old conditions and approximately a million stayed on. In the old days Chinese industrialists had all the odds against them. They were up against the competition of foreign capitalists with privileges granted under treaties, they were hampered by the incompetence of

Bridge over the Yangtze at Wuhan—the triple city of Hankow, Hanyang and Wuchang, where the 1911 Revolution started.
This bridge, over a mile long, has two decks, the lower deck carries a double track railway, the upper is a broad roadway. Built at a point where the Yangtze runs very fast and deep, it was completed in two years, under the supervision of Chinese and Soviet engineers. It provides a vital link in communications between north and south China.

the state bureaucracy, by the opposition of the Big Five families of Chinese monopolists, by corruption in public life, and by wild inflation. The 'national capitalists' receive 5 per cent interest on the capital value of their enterprises which have been nationalised, and remain to supervise the management. This arrangement, whereby the new regime was able to use their technical skill in order to rehabilitate industry, was intended to end in 1962, but was extended to 1976.

The First Five Year Plan included a number of construction projects, some of which were major achievements by international standards. For the first time the Yangtze River was bridged, at Wuhan, where the river is nearly a mile wide. It was completed in 1957, and opened up direct road and rail communications from north to south through the heart of China. This, and other projects like the Sanmen Dam over the Yellow River, were undertaken with considerable help from the Soviet Union. Up to the end of this period, there was cordial and practical collaboration between these two powers.

Second Five Year Plan – the Big Leap Forward

The Second Five Year Plan (1958–62) was more ambitious. It envisaged not just a systematic and gradual industrial expansion, but a 'Big Leap Forward'. Large investments were to be made in heavy industry and industrialisation was to proceed by leaps and bounds. Initial successes in the year of the Big Leap Forward (1958) caused an upgrading of targets for the rest of the Plan period, in the expectation that the original targets would be met within two years. Difficulties were encountered through poor organisation, inexperience, and over-zealous officials. No figures of production have been published since 1961, and it is not possible to give a useful estimate of the degree of success or disappointment with the results of the second Plan. The objectives of the Third Five Year Plan were scaled down.

It would be unwise to underestimate the capacity for spectacular achievement in the industrial sphere of a country whose resources and energies are only just being tapped. There are enormous unexploited reserves of high-grade coal and minerals, and great hydroelectric power potential; technical skills too have only just begun to be developed. A central issue of Chinese politics has been the speed at which this development can take place. The technical experts, who in general have been out of favour, counselled caution and a slower pace, while many political leaders believed that giant strides could be made immediately through the mobilisation of the dedicated energies of China's millions; this is taking place, at the local level, mainly through the agro-industrial advances of the communes.

Women and the family

The support of the peasantry for the liberation movement was stiffened by the backing of a high proportion of the womenfolk.

The life of the men in old rural China was harsh, degrading and

Welders at work on the Sanmen Gorge Dam, a great project to harness the Yellow River, no longer known as 'China's Sorrow'. The dam was designed and erected with Soviet aid.

hopeless; that of the womenfolk was worse. The woman was completely uprooted from her own family on marriage, and became a slave in the household of her husband, the frequent victim of his tyranny and that of her mother-in-law. Until old age brought veneration, she had no status and no rights. In hard times her baby daughters might be exposed or drowned, her sons sold. She herself, amongst other household chattels, might be sold for food in times of famine.

A century ago an English Baptist missionary recorded his experiences of the famine in Shansi province (1876):

It was early morning when I approached the city gate. On one side of it was a pile of naked dead men, heaped on top of each other as though they were pigs for the slaughterhouse. On the other side of the gate was a similar heap of dead women, the clothing having been taken away to pawn for food. . . . For many miles in this district the trees were all white, stripped clean for ten or twenty feet high of their bark, which was being used for food . . . [The next morning] Saw only seven persons today, but no women among them. This was explained by meeting carts daily full of women being taken away for sale. . . .

Nearly a century later an American lecturer, Jack Belden, writing of China in the 1940s, under Chiang Kai Shek, said:

The lowly position of Chinese women not only had a terrible effect on the women themselves, but also succeeded in degrading and debauching all human relations within society. The Chiang Kai Shek government in its twenty-year rule over China produced some improvements but not much . . . in the countryside, particularly the north China countryside, the position was little better than it was fifty years ago. In fact when you consider that the buying and selling of women had increased in alarming proportions during the last decade, it was almost safe to say that the lot of Chinese women was as bad as, or worse than, it had ever been. . . . In the women of China the communists possessed almost ready made one of the greatest masses of disinherited human beings the world has ever seen. And because they found the key to the heart of these women, they also found one of the keys to victory over Chiang Kai Shek.

Chiang Kai Shek's main contribution was to reinforce the subjection of women. In the 'New Life Movement' by which he hoped to revitalise the Kuomintang, he was influenced by the ideas of Mussolini's fascist movement, in which women were to be restricted to their traditional domestic role as servitors of the men.

In Honan province before the war Jack Belden 'came across a landlord who had a family of sixty-nine members. Through this family, he controlled seven hundred tenant farmers, thirty slave girls, two hundred squatters, and seven wet nurses who breast fed his numerous brood. He was able to buy and sell women because of his wealth and he was also powerful because he possessed women'.

Women of the older generation in China can remember those days. Chia Ying Lan of Luiling village recalled:

When I was twenty-two, I was sold. He (my husband) came one day and fetched me and my daughter and took us to a slave-dealer, called Yang. My husband sold us so as to get money for opium. I never saw him after that. . . . When I had been two days with Yang the slave-dealer, he sold me. He sold me and my daughter to a farmer called He Nung Kung.

I was very unhappy. Mr He was an old man. But he was kind. I wasn't ill-treated there, neither by him nor by his family. Actually, he was a nice old man. . . . I bore him a son, so everyone was kind to me. . . . Then he fell ill and died. I was thirty-five then. I had a daughter and a son. . . . I was of course a widow and a burden on the village. The landlord wanted to marry me off. . . . In order to get out of this new marriage I lied and said that I was already forty-one . . . he thought I would not be fertile any more and wouldn't have me . . . some years after that we were liberated, and the new government protected us widows and the fatherless. . . . My son is working and life is good. But I want him to marry. I have lived in bitterness all my life and now I want him to marry so that I may see a grandson before I die.

It was not only as brutal landowners but also as callous husbands and slave-owners that the rich faced their 'accusation meetings' after the liberation. The women's clamour for justice was not always gentle, and many former husbands, like the landlords, sought safety in flight.

One of the earliest acts of the People's Republic was to close all brothels (November 1949). A Marriage Law, passed in 1950, forbade arranged marriages, child brides, and bigamy; it was based on the free choice of partners and equal rights for sexes. On marriage the woman can retain her own name, and the children take the name of either father or mother. The legal age at which marriage is permitted is eighteen for women and twenty for men. Widows may remarry. The village match-maker and the dowry system have vanished.

Divorce is granted if desired by both partners and if the questions of maintenance of children and allocation of property have been settled. If only one party wants a divorce, the people's court seeks to effect a reconciliation. If that fails, the certificate of divorce is granted. In 1950, and for some time after that, there was a rush to obtain divorces for the dissolution of arranged marriages, and divorces for women who were the multiple wives of landlords. Many girl widows, who had been slaves in the households of their in-laws, were re-married. For a time, disputes relating to marriage and divorce made up 90 per cent of all the cases coming to the local court.

According to communist theory, the achievement of complete equality between the sexes is dependent upon economic equality. Women must be able to play an economically productive part in society. They have always played some productive role in agriculture in China, but the commune system has encouraged women to undertake a full share with the men. An important factor is that women are now paid independently for their work in the commune, as well as in industry. Grandmother stays at home looking after the young children, or they are cared for in creches and kindergartens. Women are also being encouraged to work in industry. The principle of equal pay for equal work is generally applied. Child care facilities

Corner of Anshan Iron and Steel
Works, in north-east China.
This region has a long history of
metal production. During the period
of Han Wu Ti, 140–87 BC, iron ore
was smelted by primitive methods.

Iron smelter.

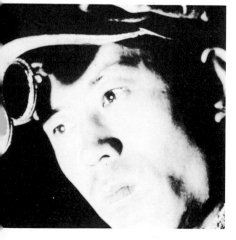

and auxiliary services like dining halls make jobs for women an economic proposition. Factories are obliged to set up creches and kindergartens where there are ten or more children of their women employees.

The quality of family life has changed considerably since the old patriarchal days. To a certain extent the conjugal family of parents and children is replacing the three-generation household; but housing shortage, as well as continued respect for family ties and for the aged, restrain this development. Old attitudes die hard, and in China as elsewhere there continues to be a tendency to regard domestic affairs as the province of the women and public life the prerogative of men, an attitude shared by both sexes. Women's associations, street committees, and cultural activities, together with the spread of literacy among all sections of the population, are helping women to overcome their diffidence and to take a full share in public life.

One striking indication of the difference between the old generation of Chinese women and the new is the size of their feet. 'Large' feet—that is, normal feet— were considered ugly and uncouth in a woman. A former beggar woman, whose feet were not bound, described the humiliation she experienced in her youth on account of her 'large' feet.

When I was seventeen I began to be ashamed of my normal feet. People used to laugh at me, saying, 'You're half man, half girl, with those hideous big feet'. . . . No one would marry me. Mothers despised me and refused to consider me as a possible wife for their sons. Finally my mother sold me to a blacksmith seven years older than me. . . .

This was the story of Wang Sui Wan, who after the liberation was elected a deputy to the National Congress.

Population

In China, losses even of millions of people, through famine and wars, resulted only in short-term depletion of the population. After a generation or so the numbers were restored, and periods of agricultural recovery were accompanied by substantial population increases.

The population of China today is about 700 million, and is expected to reach a thousand million by the end of the century. Its rapid growth has alarmed many in the west, but not in China, where additional people are regarded as a blessing, though large families are deprecated, because of the effect on the health of the mother. The Chinese are not over-anxious about their ability to support a rising population. Apart from the coastal area and the river valleys, population density is not great compared with some regions in Europe. The Chinese believe that their efforts to limit the effects of natural calamities will make it possible for agricultural production to increase at a faster rate than the population for a long time to come. There are considerable areas of land yet to be brought under cultivation. Desert regions are now being irrigated, mountain slopes terraced, and areas of thin soil protected by forest belts. Chinese agriculture is only just beginning to feel the benefit of advanced techniques. Fertilisers and agricultural machinery are still woefully lacking. Each grain of rice and ear of millet is the product primarily of human muscle and sweat. The fertiliser used is mainly human night soil. The transformation that a developed chemical industry and large-scale tractor and motor vehicle plants could generate in the countryside has still to be realised.

For a time after 1949 the Chinese were not interested in limiting the population by birth control or any other method. In the communes they said that a man's labour produced more than his sustenance. Recently young people have been encouraged to postpone marriage until their late twenties, and to have smaller families; education in planned parenthood is encouraged and birth control techniques are being advocated for young couples, with the health of the mother as the primary consideration.

Such measures are not likely to lessen to a significant degree the rate of population increase. In other parts of the world, industrialisation has been accompanied by rapid population growth in the early stages, which slowed down later. In China, it was inevitable that the elimination of famine and epidemics, the attention to public hygiene, and the extensive introduction of clinics and medical care, even at village level, would lead to an increased population.

The traditional family urge to insure its future with children, especially with sons to carry on the family name, will retain its effect for a long time. The Chinese are confident that there is elbow room for all in China. Mao Tse Tung once wrote (albeit in another context): 'China is a vast country – "When the east is still dark, the west is lit up; when night falls in the south, the day breaks in the north"; hence one need not worry about whether there is room enough to move round.'

Education

Language reform

Another task facing the new regime was education, the foundation of progress in all spheres. Despite the educational reforms at the beginning of the century, only a handful of the population was literate. Apart from the absence of schools, one of the main obstacles was the nature of the Chinese classical language, which took many years to learn and was ill-adapted to every day life. Reformers like Lu Hsun the satirist (who wrote 'The True Story of Ah Q', about a traditionalist who lives a life of illusion, and ends up by being dragged off to his execution vainly attempting to act the part of a hero) had urged the use of the vernacular instead of the restricted classical language. Today the vernacular has replaced the literary language.

The form of the written language presented another obstacle.

Derived from picture writing, it had no phonetic alphabet. The sounds as well as the outlines of each character had to be learned. To become moderately literate, some 4,000 characters had to be mastered, many requiring twenty or more strokes to write. To appreciate classical literature one had to be familiar with 10,000 characters.

The first step in language reform which was undertaken in the early years of the People's Republic was to simplify some of the basic characters. About 500 were reduced from seventeen strokes each on average to about eight strokes each, and the process is being continued. Duplicate characters for the same word were eliminated. There were some who feared that this might mean the loss to future generations of the heritage of classical literature, the loss of the written language which had formed a cultural bond in south-east Asia. But it was pointed out that all works could be printed in the revised script, and could now become available to many in place of a few. The process of simplification had moreover already occurred in some areas, for example Japan. The art of calligraphy would still be preserved, for this depended on the artist and not on the complexity of the characters.

The next stage was the introduction in 1958 of the Latin phonetic alphabet. Chinese script is an obstacle to many technical developments. A typewriter with thousands of characters has few advantages over handwriting. Without an alphabet, the construction of dictionaries and indexes is difficult. The Latin alphabet has been adopted not as a substitute for the Chinese script but to help teach Chinese more quickly. The sound of the characters can now be communicated in writing as well as orally. The Latin alphabet is taught in all schools, and public notices appear with the phonetic transcription alongside.

There are numerous spoken dialects in China, and in the past it has often been difficult for people of different regions to communicate with each other. The phonetic alphabet is helping to spread a standard pronunciation (based on the Pekingese, or mandarin form), but without eliminating local dialects. The phonetic alphabet has also simplified the work of creating scripts for the many national minorities in China who previously had no written language.

The schools

In 1949 not more than 15 per cent of the population was literate. At that time some 24 million children were receiving primary education, mostly in village or city schools set up at the beginning of the century. After a decade of the People's Republic, these numbers had been increased threefold, to nearly 90 million, with $10\frac{1}{2}$ million in secondary schools. Schools are run either by the government, or by people's communes and by factories, with financial aid from the government. Teachers, potential pupils and their parents joined forces to erect or convert buildings and to supply materials. Children themselves helped to make tables and chairs. New teachers were frequently only a week ahead of their pupils in their knowledge.

Schools for children are full-time or part-time. There is also spare-time schooling for adults who have never before been taught. The general pattern of schooling for children consists of six years primary education starting at seven years of age. The emphasis is on Chinese language and mathematics, which are regarded as the basis for further development; geography, history, nature study and physical education are also included. The six years of secondary education, where available, are divided into junior and senior middle schools of three years each. At this stage a foreign language, English or Russian, is taught, with a full range of sciences, history and geography.

Education in China is not regarded as an end in itself, for the personal satisfaction of the individual; its main purpose is the benefit of society. The old situation of an educated élite, a small class of those who did mental work and ruled others, a group too refined to soil their hands with physical labour, is no longer tolerated. Education is aimed at eradicating the distinction between mental and physical work. It is for this reason, in addition to the inadequate resources, that full-time as well as part-time schooling is combined with some kind of physical work. Primary school children, after their fourth year, do two weeks productive labour a year; in the middle school they do a month's labour annually. University and college students work from four to six weeks annually. The same provisions apply to teachers at all levels. The work done depends on the locality, and may be undertaken either in communes or factories. The Chinese maintain that these sessions away from study reinforce the effectiveness of education. In addition to eliminating the students' isolation from, and condescending attitude towards, the workaday world and the people who produce the wealth of the nation, they say that 'Students generally reflect on their learning experiences; after participation in productive labour they have greater sensitivity, new insights and deepened understanding of theoretical studies. . . . They get blisters on their hands but their skin has been darkened by sunshine, their thinking has been reddened. . . .'

The part-time schools are organised according to local circumstances; study and work alternate at daily, weekly or term intervals; they make possible some schooling for the children even in the poorest areas.

Chinese education today is an extension of, as well as a reaction against, her own cultural heritage; it is, similarly, an adaptation of, and at the same time a reaction against, Western technical advances.

In the nineteenth century the Chinese drew the conclusion that Western culture and domination were founded on military expertise, which they began to emulate. This lesson was deduced from the gunboats and from more bizarre experiences. A Chinese visitor to

Australia at the end of the nineteenth century described in his letters home some of the barbaric customs he had observed abroad, amongst them a game of football:

The game was the same as a battle; two groups of men in struggling contention. . . . They run like hares, charge each other like bulls, knock each other down rushing in pursuit of the ball and send it through the enemy's pole. . . . It is a violent game and men are often injured. But to make them bold and hardy it passes ten thousand games, for it is like fighting. . . . Men thus brave will make very good soldiers. We must adopt this game in the eight provinces. . . . We sons of Tang do not like violent things. But on earth many things are obtained by force. So we must learn some violence.

The same lesson was subsequently learned in the course of war in the Pacific.

In the sphere of higher education, the number of research institutes has greatly multiplied during the People's Republic. The explosion by China of her first atom bomb in October 1964, followed by the explosion of more advanced thermonuclear devices subsequently, have made clear to the rest of the world that the Chinese are capable of making up technical leeway in a remarkably short space of time.

Proletarian Cultural Revolution

The quantitative expansion of higher education was not at first matched by such a vigorous reorientation as took place in other spheres. Up to 1966 entrance to colleges and universities was controlled by a unified national examination. When the results appeared the best-known universities had first choice of students. In the summer of 1966 the system of selection by examination results came under strong attack from young people, an attack initiated by the girls of a Peking secondary school. They complained that the system differed little from the one dating back thousands of years. They pointed out that examination selection gave the advantage to young people from families with an intellectual background, and that those from workers' families, or the families of former poor peasants, were at a disadvantage. The system was also attacked for its encouragement of 'bourgeois individualistic' tendencies; the competition for good marks stimulated concentration on personal success, desire for individual fame, good fortune and position, rather than on collective welfare. It placed the emphasis on the memorising of formulae, the cramming of information to be forgotten immediately after the examination. Studying for examination successes tended to cut young people off from life and politics, and they came to resent the period of labour in fields or factories. The critics suggested that personal records of social and political activity should be used as criteria for selection, rather than examination performances.

In October 1964 China exploded her first atom bomb.

The Central Committee of the Communist Party of China approved these arguments and announced that the existing method of enrolment of students in higher educational establishments would be reformed, and that the 1966 enrolment would be postponed for half a year. The young people thus liberated from their studies responded eagerly to the call of Mao Tse Tung to launch a 'Great Proletarian Cultural Revolution' to eliminate the 'four olds': old ideas, old habits, old customs, old culture – to which was added, old foreign influences. The 'Red Guards' were formed; they frequently attacked the newly established authorities, including local and national officials of the Communist Party of China, accusing them of following the 'bourgeois road'. The Proletarian Cultural Revolution is an expression of the fear of reversion to traditional or to western modes of thought and behaviour. It is aimed at changing the old contempt for manual labour and servility before officials, and at removing the superstitions and fears of the past. In place of the docile acceptance of decisions made by others, Chairman Mao's 'Thoughts' are encouraging innovation, discussion, criticism, challenge. 'To dare' is to replace 'to obey'. Mao Tse Tung holds that there is nothing to fear in this nationwide agitation and ferment of discussion.

The 'Hundred Flowers' campaign of 1957 may be understood in the same context. The slogan 'Let a hundred flowers blossom, let a hundred schools of thought contend', contains a classical reference to the 'hundred schools of thought' of the Warring States period. The encouragement of discussion, criticism, and self-criticism, was designed to strengthen socialist culture and production; it was not intended to readmit western bourgeois thought or to support survivals of the traditional bureaucratic outlook, which were penalised.

Much of the early criticism in the Proletarian Cultural Revolution sprang directly from the field of education. Since 1964 the complaint that the system of entrance examinations was favouring the entrance of the children of bourgeois and intellectual families, has been accompanied by a general attack on the examination system of universities and colleges. A number of university faculties have revised their own internal examinations, introducing 'open book' examinations to replace the old 'mark-grabbing' tests. They allowed their students to refer to textbooks and reference works during the examination, and to talk among themselves. Some have experimented with the system of giving the questions in advance, the answers to be prepared by a specified date. They have tried to avoid academic questions and to pose questions for which there was no ready-made answer, in order to encourage the application of knowledge rather than simple memorising. It is said that the results of these experiments have been most rewarding, not only from the point of view of student achievement but from the general improvement in teaching methods which it stimulated.

National minorities: international relations

By 1949 most of the area of the mainland which had formed part of the Manchu empire in 1911 had been liberated from the Kuomintang or foreign occupation.

Outer Mongolia, which had been an oppressed province of the Manchu empire since the end of the seventeenth century, rose against the Manchu officials in 1911 and declared her independence. A decade of warlord struggles followed in Mongolia, terminated by a revolution in 1921. The ancient homeland of the nomads became the Mongolian People's Republic. The Kuomintang Nationalists delayed recognition of the Republic until 1945. Cordial relations were maintained between the Chinese and the Mongolian People's Republic after 1949.

With the extension of the Russian empire through the grasslands of Asia to the Pacific after the seventeenth century, the establishment of the Soviet Union (1917) and the Mongolian People's Republic (1921), ended one long phase of Chinese history. The hurricane centre from which nomad hordes swept south of the Wall into the Chinese villages was gone; there were no more nomad conquerors to threaten the Middle Kingdom, to seize the Dragon Throne. The nomads of the steppes had folded their tents and settled, building cities in the midst of their own pasturelands.

Tibet had tributary relations with China for many centuries. In the early days of the Manchu dynasty, Tibet was incorporated into the Celestial Empire as an autonomous territory. She was ruled by Dalai Lamas whose appointment needed the ratification of Peking. Fearing the advance of the British from India at the beginning of this century, the Manchus occupied Tibet (1910) and converted it into a Chinese province. The Dalai Lama fled to India, followed by Manchu forces. The revolution in China, in 1911, brought this occupation and Chinese control over the western part of Tibet to an end. A conference at Simla in India attempted meanwhile to regulate the Indian–Tibet frontier. The border proposed by Britain – the Macmahon Line – was accepted by the Dalai Lama, who had resumed control over western Tibet, but it was never ratified by China.

Western Tibet was reoccupied by Chinese forces in 1950, and Tibet became an autonomous region of the People's Republic of China, of which the Dalai Lama became a vice-chairman. In 1958, following the rising of a tribe in eastern Tibet, the Dalai Lama fled to India. Chinese forces put down the rising and extended the roads they were building to the Macmahon Line and beyond, and across other disputed territory on the borders of Tibet and India further west. In 1962 clashes between Chinese and Indian troops occurred in the Macmahon region; the Chinese pushed south and quickly overran the Indian outposts. The incident ended with the withdrawal of Chinese troops behind the Macmahon Line. The previous cordial relations between the two great Asian countries had, however, been seriously disturbed. Boundary problems between China, Burma and Nepal have been peaceably settled.

Hongkong, the island and strip of mainland territory ceded to Britain as a result of the Opium wars, on a lease which is due to expire in 1998, and the Portuguese concession of Macao, were ignored by the People's Republic when foreign concessions were annulled after 1949 and foreign properties confiscated. This quiescent approach was regarded by many as the lull before the storm.

The island of Taiwan (Formosa), which was seized from China by the Japanese at the end of the last century, has been the refuge and last stronghold of Chiang Kai Shek and the Kuomintang Nationalists since 1949. Here Chiang Kai Shek, with massive U.S. support, constantly threatened to use the island as a base for renewed attack against the People's Republic. The foreign support for the remnants of the Kuomintang, and the recognition by the United Nations of these 'Nationalists' as the representatives of China, have contributed from the earliest days of the People's Republic to a situation of tension between China and the outside world. The continued rejection of the claim by the Chinese People's Republic for a seat in the United Nations reinforced the long-established feeling in China that she could not expect goodwill or equity from foreign powers, collectively or individually.

Events after 1949 on her borders have also strengthened the conviction in China that she was threatened by the Western powers, headed by the U.S.A. In 1950, when war broke out between the north and south in Korea, U.S. troops were sent (as a United Nations force) in support of the south. When these forces advanced northwards towards the Chinese border, China came to the aid of North Korea. A cease-fire was signed in 1953; the 38th parallel remained the frontier between North and South Korea, with North Korea a People's Republic sympathetic to China, and South Korea an American ally. The war in Vietnam on China's southern border created similar suspicions. The American support for South Vietnam soon led them to within bombing distance of the Chinese frontier.

The most unpredictable aspect of China's foreign relations was the breach with the Soviet Union. After the liberation a Treaty of Friendship was signed between the Soviet Union and the People's Republic of China, and Soviet technical experts and material aid were sent to China. Differences of principle arose between the Communist parties of these countries after 1956. In 1960 the breach widened with the interruption of trade relations between the two powers and the withdrawal of Soviet experts. Among China's main grievances was the claim that the Soviet Union had not helped her to build a nuclear weapon. After this breach China became increasingly isolated in international affairs.

New Democracy

The Chinese call the political system introduced after the founding of the People's Republic the 'New Democracy', and they describe their Republic as a democratic dictatorship based on the alliance of workers and peasants, and led by the Communist Party. The 'liberation' from the Kuomintang and the warlords meant also the liberation from the old forms of control. The structural reorganisation of the government took five years. In 1954 elections were held and a National People's Congress assembled to adopt the constitution of the People's Republic. For the first time universal suffrage was introduced into China: the right to vote and to be elected was given to all citizens over eighteen years of age. Two categories were excluded from this right, the insane and those who had by law been deprived of their political rights; these were people like unreformed landlords and Kuomintang supporters, or those who had collaborated with the Japanese. Local congresses were directly elected; they are responsible for a small area of one or more villages. A group of these form a county. County congresses were elected by indirect vote – that is, by the village congresses, and so on up to provincial congresses and then the National Congress itself. The Congresses form the legislative body at each stage; they make the decisions and enunciate the laws. Executive Councils, to serve as the administrative organs, were elected by the Congresses at each level. The State Council of the National People's Congress carries out policy through its Ministries and Commissions. The Constitution provides that the National People's Congress meets annually, and that, when it is not in session, a Standing Committee acts on its behalf. At the first elections, nearly six million deputies were elected by an electorate of about 350 million to the People's Congresses at the primary level; 17 per cent of the national deputies were women.

The New Democracy in China, which includes not only the political structure but the agrarian and industrial reforms already mentioned, is seen as the means whereby the old government, economic system and culture will be totally eradicated, and the advance can be made to a socialist society. The only people who have power in the New Democracy are those who work. This power is exercised not only through the congresses, but through a number of organisations for different sections of the community – the trade unions and peasant associations; the women's federation; the youth league and the students' federation; each of these numbers many millions members.

The most powerful organisation is the Communist Party of China. When this was founded in 1921 it consisted of 57 members. At its Eighth National Congress in 1956 there were nearly 11 million members; in 1962 there were 18 million members. The Communists are the most influential people at all levels of society. They take the initiative in decision-making and are the most active in campaigning to see that the decisions are carried out. It is the Communist Party which has set the objective of transforming China from a backward agricultural country into a socialist, industrial country. The rate at which this could take place seems to have been one of the issues which has divided the Chinese Communist Party. The Ninth Congress should have been held in 1961 but by that time there was growing division in the leadership of the Party about future policy. It became clear that the division could not be resolved by debate in conference; within a few years the issue became part of the struggle for the Proletarian Cultural Revolution, in which the younger generation of China, which had never had the revolutionary experience of their parents, were mobilised as the Red Guard. According to Mao Tse Tung's theory, revolutions are not fought once and for all: the revolutionary process is a continuous one, and demands struggle at every stage if society is not to slip back into its former ways. The fact that nearly half of the Chinese population has been born since 1949 means that a new generation needs to be fired with this revolutionary zeal. Mao Tse Tung no doubt anticipates not one but 200 million youthful successors. More perhaps than other peoples, the Chinese are haunted by the ghosts of the past. The spectre that stalks China is a spawn of the old bureaucratic élite and foreign imperialism. When the Proletarian Cultural Revolution speaks of 'the fierce struggle against monsters', the Chinese understand this to include (according to their own definition) 'those in authority who are taking the capitalist road, reactionary bourgeois academic "authorities", landlords, rich peasants, counter-revolutionaries, bad elements and Rightists'.

Several political parties other than the Communist remained in existence after 1949; these joined together in a Consultative Conference which by and large supports the New Democracy.

In 1954 the first National People's Congress of China elected a number of veterans of the Chinese Communist Party to high state positions. Mao Tse Tung became chairman of the People's Republic of China, and Chu Teh, a Red Army veteran, became vice-chairman. The State Council was headed by Premier Chou En Lai, who led the Shanghai rising against the warlords, with Lin Piao, veteran of the Long March, one of the vice-premiers. The chairman of the Standing Committee was Liu Shao Chi, a veteran leader of the workers' movement, since removed from office for alleged reactionary tendencies. The widow of Dr Sun Yat Sen, Soong Ching Ling, became one of the vice-chairmen.

Chairman Mao

Mao Tse Tung, Chairman of the Communist Party of China, and Chairman of the People's Republic until 1959, when he vacated the position to concentrate on theoretical work (he was replaced by Liu Shao Chi) was born in 1893 in Hunan province in the south, in a village a few hours drive from Changsha, the provincial capital. (Mao

Mao Tse Tung, Chairman of the People's Republic of China, leader of the Chinese Communist Party since its earliest days.

found in later years that his southern dialect often hampered communication with northerners.) His father was a peasant; never very poor, he subsequently became moderately well off by dealing in surplus grain. The father was a hard and hot-tempered man; Mao Tse Tung afterwards said that there were two parties in his family – his father, the Ruling Power, on the one hand, and the Opposition, made up of himself, his mother, his brother, and sometimes the hired labourer that his father employed, on the other.

Mao Tse Tung went to the local primary school at the age of eight until he was thirteen, helping on the farm before school in the morning, and after school in the evening. The schoolteacher was a harsh man. Mao Tse Tung ran away when he was ten and wandered for several days over the hills before being found.

Father Mao was literate enough to keep his farm accounts but no one else in the family except Mao Tse Tung was literate. Son Mao disliked the formal classics, but enjoyed the old romances, especially the stories of rebellions. He wanted to continue his studies, but his father valued only his son's labour on the farm. Eventually the young Mao ran away from home to study in Changsha, where, during a period of famine, he witnessed the execution of peasants who had come to the city to ask the officials for food.

In 1911 Mao Tse Tung joined the general movement which over-threw the Manchus. He started to correspond with other students of a rebellious inclination. In 1919 he went to Peking and got a job as assistant librarian at Peking national university, and he studied in his spare time. He lived with seven other students in a two-roomed house; they could afford no fire, and had one coat between them. It was in Peking that young Mao first came into contact with Marxist literature, and here he felt the full impact of the May the Fourth Movement. The following year he returned to Changsha as lecturer at the Teachers' Training College where he had himself been a student.

When the first congress of Chinese communists was held in Shang-hai in 1921, Mao Tse Tung was one of the delegates; he was elected secretary of the newly founded Chinese Communist Party. After the split with the Kuomintang in 1927, Mao Tse Tung returned to the hills of Hunan and Kiangsi. Under his leadership the 'Autumn Har-vest' rising of peasants took place. He helped organise the peasant unions in that region, which became the first base of the Chinese soviets. Here Mao first formulated the theory of armed struggle based on the peasantry, using the villages to encircle the cities, which were then seized. His views were not at this time supported by other leaders of the Communist Party; it was not until January 1935, in the course of the Long March, that his policy prevailed.

Mao knew well the region of the Chingkang Mountains, in western Kiangsi. As a student he once spent a whole summer tramping over his native province. He had formed a kind of spartan club in those days and with other students he used to fast, to go on long hikes across the hills, swim in the coldest weather, and walk shirtless in the rain to toughen himself. Mao Tse Tung has attributed his strong constitu-tion to the hard work on his father's farm and to this toughening-up period in his youth. Except for a few weeks when he was ill he walked most of the Long March like the rank and file; his kit consisted of one change of clothes, an umbrella, notebooks, writing brush and ink box. Despite his varied life Mao Tse Tung remained a scholar. He has written many commentaries on his political and military experiences. In Yenan, after the Long March, Mao lectured to the Red Army and a number of his philosophical works date from that period. He is also an accomplished poet. Mao Tse Tung's first wife and his sister were shot by the Kuomintang, which placed a price of a quarter of a million dollars on his own head.

From the days when he returned to the hills, Mao Tse Tung has been an unorthodox Marxist, convinced that in an industrially under-developed country like China, it was necessary to rely on the rural population as the main political driving force towards revolution and not on the industrial proletariat, as the classical interpretation of

Snow: one of the best known poems of Chairman
Mao Tse Tung, in his own calligraphy.
'Our people are poor and blank, but the most
beautiful poem can be written on a blank sheet of
paper.'

Mao Tse Tung

Translation of the poem
This is the scene in that northern land;
A hundred leagues are sealed with ice,
A thousand leagues of whirling snow.
On either side of the Great Wall
One vastness is all you see.
From end to end of the great river
The rushing torrent is frozen and lost.
The mountains dance like silver snakes,
The highlands roll like waxen elephants,
As if they sought to vie with heaven in their height;
    and on a sunny day
You will see a red* dress thrown over the white,
    Enchantingly lovely!
Such great beauty like this in all our landscape
Has caused unnumbered heroes to bow in homage.
But alas these heroes! – Chin Shih Huang and Han Wu Ti
Were rather lacking in culture;
Rather lacking in literary talent
Were the emperors Tang Tai Tsung and Sung Tai Tsu;
    And Genghis Khan,
Beloved Son of Heaven for a day,
Only knew how to bend his bow at the golden eagle.
    Now they are all past and gone:
To find men truly great and noble-hearted
We must look here in the present

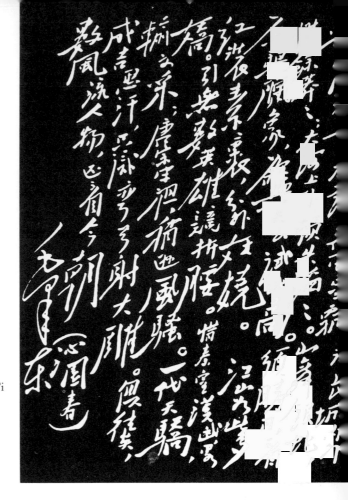

Marxism indicated. The revolution in China in fact developed many elements in the pattern of earlier peasant rebellions. Based on revolts in several different parts of the countryside, it had its main support from the poor peasants; the towns continued to be the centres of bureaucratic authority, the head-quarters of conservative military commanders and the refuge of dispossessed landlords and officials, against whom the developing strength of the industrial workers was less decisive than the struggle of the peasants.

The revolution as it happened was an epic full of peasant heroes and warrior poets, among whom Mao was not the only larger-than-life hero who fitted the role of traditional founder of a new period of Chinese history.

Red in China is the colour of joy, the colour of the bridal gown.

References

Figures in italic relate to the page number on which the references appear.

Lu Hsun, *A Brief History of Chinese Fiction*, Foreign Languages Press, Peking 1959. *14*

A. Waley, trans., *Chinese Poems*, Allen & Unwin 1946. *17*

A. Waley, trans., *The Analects of Confucius*, Allen & Unwin 1938. *23–7*

H. A. Giles, *History of Chinese Literature*, N.Y., Grove Press 1958. *25*

A. Waley, trans., *Book of Songs*, Allen & Unwin 1937. *27*

J. Needham, in *Manchester Guardian*, 29 August 1949. *27*

D. Bodde, *China's Cultural Tradition*, Holt, Rhinehart & Winston 1966. *31*

H. H. Dubbs, trans., *Hsun Tu*, Probsthain 1927. *32*

J. J. L. Duyvendak, trans., *The Book of Lord Shang*, Probsthain 1928. *33*

Chu Yuan, *Li Sao*, trans., Yang and Yang, Foreign Languages Press 1953. *34–5*

H. A. Giles, *History of Chinese Literature*. *40*

C. P. Fitzgerald, *China : A Short Cultural History*, Cresset Press 1936. *42*

H. A. Giles, *Gems of Chinese Literature*, Paragon, N.Y. 1965. *43, 45–6*

C. P. Fitzgerald, *China*. *43–4*

H. A. Giles, *Gems*. *47–8*

N. L. Swann, *Pan Chao*, N.Y. 1952. *53*

N. L. Swann, *Biography of Empress Teng*, University of North Carolina Press 1931. *53*

W. M. McGovern, *The Early Empires of Central Asia*, University of North Carolina Press 1939. *56*

H. A. Giles, *Gems*. *56*

L. Boulnois, *The Silk Road*, Allen & Unwin 1966. *57, 58*

J. Needham, *Legacy of China*, ed. R. Dawson, O.U.P. 1964. *58*

A. Waley, *Chinese Poems*. *58*

F. Hirth, *China and the Roman Orient*, Shanghai 1885. *59–60*

A. Waley, *Chinese Poems*. *62*

H. A. Giles, *History*. *62*

E. Balazs, *Chinese Civilisation and Bureaucracy*, Yale U.P. 1964. *63, 67*

H. A. Giles, *Gems*. *69, 71*

H. A. Giles, trans., *Travels of Fa Hsien*, Routledge 1923. *76*

J. Needham, in *Legacy of China*. *79*

Tung Chi Ming, *Outline of History of China*, Foreign Languages Press 1958. *83*

Yang and Yang, trans., *Courtesan's Jewel Box*, Foreign Languages Press 1957. *85*

H. A. Giles, *Gems*: Poem by Yeh Li. *85*

W. W. Yen, *Stories of Old China*, Foreign Languages Press 1958. *87*

E. Balazs, *Chinese Civilisation*. *89*

Chinese Buddhist Association, *Life of Hsuan-Tsang*, Peking 1959. *95*

S. Beal, *Life of Hiuen Tsiang*, Kegan Paul 1911. *96*

E. O. Reischauer, trans., *Ennin's Diary*, Ronald Press, N.Y. 1955. *98–9*

H. A. Giles, *Gems*. *103*

Yang and Yang. *103–4*

A. Waley, *Chinese Poems*. *104–5*

Lu Hsun, *Brief History*. *107*

Feng Yuan Chun, *Short History Chinese Classical Literature*, Foreign Languages Press 1958. *109*

H. A. Giles, *History*. *109*

J. Needham, *Science and Civilisation in China*, Vol. 1, C.U.P. 1954. *110*

A. Waley, trans., *Yuan Mei*, Grove Press, N.Y. 1956. *111*

J. Gernet, *Daily Life in China on the Eve of the Mongol Invasion*, Allen & Unwin 1962. *114–15, 122*

E. Balazs, *Chinese Civilisation*. *124*

R. E. Latham, trans., *Marco Polo*, Penguin 1958. *125*

L. J. Gallagher, trans., *China in the Sixteenth Century*, Random House 1953. *125–6*

J. Needham, *Science and Civilisation in China*, Vol. 1. *127*

H. A. Giles, *Gems*. *128*

W. W. Yen, *Stories of Old China*. *128*

G. E. Moule, *Notes of Hangchow Past and Present*, Kelly & Walsh, Shanghai 1907. *128*

E. Balazs, *Chinese Civilisation*. *128*

Courtesan's Jewel Box. *129*

N. Zhagvaral, ed., *Mongolian People's Republic*, Ulan Bator 1956. *131*

Kei Kwei Sun, *Secret History of the Mongols*, Muslim University, Aligarh 1957. *133*

J. Needham, *Science and Civilisation in China*, Vol. 1. *133*

H. A. R. Gibbs, trans., *Ibn Battutta*, Routledge 1929. *134*

M. Komroff, *Contemporaries of Marco Polo*, Cape 1929. *135*

J. Boyle, *History of the World Conqueror*, Vol. 1, Manchester U.P. 1958. *136*

C. Dawson, *The Mongol Mission*, Sheed & Ward 1955. *140–1*

L. J. Gallagher, *China in the Sixteenth Century*. *150–1*

F. Hirth, *China and the Roman Orient*. *154*

E. O. Reischauer and J. K. F. Fairbank, *East Asia the Great Tradition*, Vol. 1, Houghton and Mifflin 1958. *155*

F. Hirth and Rockhill, *Chau Ju Kua*, Taiwan 1965. *156*

J. Mirsky, *Great Chinese Travellers*, Allen & Unwin 1965. *156*

E. Bretschneider, *Mediaeval Researches*, Vol. 2, Routledge n.d. *158*

L. J. Gallagher, *China in the Sixteenth Century*. *162–3, 168*

C. H. Philips, *Historical Writing on Peoples of Asia*, Vol. 1 1962. School of Oriental and African Studies. *159*

H. A. Giles, *Gems*. *171*

H. B. Morse, *The East India Trading Company to China*, O.U.P. 1926. *169*

Lord Macartney, *Embassy to China*, 1798. (Reprinted, ed. J. L. Cranmer-Byng, Longmans 1962.) *170*

Ssu-yu Teng, *New Light on the History of the Taiping Rebellion*, Harvard U.P. 1950. *173*

A. F. Lindley, *Tiping Tien Kwoh*, London 1866. *175, 177, 179–80*

The Times, London, 12 July 1964. *180*

The Times, London, 18 July 1964. *181*

E. Balazs, *Political Theory and Administrative Reality in Traditional China* (Univ. London 1965). *182*

J. O. Bland & E. Backhouse, *China Under the Empress Dowager*, Heinemann 1910. *182*

O. Lattimore, *The Making of Modern China*, Allen & Unwin 1945. *184*

J. J. L. Duyvendak, trans., *Diary of Ching Shan*, Leiden, Brill. *185–6*

Aisin-Gioro Pu ti, *From Emperor to Citizen*, Foreign Languages Press, Peking, 1964, 1965. *191–3*

Wu Yu Chang, *Revolution of 1911*, Foreign Languages Press 1962. *193–4*

J. and A. C. Dewey, *Letters from China and Japan*, Dutton, N.Y. 1920. *195*

L. Epstein, *From Opium War to Liberation*, New World Press, Peking 1956. *197–8*

E. Snow, *Red Star Over China*, Gollancz 1938. *200*

Jan Myrdal, *Report from a Chinese Village*, Penguin 1967. *201*

P. Fleming, *One's Company*, Cape 1934. *203*

Long March. Eye Witness Accounts, Foreign Languages Press 1963. *206*

E. Snow, *op. cit. 207*

J. Myrdal, *op. cit. 209, 215–16, 220*

J. W. Stilwell, *The Stilwell Papers*, Wm. Sloane Ass., N.Y. 1948. *210*

J. L. Stuart, *Fifty Years in China*, Random House, N.Y. 1954. *213*

T. Richard, *Forty-five Years in China*, T. F. Unwin 1916. *220*

J. Belden, *China Shakes the World*, Harper & Row 1949. *220*

D. Cusack, *Chinese Women Speak*, Angus & Robertson 1958. *222*

Liao Lailung, *Yenan to Peking*, Foreign Languages Press 1954. *223*

Hwuy-Ung, *A Chinaman's Opinion*, Chatto & Windus 1927. *226*

China Pictorial, 1967, No. 4. *231*

Index